# Seeking *The* *Straight* Way

by R. M. Harnisch

To email the author, R. M. Harnisch:
salahallah7@gmail.com

Qur'an texts were from the online Qur'an Viewer 2.9

Bible quotes were taken from the King James Version, unless otherwise noted.

Copyedited by Jean Handwerk.

For a free download onto your computer of the entire Bible in your language, visit www.e-sword.org.

For a free download of the Honored Qur'an, Yusuf Ali Version in English and Arabic, please go to: Qur'an Viewer 2.93

This will give you a searchable software of the Qur'an.

For further information: www.salahallah.com

Copyright © 2015 by R. M. Harnisch

# Table of Contents

Introduction .................................................................................. 5
The Taurat and the Injeel: "…Guide to Mankind"! ............................ 7
"The People of the Book"................................................................ 12
"Glad Tidings" from Allah! ............................................................. 17
"Ransomed… with a Great Sacrifice"! ........................................... 22
"…That Allah might…purge what is in your hearts." ...................... 27
The Day the Trumpet Sounds! ....................................................... 32
"Transgress not…the Sabbath" ...................................................... 37
"Allah's Book" ................................................................................ 42
"Eschew all sin…" .......................................................................... 47
Allah's Guide to Health ................................................................. 52
Allah Revealed! ............................................................................. 57
"Allah…created the heavens and the earth in six days." ............... 62
Who is the "Comforter"? ................................................................ 69
Wise Men from the East ................................................................ 74
Ibrahim, friend of Allah ................................................................. 79
How Job (Ayub) Lost His Health and His Wealth ........................... 84
Can those hear, who are buried in the grave? ............................... 89
"A Prophet like Musa" .................................................................... 94
"The Law and the Gospel" ............................................................. 99
How Hagar Prefigured Maryam .................................................... 104
Why Allah Rejected Ancient Israel ............................................... 109
Blazing Fire ................................................................................... 114
The Throne of Allah ...................................................................... 119
How Hagar Found Allah to be Gracious ....................................... 124
Healing the disease of the Human Heart! .................................... 129
Allah, the Holy One; Isa, the Holy Son ......................................... 134
The Law of Allah ........................................................................... 139
If Scholars Lead Their Flocks Astray… ........................................... 144
The Rope of Hope… ...................................................................... 149
Jesus in the Qur'an and the Bible ................................................. 154
"Raiment of Righteousness" ......................................................... 160
The Forgiveness of Allah .............................................................. 169
Pure and Holy Wine, or the Wine of Babylon? ............................. 174
"The Hour of Judgment" ............................................................... 180
Preparation for the "Day of the Lord" .......................................... 189
Ibrahim, "Imam to the Nations" ................................................... 195
"Sincere Repentance" ................................................................... 200
The Eternal Home and Great Salvation ........................................ 205
The Baptism of Allah .................................................................... 210

# *Introduction*

The book you hold in your hands has been the work of years of research. The author has sought to gain an understanding of spiritual themes common to both the Bible and the Qur'an. He has found many similarities between the books, and he has also discovered many teachings that have been passed off as truth by scholars and educators, but which have no foundation in the Bible or the Qur'an.

Allah (God) is calling all people back to "the Straight Way." This way, or walk of life, will lead us to the eternal city that God has prepared for those who love Him. The author himself has had to make serious changes in his life as he has studied and surrendered to what God has revealed as truth. Much of what he was previously taught has had no foundation in truth. Such things we can safely leave behind, but what has been revealed as truth, we must embrace and cherish in our hearts, allowing it to transform our lives.

God wishes to purify our hearts and lives in preparation for the day of Judgment. How this is to be accomplished is revealed in the contents of this book, as the author has researched deeply into this subject.

There is a sense of urgency accompanying this book. As one observer phrased it, "The present is a time of overwhelming interest to all living. Rulers and statesmen, men who occupy positions of trust and authority, thinking men and women of all classes, have their attention fixed upon the events taking place about us. They are watching the relations that exist among the nations. They observe the intensity that is taking possession of every earthly element, and they recognize that something great and decisive is about to take place— that the world is on the verge of a stupendous crisis…." Prophets and Kings, 537.

Whether we live or die, the very best is to do so entirely within the will of Allah. Wise men, women and children seek to learn God's will for their lives, and make choices according to His far superior wisdom and love. This book reveals His will, as plainly stated in the Qur'an and the Bible, for Muslims and Christians alike. Allah loves each one equally, and has made provision to save eternally all those who accept His "straight way." The decision to accept is yours. Choose wisely for eternity.

May God grant you His Peace and Guidance as we await the Last Day.

*The author ... a learner.*

"And in their footsteps We sent Jesus the son of Mary, confirming the Law that had come before him: We sent him the Gospel: therein was guidance and light, and confirmation of the Law that had come before him: a guidance and an admonition to those who fear Allah." Sura 5.46 Al-Maeda Al-Qur'an

# The Taurat and the Injeel: "...Guide to Mankind"!

The Honored Qur'an tells us why we need to read the Taurat and the Injeel (the Bible Scriptures). Aal-E-Imran 3.3 tells us the following: "It is He Who sent down to thee (step by step), in truth, the Book, confirming what went before it; and He sent down the Law (of Moses) [Taurat] and the Gospel (of Jesus) [Injeel] before this, as **a guide to mankind**, and He sent down the criterion (of judgment between right and wrong)."

That sura states plainly that the law and the gospel were given "as a guide to mankind." The word "mankind" includes **all** people, not just a select few.

In addition, the Honored Qur'an teaches that through Isa al-Masih (Christ the Messiah), the son of Mary, the Gospel (Injeel) was sent. It was given to guide, enlighten, and admonish those who fear Allah:

"And in their footsteps We sent Jesus the son of Mary, confirming the Law [Taurat] that had come before him: We sent him the Gospel [Injeel]: therein was **guidance** and **light**, and confirmation of the Law that had come before him: a guidance and an **admonition** to those who fear Allah." Sura 5.46 Al-Maeda.

The "admonition" (Injeel) warns against faults; it reproves for wrong practices. It gives instruction and direction while we are here on planet earth. It is counsel toward right thoughts, words, and acts. Men of sound wisdom, whose ears are willing to receive Allah's instructions, will always heed admonition from Heaven, as did Moses, as recorded in the Injeel:

"They [the priests] serve at a sanctuary that is a copy and shadow of what is in heaven. This is why Moses was warned when he was about to build the desert sanctuary: 'See to it that you make everything according to the pattern shown you on the mountain.'" Hebrews 8:5.

Allah has carefully guarded His words. As it is recorded in Sura 5.48 Al-Maeda, "To thee We sent the Scripture in truth, **confirming the Scripture [the Bible] that came before it, and guarding it**…." How comforting to know that Allah protects His words and guards them, that we today may have a sure guide as to what is right and wrong.

## Taurat and Injeel Corrupted?

We should not find it amazing that there are so many positive things written about the Holy Books (Taurat and Injeel) in the Honored Qur'an. Despite that fact, though, some well-meaning people will tell you that those two books are corrupted! Imagine saying such a thing about the Holy Books sent down from Allah! It is an insult to Allah—as if He is not able to keep His words intact from evil minds! Yet these same sources that say the Holy Books of the Taurat and the Injeel have been altered or corrupted will freely quote from them when it serves their purposes, to prove their own understandings to others. They even memorize large portions of the Bible Scriptures, even though they claim the Holy Books are corrupted and tell you they are not the words of Allah! Friends, if what they say is true, why would they fill their minds with books which have been corrupted?

Others claim only portions are corrupted, and they will tell you they quote only from the uncorrupted parts. However, among themselves they disagree on what parts are corrupted! How, then, can they be sure that what they are quoting hasn't been corrupted?

All of this should tell us that people's minds have been heavily influenced by Iblis (Satan). But Allah knows what He is doing! Let us trust Him and rest upon the words sent down from Him and take these words for our own. Read again the words of Sura 5.46 Al-Maeda that the Injeel (Gospel) was sent through Isa al-Masih as guidance and admonition to those who fear Allah. Dear reader, do you fear Allah? Then these words are written for you!

## Signposts...

People today need direction. How often those who travel on the many highways look to the signposts along the way to determine the directions and distance to their intended city. In this world, we all need signposts to tell us which way to travel safely, so that we can reach our Heavenly destination. The Holy Books (the Scriptures) are signposts (guidance) which will help to keep us from going astray. Surely no one enjoys going in the wrong direction. It is very frustrating, to say the least, and sometimes we never reach our destination. Today, unfortunately, far too many are traveling in life and not even realizing they are on the wrong highway.

The Honored Qur'an tells us to "believe in Allah and in His Messenger ... **and the Scripture which He sent to those before (him)**." Sura 4.136 An-Nisa. All who refuse or deny "His messengers ... His Books" have gone far, far astray. How few among the people of Allah really believe what is here written. Here is plain counsel not only to believe in Allah, but also in the Scriptures which He sent. Friend, is it not time to search for a Bible and begin reading the instructions sent down? Is it any wonder that most of the world has indeed gone far, far astray? People have rejected guidance and light which was sent down, and have chosen instead to remain in the darkness of this world. Iblis (Satan) has indeed blinded their eyes, but Allah in mercy and in compassion is inviting us to come to the glorious light of truth as found in the Scriptures (Bible).

The Honored Qur'an says that "the truth is from your Lord." Sura 18.29 Al-Kahf. The importance of truth cannot be over-emphasized. It is through truth that Allah sanctifies His people. It is written in the Injeel, John 17:17: "Sanctify them through thy truth: thy word is truth." Allah's Word is truth. Most assuredly, Allah is wise enough and powerful enough to guard and protect His Words. Sura 6.115 Al-Anaam repeats those thoughts: "The Word of thy Lord doth find its fulfillment in truth and in justice: none can change His Words: for He is the one Who heareth and knoweth all." God is interested in giving us truth. It has been stated that in "the Gospel (Injeel): therein was guidance and light and confirmation of the Law."

Sura 5.46 Al-Maeda. Here is where truth is found.

Why does the Honored Qur'an speak so positively, confirming that the Injeel and Taurat greatly benefit us today? Remember, it says that the Taurat and Injeel are a guide for "those who fear Allah." Sura 5.46 Al-Maeda. Friends, if you fear Allah, then you will spend time in reading the Bible Scriptures, for it is true that they give guidance for mankind. In these Scriptures, the Honored Qur'an says, is found the "Criterion" between what is right and what is wrong. Sura 3.3-4 Aal-E-Imran.

The dictionary tells us that "Criterion" is the "standard" or "rule" by which something is to be tested. Thus the Honored Qur'an teaches us that the Scriptures (Bible) are the "standard" by which all matters are to be tested, whether something is right or wrong. Everything must be judged by this standard, for the prophet Isaiah (Taurat) said in chapter 8:20, "To the law and to the testimony: if they speak not according to this word, it is because there is no light in them." "To the

Law" refers to the ten commandment law, and "to the testimony" refers to the testimony of Scripture. If anyone's words or actions do not agree with what is written therein, then there is **no light** in them. Instead, they are in darkness. In the Injeel, Isa al-Masih reveals to us how we ought to live: "Man shall not live by bread alone, but by every word that proceedeth out of the mouth of God [Allah]." Matthew 4:4. Is it not obvious why the Honored Qur'an gives so much counsel that refers us to the Bible Scriptures?

## A Lamp and a Light…

In the Honored Qur'an, Sura 17.55 Al-Isra says that some prophets were given gifts. Daud (David) was given the gift of inspiration to write the Psalms (the Zabur). The Zabur says of Allah's Word, "Thy Word is a lamp unto my feet and a light unto my path." Psalms 119:105. Did you ever try to walk in the darkness of night without a light? Did you find it impossible to walk without fear of falling or stepping somewhere where you would get injured or, even worse, fall from a high place? Morally, our world is in the darkness of moonless night. If ever there was a time when we needed a lamp for our feet, it is today. So many people have departed from the right path. They have discarded the "lamp" and "light" by which we may know the right way. Why is there so much crime, lawlessness, and moral decay today? Why is society everywhere on the brink of ruin? Have not the people denied Allah, His law, His books and His messengers? Sura 4.136 An-Nisa.

People have thrown away the Bible…Here is what the Qur'an says…"And remember Allah took a covenant from the People of the Book, **to make it known and clear to mankind, and not to hide it; but they threw it away behind their backs,** and purchased with it some miserable gain! And vile was the bargain they made!" Sura 3.187 Aal-E-Imran

Therefore, everyone is now urged, whoever you may be, to read the Bible Scriptures, which in mercy have come down to us from Heaven. It is surely the "criterion" for us, teaching us what Allah says is right or forbidden.

Lastly, an incredible ayat from the Honored Qur'an—indeed, a very profound text—leads Muslims to ask those who have the Book (the Bible Scriptures): "If thou wert in doubt as to what We have revealed unto thee, **then ask those who have been reading the Book** from before thee: the Truth hath indeed come to thee from thy Lord:

so be in no wise of those in doubt." Sura 10.94 Yunus. It counsels Mohammed (PBUH) if he is in doubt to consult with those who have the Bible! Amazing, but true. The Honored Qur'an points to the Bible, dear friends. Before opening its pages, always ask (*du'a*) Allah to teach you the correct understanding as you read. Allah blesses those who sincerely are learners and seekers for righteousness. Taurat Jeremiah 29:13 contains Allah's promise: "And ye shall seek me, and find me, when ye shall search for me with all your heart." Those who seek Allah must seek with all the heart. Allah will never disappoint anyone who seeks His Word and reads what is written. Seek for His Holy Books as you would for valuable hidden treasure. Today Allah is leading millions to trust in His Holy Books sent down. May Allah bless you abundantly.

# "The People of the Book"

Greetings, dear friend of Allah. Frequently the Honored Qur'an points out a group called "the People of the Book." You probably have encountered those words before. Who are these people? There can be no doubt that they must be very special to Allah, to receive special mention, so let's look closely in the Honored Qur'an to see **who** they are and **how to recognize** them!

Sura 3.113-115 Aal-E-Imran informs us: "Not all of them are alike: of the People of the Book are a portion that stand (for the right): They rehearse the Signs of Allah all night long, and they prostrate themselves in adoration. They believe in Allah and the Last Day; they enjoin what is right, and forbid what is wrong; and they hasten (in emulation) in (all) good works: **They are in the ranks of the righteous**. Of the good that they do, nothing will be rejected of them; for Allah knoweth well those that do right."

The "People of the Book" (the "Book" meaning the Bible) are generally known as "Christians." However, the Honored Qur'an makes a distinction among Christians, teaching that "**they are not all alike**." "A portion" of them is different from the others; they are "among the righteous." Who is this unique group of people to whom the Honored Qur'an calls attention in such a remarkable manner? Notice the identifying characteristics of this "portion" or group from Sura 3.113-115 Aal E-Imran:

1. This group is not like other Christians.
2. This portion stands for the right,
3. ...rehearse the signs of Allah,
4. ...prostrate [bow] themselves in adoration,
5. ...believe in Allah and the Last Day,
6. ...enjoin what is right [instruct with authority what is right]
7. ...forbid what is wrong, and ... hasten in emulation [strive for that which is praiseworthy] in all good works, and
8. ...are **in the ranks of the righteous.**
9. **Nothing will be rejected of them.** [They are known by Allah.]

If the Honored Qur'an says that this **unique portion** is "among the righteous," is it not obvious that what they believe and teach from the Taurat, Zabur, and Injeel is truth? If Allah Himself finds them to be among the righteous, then we dare not find fault with them at all! Instead, could we learn from them? They hold to "the Book" (Bible Scriptures) which the Honored Qur'an purposely directs us to in Sura 5.46 Al-Maeda: "…We sent Jesus the son of Mary, confirming the Law [Taurat] that had come before him: We sent him the Gospel [Injeel]: therein was guidance and **light**, and confirmation of the Law [Taurat] that had come before him: A **guidance** and an **admonition** to those who fear Allah."

The Honored Qur'an speaks of the Taurat and Injeel, (Bible Scriptures) as giving (1) guidance, (2) admonition, and (3) light. This makes it very clear that the Taurat and Injeel are from Allah. The Injeel came to us through Isa al-Masih (Christ the Messiah), and is for those who fear Allah. This unique group from among the "People of the Book" believe that it is their duty to submit to Allah without reserve, with unquestioning submission. They have high moral values based upon the Bible Scriptures. They honor Allah (God) as Supreme and reject any teachings that give Him human "partners" such as Mary or other so-called adored saints that most Christians accept. The Injeel (James 2:19) says: "Thou believest that there is <u>one God</u>; thou doest well." In Mark 12:29 Isa al-Masih Himself said, "The Lord our God is one Lord."

Those in this distinct group also do not bow to idols in their worship, as most other Christians do. They know that worshipping idols or images is strictly forbidden by Allah, as written in the Taurat, Exodus 20:4-5: "Thou shalt not make unto thee any graven image, or any likeness of anything that is in heaven above, or that is in the earth beneath, or that is in the water under the earth: Thou shalt not bow down thyself to them, nor serve them." The Honored Qur'an goes on to say that these people, in their worship of Allah, "prostrate" themselves. They bow down before Allah as Daud recorded it in the Zabur (Taurat), Psalms 95:6: "O come, let us worship and **bow down**: let us kneel before the LORD our maker."

In addition, Sura 3.114 Aal-E-Imran tells us that they "forbid what is wrong." This "portion" of the 'People of the Book' forbid the eating of unclean foods (*haram*) such as "swine's flesh" (pork) and others.

Taurat Leviticus 11:7 says, "And the swine..., he is unclean to you." They forbid the use of alcohol, tobacco, and other harmful (*haram*), health-destroying substances. Gambling and pornography are also strictly prohibited. They honor the ten commandment laws of Allah as recorded in Taurat Exodus 20. These people believe that we are living in the "last days" of earth's history.

## SEVENTH-DAY ADVENTISTS

Who is this exceptional "portion" of the "People of the Book" about whom the Honored Qur'an speaks so highly? Allow me to introduce to you a group of people known among the "People of the Book" as "Seventh-day Adventists." Below is a brief description of what they believe. Compare for yourself whether their beliefs and practices fit the description outlined in Sura 3.113-115. Are these the "portion" of the People of the Book which are among the righteous?

1. Seventh-day Adventists serve One God (Allah) and they do not attribute human partners to Allah such as the Virgin Mary and other reverenced, supposed saints. Injeel James 2:19 says, "Thou believest that there is one God; thou doest well...."

2. They believe in entire submission to Allah with their whole soul. Injeel Luke 10:27 teaches, "And he answering said, Thou shalt love the Lord thy God [Allah] with all thy heart, and with all thy soul, and with all thy strength, and with all thy mind; and thy neighbor as thyself."

3. They do not worship or serve Allah with idols or images. Exodus 20:4-5 states, "Thou shalt not make unto thee any graven image, or any likeness of any thing.... Thou shalt not bow down thyself to them, nor serve them: for I the LORD thy God [Allah] am a jealous God...." Although most Christians bow to images in their worship, this is strictly forbidden in the Holy Scriptures.

4. They believe in the Judgment of Allah and because they place much emphasis upon Bible prophecy, they know the investigative phase of the Judgment is now happening. See Taurat Daniel 8:14. Out of love for Allah, knowing that they are living in these last vital hours of earth's history, Seventh-day Adventists have a high regard for the poor and unfortunate of this world, and hold a solemn responsibility toward them.

## The Seventh Day

5. They believe that the seventh day of the week (Saturday, the last day of the calendar week) is special, set aside by Allah. They honor and "keep holy" that day by gathering together to worship the Creator (Allah). That day is called the "Sabbath" or "Rest Day." In Arabic, it is "al-Sabt."

Seventh-day Adventists teach and follow all of the commandments of Allah as given in Taurat Exodus 20, including the true Sabbath, or rest day, of Allah. Exodus 20:8-11 says, "Remember the sabbath day, to keep it holy. Six days shalt thou labour, and do all thy work: But the seventh day [Saturday or al-Sabt] is the sabbath of the LORD thy God [Allah]: in it thou shalt not do any work, thou, nor thy son, nor thy daughter, thy manservant, nor thy maidservant, nor thy cattle, nor thy stranger that is within thy gates: For in six days the LORD made heaven and earth, the sea, and all that in them is, and rested the seventh day: wherefore the LORD blessed the sabbath day, and hallowed it [made it sacred]." They believe that Allah is the Creator, having created the earth and all that is in it in six 24-hour days and rested upon the seventh.

In full accord, Sura 10.3 Yunus teaches: "Verily your Lord is Allah, who created the heavens and the earth in six days, and is firmly established on the Throne (of authority), regulating and governing all things. No intercessor (can plead with Him) except after His leave (hath been obtained). This is Allah your Lord; Him therefore serve ye: will ye not celebrate His praises?"

Most Christians think to "keep holy" Sunday. Yet, God never hallowed (made sacred) the first day of the week. That substituted day was brought into the worship of the Creator many years ago by the Roman Catholic Church, through the influence of pagan sun worship, but it is rejected as forbidden by Allah. Allah recognizes only one day of the week as the Sabbath. It is the seventh day, known today as Saturday or al-Sabt.

## How Should the Sabbath be Kept?

Just imagine spending the entire day, the seventh and last day of the week, in total dedication to Allah! Would it not be the best day since it is spent in worship and praise to Allah, in company with others who worship Allah? All business and worldly affairs, all distractions, are set aside; it is a time to take the family to worship Allah and to spend time together as a family, perhaps in a quiet walk in nature. Truly this is a blessing few realize. Would this not include loving Allah with all the heart?

Keeping the Sabbath each week reminds all believers that Allah is the Creator of this earth and all things therein. Keeping the seventh day of the week holy, as Allah directs us, keeps ever in mind that fact that we did not come from apes or evolution, but from the One Supreme Creator of heaven and earth!

Lastly, #6, these people are followers of Isa al-Masih, the son of Mary (Christ the Messiah). The Honored Qur'an has very positive statements to make of those who follow Isa al-Masih: "Behold! Allah said: 'O Jesus! I will take thee and raise thee to Myself and clear thee (of the falsehoods) of those who blaspheme; <u>I will make those who follow thee superior</u> to those who reject faith, to the Day of Resurrection…"Sura 3.55 Aal-E-Imran.

Isa al-Masih was the holy or righteous son of Mary born through the "Ruh Allah." To Maryam it was announced… "He [angel] said: "Nay, I am only a messenger from thy Lord, (to announce) to thee the gift of a holy [Righteous] son." Sura 19.19 Maryam

This Righteousness Isa al-Masih is willing to give to all who trust Him.

The reader is invited to become acquainted with a Seventh-day Adventist and learn more about this special portion of the People of the Book to which the Honored Qur'an refers. Are not Muslims and Seventh-day Adventists brothers?

# "Glad Tidings" from Allah!

Truly even one word from Allah would be glad tidings! How grateful people ought to be to receive anything from Allah. He is so merciful and kind to be concerned with mankind. The Honored Qur'an tells us that He sent us a "Word" from Himself; His name was Christ Jesus (Isa al-Masih).

"Behold! the angels said: 'O Mary! Allah giveth thee glad tidings of a Word from Him: his name will be Christ Jesus, the son of Mary, held in honour in this world and the Hereafter and of (the company of) those nearest to Allah.'" Sura 3.45 Aal-E-Imran.

Surely these are indeed "glad tidings." That the great Allah, Maker of the universe, would even stoop to communicate to fallen man is a wonder to consider! This could only be because of the deepest love and infinite pity that He has for each and every one of us! Allah is so concerned for us that in mercy He chose to send Someone who is held in honor— One nearest to Himself.

Sura 5.46 Al-Maeda continues the "glad tidings," twice telling us that Jesus (Isa al-Masih Ibn Maryam) was sent from Allah to confirm the Law (Taurat ). It says Heaven also sent the Gospel (Injeel) to us through Jesus. "Therein is guidance and light." Sura 5.48 Al-Maeda adds the fact that the Scripture (Bible) was "guarded." Thus it appears that the Honored Qur'an is directing seekers of truth to the Word from Allah, the Bible Scriptures.

## Nearest to Allah!

To this guidance and light I also point the reader. The Injeel says in Hebrews 1:3 that Isa al-Masih (Christ the Messiah) "is the **express image** of His [Allah's] Person, and upholding all things by the Word of His power, …sat down on the right hand of the Majesty on high." How true that Isa al-Masih (Christ the Messiah), after living here on earth, sat down at the right hand of God [Allah] and is "nearest to Allah." Sura 3.45 Aal-E-Imran. We are fallen, sinful beings. In our sinful condition we cannot see Allah and yet live. Nevertheless, we need to have an understanding of what Allah is like, in order to believe in Him and love Him. In the Injeel, John 1:18 tells us that "no man hath seen God

[Allah] at any time." It tells us that only Christ (Isa al-Masih), "which is in the bosom of the Father, he hath declared him." Mortals cannot look upon Allah in His glory and live, yet Allah in His Mercy sent One who was "in the bosom" of Himself and who is closest to Himself. He was sent as the "express image" of the character of Allah.

How privileged we are to be able to see for ourselves what Allah is like. In the life of Isa al-Masih we may behold the kindness and compassion of Allah's love towards humanity expressed most fully. Isa's own words in the Injeel were, "If ye have seen me, ye have seen the Father." John 14:9. We can understand what Allah is like from the life of Isa al-Masih.

## A Remarkable Man

Is it any wonder that the Honored Qur'an has in itself more than 90 ayats which speak directly about Isa (Christ the Messiah)? Fifteen suras in the Honored Qur'an also speak of Him. It appears that Mohammed must have been directed as to the importance of understanding who Isa al-Masih (Christ) is, or he would not have spoken of Him in so many suras in the Honored Qur'an. We should be considered most blessed if we spend time to become acquainted with this remarkable Man, whose life is recorded in the Injeel (Gospel). There we may read how Isa al-Masih went about healing diseases and sickness of every sort. Even those with dreadful leprosy were made whole. He healed old and young-- men, women and children. The blind received sight; the deaf were made to hear again; and the crippled were given ability to walk. The dead were even brought back to life. What rejoicing this caused among men of that day! As Isa al-Masih walked the dusty paths of village after village, His compassion for fallen man was clearly seen. As He said, He had come to reveal what Allah is like. In Isa al-Masih (Christ the Messiah) we see a picture of Allah which had never before been revealed in such depth. The Honored Qur'an continues to tell us that those who follow Christ (Isa al-Masih Ibn Maryam), Allah will make "superior to those who reject faith." Sura 3.55 Aal-E-Imran.

Friends, is it not important then to research into the life of this Man sent by Allah? If the Honored Qur'an says that those who follow Isa al-Masih will be made "superior to those who reject faith," then it is most proper for us to know about Isa (Christ Jesus) and also be a follower of Him.

With assurance, the Honored Qur'an states that those who are the disciples (followers) of Isa (Christ the Messiah), helpers of Allah, would be called "Muslims." Sura 3.52 Aal-E-Imran. We all know that a "Muslim" is someone who is surrendered and submitted to Allah. This submission is to be without question or reservation on our part. This submission must also be to the Word (Isa al-Masih) sent to us from Allah. If you recall, Sura 3.45 Aal-E-Imran tells us that Allah sent "a Word from Him: his name will be Christ Jesus." Allah, the Holy One, would not have done all that was necessary to send His Word to us in the person and life of Isa al-Masih if it were not important for us to receive Him.

Suppose you should be so honored that the king of a country sends a representative of himself to you—someone who is very near the king. When this representative arrives and seeks to speak with you, what would happen if you should ignore this individual? Would it not terribly insult the king? Listen, dear friend of Allah. In a similar way, the God of Heaven and earth has indeed sent His Word to us, in the form of Isa-al Masih (Christ Jesus). He was not just any person. The Word (Isa al-Masih) is nearest to Allah and comes from the "bosom" or "heart" of the Father (Allah). We must pay special attention to Someone so important, so loved by the Father, and from the very heart of Allah, or we will be found to have greatly insulted Allah.

### Allah Himself Has Instructed Man

When Isa-al Masih was baptized at the river Jordan as an example for us, the Scriptures tell us "and lo, a voice from heaven"—the voice of Allah Himself-- was heard, saying "This is my beloved Son, in whom I am well pleased." (Injeel) Matthew 3:17. Some years later, Allah again spoke to mortal man about Isa al-Masih. "A voice out of the cloud" said, "This is my beloved Son, in whom I am well pleased; hear ye him." Matthew 17:5. Those last three words—"hear ye him"-- how important that we listen to what Allah has said to us through Isa al-Masih!

The Gospel (Injeel), which the Honored Qur'an in Sura 3.3 Aal-E-Imran says was sent down from Allah, contains passages of Scripture which repeat some of the same thoughts as found in Sura 3.45 Aal-E-Imran. That Sura speaks of Isa al-Masih (Christ the Messiah) as "the Word from Allah." Notice what it is says in Injeel John 1:1: "In the beginning was the Word, and the Word was with God [Allah], and the Word was God [Allah]." The verse continues, telling us that "the

Word was made flesh and dwelt [lived] among us" (verse 14). It is this Word who showed us what Allah is really like. He was clothed in human flesh, His divinity hidden, so that we could see and have a better understanding of the character of Allah and the principles of the kingdom of heaven.

Isa al-Masih is not a physical son from Allah, as men today have children. No, no, for that could not be. Yet for the Word to dwell among men, He had to become one with them. Therefore, He was born of a virgin, who had never known or been touched by a man. Remember, nothing is too difficult for Allah! He can simply speak and it appears. Read again Sura 3.46 Aal-E-Imran: Zabur Psalms tells us, "For He spoke, and it was done; He commanded, and it stood fast." Allah needs only to speak, and it comes to pass. There is power in His Word. This is also confirmed by the Qur'an. Sura 16.40 Al-Nahl "for to anything which we have willed, We but say the word, "Be", and it is." Also Sura 36.82 Ya-Seen "Verily, when He intends a thing, His Command is, "Be", and it is!"

### GOD'S (ALLAH'S) SON?

You may have heard someone being called a "son of the road." Does the road have a son? No, of course not. That saying refers to a person who is a traveler. So do not be discouraged when you hear the phrase "Christ, the Son of God." It does not mean that God (Allah) had a son in the way humans conceive and bear children, for this cannot be. Rather, Allah inspired the writers of the Scriptures to use the word "Son" to convey to humans, in a way humans could understand, the close relationship that exists between the "Son" and Allah, the Father. Therefore, it is through Isa (Christ), living in human form here on earth, that Allah's character has been revealed the best. No one could possibly represent Allah better than One so close to Him. And the clearest and best way for Allah to communicate to mankind is through Someone who is like us! Therefore He sent Isa al-Masih ibn Maryam, the Word from Allah. "Hear ye Him."

### THE BURNING BUSH

Dear friend, do not think for a moment that Allah is limited and cannot do this. Remember the story of Moses and the bush that burned, yet the bush was not consumed? Allah spoke to Moses from the fire:

"But when he [Moses] came to the (Fire), a voice was heard from the right bank of the valley, from a tree in hallowed ground: 'O Moses! Verily I am Allah, the Lord of the Worlds....'" Sura 28.30 Al-Qasas. If Allah can come in the form of a bush on fire, can He not also come in the form of man and reveal Himself to us and speak to us? Most assuredly, nothing is too difficult for Allah! We dare not limit Him!

May Allah bless you abundantly as you seek to do His will and as you choose to submit to what He has revealed to you. Truly the Word from Allah in Christ the Messiah is "glad tidings." "Hear ye Him!"

Before opening the pages of the Holy Books, always ask Allah to teach you the correct understanding as you read. Allah blesses those who sincerely are learners and seekers for righteousness. Jeremiah 29:13 says, "And ye shall seek me, and find me, when ye shall search for me with all your heart." Those who seek Allah must seek with all the heart.

"O ye who believe! seek help with patient Perseverance and Prayer; for Allah is with those who patiently persevere." Sura 2.153 Al-Baqara. May you be blessed with His Glad Tidings today!

# "Ransomed... with a Great Sacrifice"!

### IBRAHIM CALLED OUT

One of the best examples of submission to the Word of Allah occurred when Ibrahim was called to leave his home, his kindred, and his country. He was to travel toward an unknown destination that Allah, in time, would show him. Ibrahim implicitly obeyed when Allah spoke to him. This event is recorded in the Honored Qur'an and in Taurat Genesis 12, starting in verse 1: "Now the LORD had said unto Ibrahim, Get thee out of thy country, and from thy kindred, and from thy father's house, unto a land that I will shew thee." Ibrahim's response is recorded in Genesis 12:4: "So Ibrahim departed, as the LORD had spoken unto him … and Ibrahim was seventy and five years old when he departed out of Haran."

By this time Ibrahim was no longer a young man; he was settled and wealthy. But when he heard the voice of Allah, he obeyed without questioning. Ibrahim was not told where he would go, but only that he was to pack his belongings, gather his household and leave. This he did, setting aside his own preferences because he was fully confident in Allah's leading. You see, Ibrahim had developed a relationship with Allah; he understood that His way is best. Therefore, he simply took Allah at His Word and submitted to His wishes. We, too, would do well to render that same submission to Allah as Ibrahim rendered.

### IBRAHIM CALLED TO SACRIFICE

Chapter 22 of Taurat Genesis contains another record of Ibrahim. Many years after leaving his home and kindred, he was directed by Allah to sacrifice his son. Many details are revealed about what happened then. Is this account important? Yes! Why else would Sura 26.69 tell us to "<u>rehearse</u>" the story of Ibrahim? The Honored Qur'an has a very positive statement about Ibrahim. Sura 26.69 Ash-Shuara states, "And rehearse to them (something of) Ibrahim's story." It is evident that this account is most important for us to know and understand, for it has a lesson to teach us. We are most blessed to know the story.

In Taurat Genesis 22:2 it is written, "And he (Allah) said, Take now thy son, thine only son…." Then came these most unexpected, extremely painful words: "…Whom thou lovest, and get thee into the land of Moriah; and offer him there for a burnt offering upon one of the mountains which I will tell thee of."

Ibrahim was in the habit of communing with Allah. As a result, there had developed such a relationship between Allah and Ibrahim that Ibrahim recognized Allah's voice when he heard it. And the love Ibrahim had towards Allah was such that when Ibrahim heard His voice, he trusted and obeyed from his heart, even when he did not understand Allah's purposes. As Ibrahim had in the past, he again moved to obey. This story is briefly recorded in As-Saaffat Suras 37.102-107. It could not have been an easy task for him to carry out that command! His tender heart must have been pained beyond description! Yet the Word from Allah rang clear in his memory.

## Ibrahim Among the "Hanif"

The "Hanif" are truly sincere and most devoted to Allah. They are the purest in their worship of Allah. The biblical account in Genesis 22:3 says that after Ibrahim was told to sacrifice his son, he "…rose up early in the morning, and saddled his ass, and took two of his young men with him, and …his son, and clave [split] the wood for the burnt offering, and rose up, and went unto the place of which Allah had told him." This humble obedience is why Ibrahim is considered to be among the "Hanif." When Ibrahim received Allah's command, he obeyed without delay, acting willingly upon what he was instructed to do. Is it not true that today, those who are obedient to the voice of Allah, those who yield unquestioning submission to Him, are also among the "Hanif"?

## Ibrahim Called to Mount Moriah

This task Allah had asked Ibrahim to carry out was no small feat. The Taurat tells us it took three days to make that journey to the land of Moriah. They must have been three long, painful days, since Ibrahim believed he would return from the place of sacrifice without his beloved son. And what would he tell the boy's mother? One wonders if Ibrahim found any rest during the nights while others slept. Surely Ibrahim wrestled with Allah in prayer over this issue.

Taurat Genesis 22:4-8 continues the story: "Then on the third day Ibrahim lifted up his eyes, and saw the place afar off. And Ibrahim said unto his young men, abide ye here with the ass; and I and the lad will go yonder and worship, and come again to you." No other person was to witness this event before Allah. "Ibrahim took the wood of the burnt offering, and laid it upon ... his son; and he took the fire in his hand, and a knife; and they went both of them together." Before long the son of Ibrahim spoke saying, "My father, ...behold the fire and the wood: but where is the lamb for a burnt offering? And Ibrahim said, My son, God will provide himself a lamb for a burnt offering: so they went both of them together."

They arrived at the site; the altar was built; the wood was placed upon the altar. Then the aged father had to tell his dear son, "You are to be the sacrifice." Imagine! This was the beloved son of Ibrahim in his old age! Yet the son submitted fully to what Allah had asked of Ibrahim. Without verbal protest or physical resistance, he allowed himself to be bound and placed upon the altar.

Ibrahim raised the knife in his hand and was about to slay his son, when his hand was stayed. A voice from heaven called: "Ibrahim, Ibrahim." He answered, "Here am I." Genesis 22:9-11. The story continues in verses 12-13: "And He [Allah] said, lay not thine hand upon the lad, neither do thou anything unto him: for now I know that thou fearest God, seeing thou hast not withheld thy son, thine only son from me. And Ibrahim lifted up his eyes, and looked, and behold behind him, a ram caught in a thicket by his horns: and Ibrahim went and took the ram, and offered him up for a burnt offering <u>in the stead [place] of his son</u>."

## IBRAHIM'S SON RANSOMED

How was Ibrahim's son ransomed? The Honored Qur'an says that it was done with a momentous or great sacrifice! Sura 37.107 tells us: "And We ransomed him with a <u>momentous sacrifice</u>." Was the ram caught in the thicket really a "momentous" or great sacrifice? We know it cannot be. Therefore, we know there is more to this story. Could it be that the ram provided by Allah pointed to the future "great Sacrifice"? Did it represent Him whom Allah would send to be the sin offering for the entire world?

In a sense, Ibrahim's son represented all of humanity. We all should die eternally, because of our sins. However, we may be relieved of that fate and live eternally, thanks to the ransom provided by Allah, that ram-lamb that was sacrificed in our stead about 2,000 years ago. His name is Isa al-Masih, Christ Jesus, the son of Maryam— sent from Allah to be the atonement on behalf of mankind. Man had disobeyed Allah and deserved destruction, yet Allah would provide a solution. The sinful race could be ransomed only by the magnificent sacrifice of Him Who was sent from Allah.

## Ibrahim Called Blessed by Allah

Because Ibrahim obeyed Allah's voice in this matter, the account in Genesis 22:16-18 (Taurat) says he was blessed by Allah. And not only was he blessed, but "in his seed" (his descendants, and one in particular—Isa al-Masih) everyone on the earth would be blessed. "I [Allah] will bless thee…. I will multiply thy seed as the stars of heaven, and as the sand which is upon the sea shore… and in thy seed shall all the nations of the earth be blessed; because thou hast obeyed my voice."

Genesis 26: 5 tells us again why Ibrahim was blessed by Allah: "…Because that Ibrahim obeyed my voice, and kept my charge, my commandments, my statutes, and my laws…." Some would argue that the ten commandments were not given until Moses' time at Mt. Sinai, long after Ibrahim. However, this account in Genesis forever settles the fact that even Ibrahim obeyed Allah's ten commandments and other instructions. If we wish to have the blessing of Allah, we, too, must be willing to render obedience to Allah's Word and His commandments, with the same surrendered will with which Ibrahim obeyed. Most assuredly, we also will be blessed by Allah.

All the verses in the Old Testament Scriptures (Taurat) that speak about sacrificing of animals were to lead us to look forward to the "great Sacrifice," the "momentous sacrifice" which was to be sent from Allah. Yet when Isa al-Masih Ibn Maryam finally came to mankind, few believed that He was truly the Messiah, the sin offering, the ransom, the Saviour of this doomed world that had fallen deeply into sin.

## Mount Moriah and the Ransom

Why did Allah ask Ibrahim to travel to Mount Moriah? That mountain was where the temple would later be built, but it was also the same mount upon which, many years later, Isa al-Masih would give

His life as a sacrifice for the human race. He died in the very place where, centuries before, Ibrahim's hand had been stayed, sparing his beloved son. But for Isa al-Masih, Allah's own hand was not to be drawn back. He (Isa al-Masih), who was nearest to Allah, became a sacrifice on behalf of humanity. His life was yielded for us. Father Ibrahim's experience with his son was a foreshadowing; it foretold what was to come. In Ibrahim's day, a ransom was found: the ram in the thicket. But of Isa al-Masih, the Injeel says, "Even as the Son of Man [Isa] came … to give His life a ransom for many." Matthew 20:28.

Anciently, wise people of the East knew that a ransom would come on behalf of mankind. A ransom is the price required to be paid for someone to be released from bondage or captivity. In this case, sinners needed to be rescued or pardoned from sin, because "the wages of sin is [eternal] death." Romans 6:23. In the Holy Books we read, "…Deliver him [man] from going down to the pit [destruction]: I have found a ransom." Job 33:24.

Someone had to pay the price on mankind's behalf, or we sinful humans surely would have only the pit [destruction] to look forward to. It is written in the Injeel that Allah provided a sacrifice, that ransom: "But this man [Isa al-Masih], after he had offered one sacrifice for sins for ever [Himself], sat down on the right hand of God [Allah]." Hebrews 10:12. "And He [Isa al-Masih] is the propitiation [the reconciliation to God] for our sins: and not for ours only, but also for **the sins of the whole world**." 1 John 2:2.

Dear friend of Allah, will you not accept this sacrifice, this ransom from Allah, on your behalf? For you, Allah gave Isa al-Masih, the Messiah, as the "momentous sacrifice." He is our Saviour from sin. We would be wise to accept this gracious offer today! Any wonder that Isa al-Masih is the "Great" or "Momentous" Sacrifice to save a world perishing in sin.

# "...That Allah might...purge what is in your hearts."

What has happened to the human heart? Why has it become so cold and unfeeling? Why is there so much deceit, corruption and lawlessness in the entire world today? No area or people is excluded, and even seemingly good religious people are not exempt from participating in such activities. This heart problem is not physical in nature, but it is certainly a sickness or disease that can be fatal. Also, where did this deadly disorder or disease originate? Did Allah possibly make the human heart corrupt? Or did men choose to have it that way? These are some of the questions for which we seek answers.

We know that Allah will give us answers from the Holy Books which were sent down. Before opening the sacred pages of the Holy Books, it is extremely wise to ask for counsel from One (Allah) who alone is able to give us correct understanding.

Our first ayat from the Honored Qur'an is: "It is He Who sent down to thee (step by step), in truth, the Book, confirming what went before it; and He sent down the Law (of Moses) [Taurat] and the Gospel (of Jesus) [Injeel] before this, as a guide to mankind, and He sent down the Criterion (of judgment between right and wrong)." Sura 3.3 Aal-E-Imran.

The Honored Qur'an tells us that the Law (Taurat) and the Gospel (Injeel) serve humanity as a guide. Allah has given light and guidance in what the honored Qur'an calls "Allah's Book," which refers to the Taurat of the Bible Scriptures that was given to Moses. Sura 5.44 Al-Maeda. However, Allah did not stop there. He also gave us the Injeel (Gospel) as guidance, light, and admonition, confirming what was sent previous in the Law or "Allah's Book." Allah's Book has the answers we need to these difficult questions. We find that the Honored Qur'an again and again points us to the Holy Books of the Bible Scriptures (Sura 3.3; Sura 5.44-48; Sura 21.48-49).

## How the Human Heart Became Diseased

Many of you know of the story of Adam, the first human created by Allah. The entire account is recorded in the Taurat (Genesis 1:26-

31). Allah had created Adam and his wife perfect and holy. He placed them in a beautiful garden-- lovely beyond anything we have ever seen. The holy pair enjoyed the bliss and tranquility of that blessed place. Nothing disturbed their peace there. Their natures were pure; their thoughts were holy. In this beautiful garden Allah gave them all needful things to make and keep them happy and perfectly content. They were given unrestricted access to all the many and varied trees; they could eat from all which were for food... **except one**. Only one tree was withheld from them. They were forbidden to eat from "the tree of the knowledge of good and evil" in the midst of the garden. Taurat Genesis 2:15-17 reveals Allah's instructions to them: "But of the tree of the knowledge of good and evil, thou shalt not eat of it: for in the day that thou eatest thereof thou shalt surely die."

This prohibition was simply a test to see if man could be trusted. All went well for that holy pair in the garden of bliss-- until they disobeyed. They yielded to the temptations of the serpent, and the command of Allah not to eat from the forbidden tree was violated. "In the result, they both ate of the tree, and so their nakedness appeared to them: they began to sew together, for their covering, leaves from the Garden: thus did Adam disobey his Lord, and allow himself to be seduced." Sura 20.121 Ta-Ha.

Thus the holy pair fell. Because of his disobedience, Adam's thoughts were no longer naturally pure, as they once were. Instead, they became evil. From that fateful day to ours, disobedience toward Allah, which is sin, has cursed the human race. Since we all are the children of Adam, his descendants, we have inherited his fallen nature. The Taurat tells us our true condition: "The [human] heart is deceitful above all things, and desperately wicked: who can know it?" Jeremiah 17:9.

## How Healing Comes

We thus know our hearts (minds) cannot be trusted; we cannot look within ourselves, thinking we can improve our human nature ourselves. We would deceive ourselves and continue to sin. No human power can remedy the sin condition in the heart of man; we are helpless to change ourselves. But is man left without hope? Not at all! Allah, in His mercy and compassion toward us, does not leave man in this hopeless condition. Allah has promised help. Read for yourself these comforting words: "...That Allah might test what is in your breasts and

**purge** what is in your hearts. For Allah knoweth well the secrets of your hearts." Sura 3.154 Aal-E-Imran.

It is Allah who takes the initiative to help man. Allah is continually pressing upon the human heart the need for cleansing from the defilement of sin. However, man must desire this purging, this cleansing, from Allah. Man must ask Allah for it, and seek for it with all his ability.

How is this cleansing of the human heart accomplished and through whom? The Honored Qur'an talks about One who was sent down from Allah—One special person who was nearest to Allah. His name was Isa al-Masih Ibn Maryam. "Behold! the angels said: 'O Mary! Allah giveth thee glad tidings of a Word from Him: his name will be Christ Jesus, the son of Mary, held in honour in this world and the Hereafter and of (the company of) those nearest to Allah.'" Sura 3.45 Aal-E-Imran.

We read that Isa al-Masih, when He was sent to this earth, went about having compassion upon the people, healing their physical diseases. Could it be that this One sent down from Allah could also heal the disease of the heart? Could Allah also have a solution to this problem of evil and sin in the human heart? The Injeel reports that all who went to Isa al-Masih for healing of physical and mental problems received help. Not one was turned away. We read in the Holy Books (Injeel) Mark 1:41: "And Jesus [Isa al-Masih], moved with compassion, put forth his hand, and touched him [one with leprosy], and saith unto him, I will; be thou clean." Could it be that Allah also has made available to us the cure for the disease of the human heart through the same person of Isa al-Masih? The Injeel tells us it is so. In 1 John 1:7 we read, "But if we walk in the light, as he [Isa al-Masih] is in the light, we have fellowship one with another, and the blood of Jesus Christ [Isa al-Masih] his Son cleanseth us **from all sin**."

## CAN WE HAVE THE CLEANSING NOW?

This cleansing we can experience here and now. You see, Allah knows what is in our sinful hearts. He knows of every evil act, word or thought, whether it be lying, dishonesty, adultery or any other sin. And Allah is seeking even now to cleanse us from these evil habits and practices that hold us in the iron grips of sin. Allah has the solution and has promised to release us from this malady of sin. That is why Isa al-Masih is called the "Messiah," the "Saviour" from sin. Not only did Isa pay the ransom for sin, but also this Person sent from Allah has promised to give us new hearts, to cure the disease in our fallen, corrupt hearts. We receive help only by going to Allah and to Him whom Allah sent down. Again from the Injeel, in 1 Timothy 2:5-6: "For there is **one God**, and one mediator [*Shafi*] between God and men, **the man Christ Jesus** [Isa al-Masih]; Who gave himself **a ransom** for all…."

### How Thorough Is This Heart Purging?

This cleansing affects even our very thoughts!

2 Corinthians 10:5 says, "Casting down imaginations, and every high thing that exalteth itself against the knowledge of God [Allah], and bringing into captivity every thought to the obedience of Christ [Isa al-Masih]." Imagine even our very thoughts purged! What relief, what joy, what blessing!

The Injeel reports in Acts 3:26 that "unto you first [Israelites] God having raised up his Son Jesus [Isa al-Masih] sent him to bless you, in turning away every one of you from his iniquities [sin]." Long ago, people didn't want such a Saviour; they chose instead to remain in sin and to retain the disease of the fallen heart. In fact, in those days, the men who proclaimed this message of freedom were hated by the Jews—so much so that many were put into prison and even put to death. Such was the hatred against those who accepted Him whom Allah had sent to this earth.

Fearlessly, though, did the followers of Isa al-Masih speak and declare that "neither is there salvation in any other: for there is none other name under heaven given among men whereby we must be saved." Injeel Acts 4:12. With all respect and due consideration, then, is it any wonder that the Honored Qur'an speaks of the Injeel, that it was the "gospel" or good news which was sent down from Allah through Isa al-Masih? Why would the Honored Qur'an mention Isa al-Masih specifically by name in fifteen suras, as well as refer to him over ninety times? Surely the news in the Injeel is "glad tidings from Allah." Sura 3.45 Aal-E-Imran.

### How Your Heart Can Receive the Blessing

The old heart of sin finds no human cure. Try as we might with good deeds, by giving to the poor, and by praying often and long, we cannot purge our hearts or lives. Even washing our bodies will only clean the outsides, and soon they will be defiled again through sweat and dust. But Allah's cleansing is much deeper. His cleansing reaches to the heart, which represents the mind, the seat of the will. Allah alone has promised to cure our diseased hearts by granting us new hearts. Taurat Ezekiel 36:26 says, "A new heart also will I give you, and a new spirit will I put within you: <u>and I [Allah] will take away the stony [hard and corrupted] heart out of your flesh</u>, and I will give you an heart of flesh."

How can we receive these "new hearts"? Simply by asking Allah! Go to Him in private prayer (*du'a*) or when you are in the mosque. Allah is gracious, kind, and compassionate toward all the children of men, yet He does not force Himself upon us. He has said in the Honored Qur'an: "Let there be no compulsion in religion: Truth stands out clear from Error: whoever rejects evil and believes in Allah hath grasped the most trustworthy hand-hold, that never breaks. And Allah heareth and knoweth all things." Sura 2.256 Al-Baqara.

Allah will not impose Himself upon us. That is because He wants willing followers that choose His ways. Therefore, He must be asked. Each individual alone must make that decision to ask. Man must choose who will be his Master-- either Allah, through Isa al-Masih, or Satan [Iblis] the fallen one, who is a great deceiver. All the powers of heaven are involved with helping you make the best decision. Ask today! Take hold of that "most trustworthy hand-hold."

# The Day the Trumpet Sounds!

In the Injeel, Isa al-Masih tells us He will "come again" to this earth. John 14:28. Are you among the many in Islam who believe the time of His Second Coming is soon? When Isa al-Masih does return, how can we be certain that whom we see and hear is really Isa al-Masih? Could such a glorious event and such a holy Person be counterfeited? Who would try, and why?

### THE COUNTERFEITS OF IBLIS...

Remember that Iblis (Satan) has tried to counterfeit everything Allah has done. For example, Taurat Genesis 1:1 says that "in the beginning Allah [God] created the heaven and the earth." The Honored Qur'an states the same thing: "It is Allah Who has created the heavens and the earth, and all between them, in six Days, and is firmly established on the Throne (of Authority): ye have none, besides Him, to protect or intercede (for you): will ye not then receive admonition?" Sura 32.4 As-Sajda.

Yet we find that many, even among believers, say that this is not so. They have been taught, and now claim, that the earth, mankind, and both land and sea animals have "evolved" over millions or perhaps billions of years to get to the point they are now. To believe that Allah created all things in nature around us within six days is unthinkable for them.

Likewise, Taurat Genesis 1:26 records Allah's words, "Let us make man in our image...." Yet despite this clear language, many otherwise-intelligent people believe that over a very long period of time, apes gradually developed ("evolved") into humans. This, too, is a lie of Iblis (Satan). The Word from Allah makes it plain that the first humans were created fully human, even "in the image of God." This was not magic from Heaven, but simply God speaking and it appears. Allah has to simply say "Be" and it is. His Words have power to create and that power is instant.

"For to anything which We have willed, We but say the word, "Be", and it is." Sura 16.40 An-Nahl

Those who believe in counterfeit teachings have set aside the Word of Allah for the pleasing fable of "evolution." They have accepted a counterfeit teaching, instead of the real truth. And this counterfeit theory of evolution ("evil-lution") that attempts to replace Allah's six-day creation has led man astray—away from Allah-- for many years now. It is very apparent that Iblis (Satan) hates the Word from Allah. He hates the Holy Books and those sent from Allah.

Because of Iblis' past deceptions such as evolution (evil-lution), we can be certain he will also try to counterfeit the Second Coming of Isa al-Masih! But Allah, in His goodness, compassion, and great mercy, has already sent down truth ahead of time, so that we may know the tricks or deceptions of Iblis (Satan). (Injeel) Matthew 24:4 says, "And Jesus answered and said unto them, Take heed that no man deceive you." Five times in the Injeel we are warned not to be deceived! The Honored Qur'an confirms Iblis as the "chief deceiver." Sura 31.33 Luqman; Sura 35.5 Fatir.

The success of any counterfeit lies in its ability to precede or replace the true. Those who do not know what the true is can easily be deceived by something closely resembling it. I once was given a counterfeit monetary note from a taxi cab driver. I did not examine the note closely until later that evening, when I noticed something was different about one note I had received from him. It was indeed a counterfeit; I had been deceived! Fortunately, the amount of money was small, so the matter was not very significant to me. However, the great Second Coming of Isa al-Masih has immense significance to every human being.

To defeat Allah's purposes, Iblis (Satan) will cause the false to precede the true. To millions it will appear that Isa al-Masih is coming to earth the second time, but the whole scene will be Iblis's counterfeit. In that way, Iblis will attempt to deceive all that believe in Isa's Second Coming to earth, and to lead them to depart from the straight path of Allah.

## The Truths of Allah…

The Holy Books, the Bible Scriptures, tell us that the true people of Allah will be expecting Isa al-Masih (Christ the Messiah) to return. They will "look for" Him, as foretold in the Injeel Hebrews 9:28: "So Christ [Isa al-Masih] was once offered [the ransom] to bear the sins of many; and unto them that look for him shall he appear **the second time**…."

Allah, in His mercy, has given warnings ahead of time, so that we need not be deceived by any counterfeits. The Injeel (Gospel) warns us that many men shall claim themselves to be Isa al-Masih, and many will be ensnared by their lies. Injeel Matthew 24:5 states what verse 24 repeats: "For **many** shall come in my name, saying, I am Christ; and shall deceive many…. There shall arise false Christs, and false prophets, … if it were possible, they shall deceive the very elect."

2 Corinthians 11:13-14 also mentions those deceivers, and adds Iblis' deception: "For such are false apostles, deceitful workers, transforming themselves into the apostles of Christ. And no marvel; for **Satan** [Iblis] himself is **transformed into an angel of light**."

Iblis (Satan), a false Christ, will present himself to the world as Isa al-Masih, intending by his assumed grandeur and pretended compassion to deceive all people and gain their allegiance before the true Christ arrives. But Injeel Matthew 24:30 gives us details about the arrival of the true or "real" Christ: "And then shall appear the sign of the Son of man in heaven: and then shall **all the tribes** of the earth mourn, and they shall see the Son of man coming in the clouds of heaven with power and great glory."

Why do "all tribes of the earth mourn?" Because they have accepted the false, counterfeit Christ. When the real or true Christ appears in the clouds with power and great glory, they realize they made a grave mistake, but alas! It is too late for them! Dear friends, it is not yet too late for us. We can know truth!

## How will Isa al-Masih return?

In the Revelation of Isa al-Masih given to Yahya (John, on the Isle of Patmos) we learn about the true return of Isa al-Masih: "Behold, he (Isa al-Masih) cometh with clouds; and **every eye shall see him**, and they also which pierced him: and all kindreds of the earth shall wail because of him…." Injeel Revelation 1:7. We are assured that "every eye shall see him" as He comes with "clouds" (huge gatherings of angels). But it also says that "all kindreds of the earth shall wail." Why? Because everywhere on earth will be people deceived by the counterfeit.

The Second Coming of the true Isa al-Masih will be as brilliant as lightning. Injeel Matthew 24:27 tells us, "For as the lightning cometh out of the east, and shineth even unto the west; so shall also the coming of the Son of man [Isa al-Masih] be."

The Second Coming of Isa will be seen all over the world. You will not need to go to your television or internet or iPod to see this event. Wherever you are when it occurs, you will see it.

Another amazing feature of this event will be a resurrection of the dead from their graves. "The trumpet shall be sounded, when behold! from the sepulchres (men) will rush forth to their Lord!" Sura 36.51 Ya-Seen.

1 Thessalonians 4:16 first tells us about the sounds: "For the Lord [Isa al-Masih] himself shall descend from heaven with a shout, with the voice of the archangel, and with the trump [trumpet] of God [Allah]...." This event will not only be seen by every eye, but every ear will hear a shout, a great voice speaking, and a trumpet call. And then: "...**The dead in Christ shall rise** first." Yes! This is the resurrection of true believers from their graves. They "rise" from their dusty graves, having been given life again.

1 Thessalonians 4:17 tells what will happen next: "Then we which are alive and remain shall be caught up together with them [those righteous ones who are raised from their graves] in the clouds, to meet the Lord in the air: and so shall we ever be with the Lord." What joy and peace! And don't miss this critical point: The resurrected ones and the righteous living ones rise "to meet the Lord in the air." The Holy Scriptures specifically state that when Isa al-Masih comes this second time, He will not land upon the earth and walk about as He did the first time, long ago. This time, He comes to gather the believers to Himself "in the air." This is a rescue mission from off this planet, which has become corrupted due to the counterfeits and deceptions of Iblis (Satan).

## Signs of Isa's Return...

How can we be sure that His coming is soon? Will there be signs of its nearness? Yes. One of the signs Isa al-Masih named is that life on earth will be as it was in the days of Noah before the Flood, and as in the days of Lot in Sodom. Injeel Luke 17:26-30: "And as it was in the days of Noe [Noah], so shall it be also in the days of the Son of man. They did eat, they drank, they married wives, they were given in marriage, until the day that Noe [Noah] entered into the ark, and the flood came, and destroyed them all. Likewise also as it was in the days of Lot; they did eat, they drank, they bought, they sold, they planted, they builded; But the same day that Lot went out of Sodom it rained fire and brimstone from heaven, and destroyed them all. Even thus shall it be in the day when the Son of man [Isa al-Masih] is revealed."

Just how wicked and evil was it back in those days before the Flood? Taurat Genesis 6:5: "And GOD [Allah] saw that the wickedness of man was great in the earth, and that every imagination of the thoughts of his heart was **only evil continually**."

Every thought and motive was evil! Does this not describe our day as well? Wherever one goes, it is rare to find a person who is honest, or a person who is truly seeking the way of Allah with his whole heart! Truly the wickedness described in the Injeel about the pre-Flood days is being repeated today. War abounds around the planet, it seems. Therefore, we can soon-- very soon-- expect the return of Isa al-Masih to end this terrible evil and rebellion against Allah.

"And the Day that the Trumpet will be sounded - then will be smitten with terror those who are in the heavens, and those who are on earth, except such as Allah will please (to exempt): and all shall come to His (Presence) as beings conscious of their lowliness." Sura 27.87 An-Naml.

Will you and I be ready for that day? Will we heed the warnings to avoid the counterfeits of Iblis? To prepare for this event, we must trust our lives to One Who was sent down, to Isa al-Masih Ibn Maryam. He is your personal Saviour from sin; He will keep you from being deceived. May Allah grant unto you His Eternal Peace!

# "Transgress not...the Sabbath"

Here is an excellent question for study: Should Muslims honor the Sabbath day "Al-Sabt" as the day of rest upon which one refrains from any work? Many in Islam believe that the Ten Commandments, which were written with the "finger of Allah," are to be obeyed. What many have overlooked, however, is the fact that one of these Ten Commandments has been largely forgotten! Even the majority of Christians who claim they are the people of the Book (Holy Books of the Bible) do not give heed to one of the commandments as written in the Taurat. In fact, many of them look upon these ten sacred Laws for humanity with disinterest, scorn or even with hatred.

Let us first take a close look at what the Ten Commandments really are, and then determine whether we are to live by these laws today. We know they are written specifically in the Taurat in both Exodus Sura 20 and Deuteronomy Sura 5 of the Holy Books given to Moses.

"**We gave Moses the Book** [Taurat] and followed him up with a succession of messengers; We gave Jesus the son of Mary Clear (Signs) and strengthened him with the holy spirit. Is it that whenever there comes to you a messenger with what ye yourselves desire not, ye are puffed up with pride?- Some ye called impostors, and others ye slay!" Sura 2.87 Al-Baqara

What we find interesting is that to Moses, Allah did not send a message through an angel, to Moses Allah spoke direct. Hence the Message given to Moses was therefore something which Allah Himself felt was so important that He Himself would communicate to Moses.

"Of some messengers We have already told thee the story; of others We have not;- and **to Moses Allah spoke direct**;-" Sura 4.164 An-Nisa

Remember that the Honored Qur'an has revealed that both the Taurat (Law) given to Moses and the Injeel given to Isa al-Masih (Christ the Messiah) were "for our admonition." They are "guidance and light," and are the "criterion" of the judgment. See Sura 2.53 Al-Baqara; Sura 3.3 Aal-E-Imran; Sura 21.48 Al-Aniva; Sura 10.94 Yunus; Sura 5.44 Al-Maeda. These suras are only some of the many references made in the Honored Qur'an to the Holy Books of the Bible Scriptures (Taurat and Injeel).

## Example of Ibrahim

Many today feel that Ibrahim, from long ago, was a man who honored Allah with all his heart. He has therefore become a model or pattern for us to follow. The Holy Books (Bible Scriptures) tell how Ibrahim viewed Allah's Ten Commandments. Taurat Genesis 26:5 says, "…Abraham [Ibrahim] obeyed my voice, and kept my charge, **my commandments**, my statutes, and my laws."

This verse in the Taurat tells us that the Ten Commandments of Allah were faithfully followed by Ibrahim, who lived long before Moses' time. That fact proves that men of ancient times certainly knew of that law, which Allah repeated to Moses centuries later in the towering heights of Mount Sinai. If Ibrahim is considered to be the "Hanif" of those who are in sincerity drawing close to Allah, then we would do well to follow the example of Ibrahim by also keeping the Ten Commandments Laws of Allah. Simply put, Ibrahim obeyed the fourth commandment by keeping the seventh day of the week as "Al-Sabt," as the "day of rest" in honor of Allah.

## "The Finger of Allah"

The story of the Ten Commandment Laws is recorded in the Taurat in Exodus 20 given to Moses. As the children of Israel who had been delivered from Egyptian bondage encamped in the wilderness of the desert, Moses (Musa) was instructed by Allah to climb up to Him on Mount Sinai. It is while Moses was up there that he was given two tables of stone upon which were written the Ten Commandments, or Ten Words, by the finger of Allah. Taurat Exodus 31:18; Deuteronomy 9:10.

The Holy Qur'an refers to this event: "And for their Covenant we raised over them (the towering height) of Mount (Sinai); and (on another occasion) We said: 'Enter the gate with humility;' and (once again) We commanded them: 'Transgress not in the matter of the Sabbath.' And we took from them a solemn Covenant." Sura 4.154 An-Nisa.

## Allah's Messenger a Hypocrite?

That subheading above asks a question for which most of you surely already know the answer: Of course not! If the ancient desert prophet (Musa) was told to say to the people, "Transgress not in the matter of the Sabbath," then would he not be considered a hypocrite if he did not abide by the Sabbath himself? In other words, the prophet surely would not ask people to abide by one of Allah's Laws if he himself did not abide by the same law! That reasoning is proof enough that the desert prophet also must have obeyed the fourth commandment

That commandment instructs us to rest upon the seventh day of the week in honor of Allah. It serves to remind us that Allah created all things in six days. In the clearest words of the Honored Qur'an, it is written that the Sabbath is not to be transgressed. In fact, in the following sura a "curse" was pronounced by Allah upon those who were "Sabbath breakers:" "O ye People of the Book! believe in what We have (now) revealed, confirming what was (already) with you, before We change the face and fame of some (of you) beyond all recognition, and turn them hindwards, or curse them as We cursed the Sabbath-breakers, for the decision of Allah must be carried out." Sura 4.47 An-Nisa.

## EXAMPLE OF ISA AL-MASIH

Perhaps from One who was closest to Allah, we can learn the truth about the Sabbath—that is, whether it is still in effect today! We have the example of Isa al-Masih, who was sent down from Allah, who was the Word from Allah.

To Isa al-Masih was given the Injeel. Sura 3.45 tells us that the Word from Allah came through Isa al-Masih, who was held in Honor in heaven.

"Behold! the angels said: "O Mary! Allah giveth thee glad tidings of **a Word from Him: his name will be Christ Jesus, the son of Mary**, held in honour in this world and the Hereafter and of (the company of) those nearest to Allah;" Sura 3.45 Aal-E-Imran

From the lips of Him Who was sent down, we learn that Isa on the Sabbath day taught those who had gathered together in the synagogue. Injeel Mark 1:21 says, "And they went into Capernaum; and straightway **on the sabbath day** he [Isa al-Masih] entered into the synagogue, and taught."

Some argue that the Sabbath was made only for the Jews, but the Word from Allah reveals the truth of the matter: Injeel Mark 2:27 says, "And he said unto them, The sabbath was made **for man**, and not man for the Sabbath."

Some prefer to twist or misinterpret that quoted verse above to read or mean "Jew" instead of "man." But there it is in plain language:

Isa al-Masih, who was sent down from Allah and who was among those nearest to Allah, and held in honor (Sura 3.45), has indeed told us that **"the Sabbath was made for man."** (That word "man" means all of mankind.) Besides, it was at Creation that the first Sabbath was kept by Allah Himself—long before there was a Jew. Yet how many of the believers accept and honor this message from Allah? Do men not find their own business more important than the business of Allah-- even on His Holy Day, the seventh of the week (Saturday), which is called "Al-Sabt"?

Many treat the Holy Books like shoppers who go to a store and select only some things, and refuse the rest. Is this not what has happened in our world today? Where is the earnest seeker for truth? Who among men place the affairs of Allah foremost, and seek with all their hearts to know His will? Injeel Luke 4:4 reads, "Man does not live by bread alone but by <u>every word</u> of God [Allah]." Clearly, it is not left to man to "pick and choose."

### DOES ALLAH CHANGE?

We have the record that upon the heights of Mount Sinai, the Words of the Ten Commandments not only were written upon stone by the finger of Allah, but also **the Words** were spoken by Allah Himself! Taurat Deuteronomy 5:22 tells us, "These words the LORD [Allah] **spake** unto all your assembly in the mount [Sinai] out of the midst of the fire, of the cloud, and of the thick darkness, **with a great voice**: and he added no more. **And he wrote** them in two tables of stone, and delivered them unto me [Moses]."

Notice that no one can alter the words from Allah.

"…there is none that can **alter the words (and decrees) of Allah**…." Sura 6.34 Al-Anaam

Moses was a man given a special mission from Allah direct, not through an angel.

"(Allah) said: "O Moses! I have chosen thee above (other) men, **by the mission I (have given thee) and the words I (have spoken to thee)**: take then the (revelation) which I give thee, and be of those who give thanks." Sura 7.144 Al-Araf

It is through the Words from Allah that truth is established here upon earth. "And **Allah by His words doth prove and establish His truth**, however much the sinners may hate it!" Sura 10.82 Yunus

Allah has established truth and given directions for mankind in revealing to us His Words. We are always safe in following the Words given us by Allah.

Exodus 20:1 reads, "And God [Allah] **spake** all these words, saying...." Thus Allah not only wrote the Words, but He also spoke the Words, so that we would make no mistake. Below is the Sabbath Law, quoted just as Allah spoke it at Mt. Sinai:

Taurat Exodus 20:8-11: "Remember the sabbath day, to keep it holy. Six days shalt thou labour, and do all thy work: But the seventh day is the sabbath of the LORD thy God: in it thou shalt not do any work, thou, nor thy son, nor thy daughter, thy manservant, nor thy maidservant, nor thy cattle, nor thy stranger that is within thy gates: For in six days the LORD made heaven and earth, the sea, and all that in them is, and rested the seventh day: wherefore the LORD **blessed** the sabbath day, and **hallowed** it." Please notice, dear reader, that Allah "blessed" the day and "hallowed it" (made it sacred).

Will Allah alter or change the Laws which have gone out of His mouth? To this we simply answer by the Word from Allah. Zabur Psalms 89:34 states, "My covenant will I not break, nor alter the thing that is gone out of my lips."

## What God Blesses is Blest Forever!

Injeel I Chronicles 17:27 states, "Now therefore let it please thee to bless the house of thy servant, that it may be before thee for ever: **for thou blessest, O LORD, and it shall be blessed for ever.**" Now it is our choice whether we will follow and render full submission to Allah's will, or whether we will be like the unbelievers who disregard His will. That you may be found among the faithful is our wish for you, dear reader. Remember, a Muslim is one who is submitted to Allah's Word without question. Would this not include observing the Sabbath day of rest? God has promised: "...Them that honour me I will honour...." I Samuel 2:30.

The Sabbath, which each week commemorates the creation of God, will be kept in eternity. The ancient prophet Isaiah foretells, "...From one Sabbath to another shall all flesh come to worship before me, saith the Lord." Taurat Isaiah 66:23.

It is important to understand the will of Allah here and now, and to follow His counsel here, in preparation for following Him in the hereafter. Join in that Sabbath rest, and you will be abundantly blessed.

# "Allah's Book"

### Is the Bible the Word of Allah?

Can the Bible be trusted? Is it the Word from Allah? These are important questions that we are often asked today by many people. Muslims around the world are asking, "Are the Bible Scriptures truly sent from Allah? How can we know? Is there any proof?"

Before we search for answers, I invite the reader to send a prayer *(du'a)* to Allah, for Allah knows best. He will provide the answers for which sincere people the world over are asking. Allah will always answer important questions that are motivated by an earnest desire to know truth.

### What Does the Honored Qur'an Say?

Sometimes we may find an answer to a question by asking another question. In this case, we would ask, "'How does the Honored Qur'an regard the Holy Books of the Bible Scriptures? What does It say about the Taurat and the Injeel (the Bible Scriptures)?" For the answer, we invite the reader to turn to the Honored Qur'an and find the following passages:

"And remember **We gave Moses the Scripture** and the Criterion (between right and wrong): There was a chance for you to be guided aright." Sura 2.53 Al-Baqara.

"It is He Who sent down to thee (step by step), in truth, the Book, confirming what went before it; and **He sent down the Law (of Moses)** [Taurat] **and the Gospel (of Jesus)**[Injeel] before this, **as a guide to mankind**, and He sent down **the Criterion** (of judgment between right and wrong)." Sura 3.3 Aal-E-Imran.

The Honored Qur'an mentions only one "Criterion" for the Judgment, and that is the Holy Scriptures, the Taurat. Remember that if no law was violated, then there would be no need for the Judgment! But mankind has sinned and violated repeatedly Allah's Holy and Just laws.

In the Taurat we find the basis for the judgment, called the Ten Commandments. This is the foundation of the government of Heaven. It is the Holy and Just Law of Allah. It is found recorded in the Taurat in Exodus chapter 20:1-17.

"In the past We granted to Moses and Aaron **the Criterion** (for judgment) [Taurat], and a **Light** and a **Message** for those who would do right." Sura 21.48 Al-Anbiya.

Here the Honored Qur'an reveals that the Taurat is "a Light and a Message for those who would do right." How dare anyone disregard this admonition? Would it not be a fearful thing to suggest that the Taurat is not Allah's Word? How would anyone stand in the great Judgment with thinking that is contrary to what is written here?

"If thou wert in doubt as to what We have revealed unto thee, then ask those who have been reading the Book [the Holy Books of the Bible Scriptures] from before thee: the Truth hath indeed come to thee from thy Lord: so be in no wise of those in doubt." Sura 10.94 Yunus.

In this passage the Honored Qur'an instructs the desert prophet to "ask" those who have been reading the Book (Bible Scriptures) "from before thee." Why does the Honored Qur'an, which tradition tells us came from Allah, direct our attention to those who honor the Bible?

"It was We who revealed the Law (to Moses): therein was **guidance** and **light**. By its standard have been judged the Jews, by the Prophets who bowed (as in Islam) to Allah's will, by the rabbis and the Doctors of Law: **for to them was entrusted the protection of Allah's Book**, and they were witnesses thereto: therefore fear not men, but fear Me, and sell not My Signs for a miserable price. If any do fail to judge by (the light of) what Allah hath revealed, they are (no better than) Unbelievers." Sura 5.44 Al-Maeda.

These are just some of the many ayats listed in the Honored Qur'an which testify that the Taurat, Zabur, and the Injeel were sent down from Allah and are for all people (mankind). In the ayat we just read, the Tauratis called "Allah's Book."

## Words of the Prophets

All the prophets that were called of Allah were bound by the same laws that were given by the former prophets. "And the spirits of the prophets are subject to the prophets." 1 Corinthians 14:32. Throughout human history, God has generally used one means of communication with man. He has spoken to us through the prophetic gift given to the prophets of old:

"…Now to him who is able to establish you by my gospel and the proclamation of Jesus Christ, according to the revelation of the mystery hidden for long ages past, but **now revealed and made known through the prophetic writings by the command of the eternal God,** so that all nations might believe and obey him...." Romans 16:25-26 NIV.

"Beloved, ...remember the words having been spoken before by the holy prophets...." 2 Peter 3:1-2.

## Altered or Corrupted?

Some would be quick to argue that the Bible has been altered or corrupted, so that it no longer can be trusted. In response to that charge, we ask a simple question: If the Bible had been altered before the time of Mohammed (PBUH) to the point that it could no longer be trusted, then why was the desert prophet pointed to it as a trustworthy source of divine revelation? Would Allah direct the desert prophet to a false or corrupted book?

"And remember Allah took a Covenant from the People of the Book, **to make it** [the Book] **known and clear to mankind**, and not to hide it; but they threw it away behind their backs, and purchased with it some miserable gain! And vile was the bargain they made!" Sura 3.187 Aal-E-Imran.

Here's another question: If the Bible Scriptures have been corrupted since the time of the desert prophet, then where are the manuscripts which are true, to prove the supposedly false ones false? No one has been able to show such manuscripts, because there are none. The Bible Scriptures that were available in the time of Mohammed (PBUH) are the same ones which are still available today. Remember, Allah is well able to keep His Words from being corrupted, so that man today may know Allah's will.

"...no change can there be in the words of Allah..." Sura 10.64 Yunus

Besides all this, who would be able to undertake the task of finding all the Bible manuscripts, to bring them together to alter and falsify them? Think seriously about this, dear reader!

The counsel in the Injeel still stands true today. Injeel Luke 4:4 says, "And Jesus [Isa al-Masih] answered him, saying, It is written, That man shall not live by bread alone, but <u>by every word of God</u> [Allah]."

Doubt not; we can safely trust His Word.

## The Value of the Word

I have a personal testimony of what Allah's Word, the Bible, has done for me. Studying this Book changed my life. I've learned that in the pages of the Bible is a power, an energy, that is given to those who take the time to become familiar with its contents. The changes in our lives become very apparent. He who submits to the Words of Allah will find that he acquires new tastes, new thoughts, new feelings, and new motives directing his life. All of this happened to me, and will happen to you when you submit to Allah and to His Word sent down.

Injeel John 6:63: "It is the spirit that quickeneth; the flesh profiteth nothing: **the words** that I speak unto you, they are **spirit**, and they are **life**." Here Isa al-Masih said plainly that His words are "spirit" and "life." They are the "way" to everlasting "life."

Wise men from the East in ancient times saw the value of Allah's Word. Ayub or Job 22:22 counsels us today: "Receive, I pray thee, the law from his mouth, and **lay up his words in thine heart**."

Job (Ayub), the ancient prophet of Allah from long ago, also tells us of his desire and respect for the Word of Allah: "…Neither have I gone back from the commandment of his lips; I have **esteemed the words of his mouth more than my necessary food**." Taurat Job 23:12.

## Allah is Well Able to Keep His Word Undefiled.

Dear friends, we need not fear that Allah's Word has been corrupted. Is Allah not infinite in power? Can He not be trusted to keep His Word complete for us today? After all, it is Allah who sustains all of nature; it is He who provides for all the multitudes of people on earth. It is Allah who keeps galaxies in orbit and keeps unnumbered millions of stars swirling in outer space, to keep them from crashing into each other. How simple a matter for Him to also keep intact His Word sent down! Indeed, it is an "easy" thing for Allah (Sura 35.11 Fatir). "The word of thy Lord doth find its fulfilment in truth and in justice: **None can change His words:** for He is the one Who heareth and knoweth all." Sura 6.115 Al-Anaam.

## Traditions Contrary to Allah's Word

Unfortunately, many have made the Word of Allah of none effect through human teachings called "traditions" that have been handed down without any foundation in the Holy Books. All too many listen to scholars who teach about the Taurat and Injeel contrary to what has been revealed about them in the Honored Qur'an. We need to be very careful lest these words of warning apply to us: "...Making the word of God (Allah) of none effect through your **tradition**...." Injeel Mark 7:13.

That specific warning from Isa al-Masih applies to us today as much as to those of that day. May we heed it, and be spared the consequences of not heeding. How dreadful the day, when we should find that we have made of none effect the Words of Allah!

Friends, now more than ever, it is time to give special attention to the Word sent down to us in the Taurat and Injeel. Daily we need to let that Word sink deeply into our souls. May Allah change your life so that you, too, can testify that these are indeed the Words from Allah. These words will prepare us to face the future unafraid, and to stand through the Judgment!

Injeel 2 Timothy 3:16-17 reads, "All scripture is given by inspiration of God [Allah], and is profitable for doctrine, for reproof, for correction, for instruction in righteousness: That the man of God [Allah] may be perfect, throughly furnished unto all good works."

"The grass withers, the flower fades; but the Word of our God shall stand forever." Taurat Isaiah 40:8.

The promise of Allah is that His words will stand the test of time and are forever. In fact, the Word of Allah, as is recorded in the Taurat, Zabur, and the Injeel, is the test or standard as to whether or not any messenger teaches truth. Taurat Isaiah 8:20 teaches, "To the Law and to the Testimony: if they speak not according to this word, it is because there is no light in them."

"believe in Allah...and His words..." 7.158 Al-Araf.

# "Eschew all sin..."

May the peace of Allah be upon you, and may He guide your life. Our topic in this study is the Law of Allah, the "Sharia of Allah" (the Ten Commandments). Many are saying that the Law of Allah, as written in the Ten Commandments, is no longer binding upon mankind today. Some, even among those who claim to be believers, even go so far as to say that Allah has no law-- that He has abolished it! Can humans really live without laws?

## A NATION WITHOUT LAWS

Can we imagine a nation, let's say, without traffic laws? Or a nation dismissing all police officers from their law enforcement duties? Even worse, just suppose that a nation chooses to do away with all law. Each man would become free to do whatever he wishes! Would this not cause extreme chaos? Nothing and no one would be safe! Life would turn into a massive scene of horror. Thieves would take that which is another's without respect for property or life. Surely such an existence would be most undesirable—even unthinkable. Yet, for some reason, some people think that the Ten Commandment Law of Allah is no longer binding!

Imagine telling someone, "Allah doesn't mind if I have other gods." How can that even be believed? Or this: "Allah doesn't mind if I steal my neighbor's belongings or lie to him or even take his wife from him." A society based on those standards would surely come quickly to a tragic end.

Friends, has it ever dawned upon mankind that the reason this world is in such difficulty is that far too many have set aside the Law (*Sharia* of Allah), the Ten Commandments of Allah, as found in the Taurat?

Sura 2.93 Al-Baqarat reminds us of the Law given:"And remember We took your Covenant and We raised above you (the towering height) of Mount (Sinai): (Saying): 'Hold firmly to what We have given you, and hearken (to the Law)....'" Would the Honored Qur'an tell its readers to "hold firmly to what was given you and hearken to the Law" (of Ten Commandments) and then later say it is no longer binding?

Would Allah not offer us knowledge of His guidance and Law in divine compassion, knowing what our end would be without His law?

Is it not time to be honest with ourselves, to accept what the Honored Qur'an says in reference to the Law of Allah? In irrefutable clarity, it instructs us to eschew (avoid) all sin. "Eschew **all sin**, open or secret: those who earn sin will get due recompense for their 'earnings.'" Sura 6.120 Al-Anaam.

## Lessons from Job (Ayub)

Long ago, ancient Arabs from the East were well aware of what it means to "eschew sin." These God-fearing men were recognized in the Taurat (Holy Books). The Book of Job (Ayub) 1:1, for example, speaks of a man named Job an Arab: "There was a man in the land of Uz, whose name was Job; and that man was perfect and upright, and one that feared God [Allah], and **eschewed evil** [sin]." He was noted by Allah as being the "greatest [most prosperous] of all men of the east." Job 1:3. How would this great man have known what evil (sin) is, if he was not instructed in the Law of Allah? Even today, how are we to know what sin is, unless we look at the Law of Allah? Moreover, what is sin? How is it defined, so that we understand what is being discussed here?

The Holy Injeel defines exactly what sin is. Persons lead by the Spirit of Allah, to them was revealed the sacred words. Injeel 1 John 3:4 states, "Whosoever committeth sin transgresseth also the law: for **sin is the transgression of the law.**" It is obvious, therefore, that a knowledge of Allah and His Law is necessary for us to even understand what sin is. And it is also vital to know what sin is, since it is mentioned well over 70 times in the Qur'an and well over 700 times in the Bible. We need to know that sin—transgression of Allah's Law-- is to be "feared." Sura 4.25 An-Nisa.

On the other hand, obedience to the Law brings peace. This Law, the Ten Commandments, was given for man's happiness. If men everywhere obeyed, revered, and respected this Law, how happy and peaceful our world would be. Allah would be honored supremely; everyone's possessions would be respected; each life would be sacredly guarded. Life on this planet today would be far different, if all held in high regard the Ten Commandments of Allah.

## Allah's Special Ten

In the event the reader is unaware of the Ten Commandments of Allah given to humanity from heaven, we want to include them in this study. We already know that the Law was given long before the time of Moses, for the Taurat says that Ibrahim, the *"khalil* of Allah," obeyed Allah's Laws. The Honored Qur'an calls Ibrahim the "Imam to the nations." Sura 2.124 Al-Baqara. He is an example of someone following God's Laws. Taurat Genesis 26:5 states: "Because that Abraham obeyed my voice, and kept my charge, **my commandments**, my statutes, and **my laws**...." Here we see one from ancient times who was faithful to Allah, one who kept and respected Allah's Laws. Should we not follow the example of Ibrahim, who is among the *Hanif*?

Centuries later, because mankind had forgotten, Allah repeated the Law to Moses upon the towering heights of Mount Sinai. To impress upon the mind of the people the importance and permanence of His Law, Allah Himself spoke the words and Himself wrote them upon tables (tablets) of stone. He would not commit to man this most important task. It was His own handwriting that would be seen.

Below is a list of Allah's Ten Commandments as recorded in Taurat Exodus 20:1-17: "And God spake all these words, saying, I am the LORD thy God, which have brought thee out of the land of Egypt, out of the house of bondage.

1. "Thou shalt have no other gods before me.
2. "Thou shalt not make unto thee any graven image, or any likeness of any thing that is in heaven above, or that is in the earth beneath, or that is in the water under the earth: Thou shalt not bow down thyself to them, nor serve them: for I the LORD thy God am a jealous God, visiting the iniquity of the fathers upon the children unto the third and fourth generation of them that hate me; And shewing mercy unto thousands of them that love me, and keep my commandments.
3. "Thou shalt not take the name of the LORD thy God in vain; for the LORD will not hold him guiltless that taketh his name in vain.
4. "Remember the sabbath day, to keep it holy. Six days shalt thou labour, and do all thy work: But the seventh day is the sabbath of the LORD thy God: in it thou shalt not do any work, thou, nor thy son, nor thy daughter, thy manservant, nor thy

maidservant, nor thy cattle, nor thy stranger that is within thy gates: For in six days the LORD made heaven and earth, the sea, and all that in them is, and rested the seventh day: wherefore the LORD blessed the sabbath day, and hallowed it.

5. "Honour thy father and thy mother: that thy days may be long upon the land which the LORD thy God giveth thee.
6. "Thou shalt not kill.
7. "Thou shalt not commit adultery.
8. "Thou shalt not steal.
9. "Thou shalt not bear false witness against thy neighbour.
10. "Thou shalt not covet thy neighbour's house, thou shalt not covet thy neighbour's wife, nor his manservant, nor his maidservant, nor his ox, nor his ass, nor any thing that is thy neighbour's."

Thus ends the ten brief laws of Allah from Taurat Exodus 20. They are also listed in Taurat Deuteronomy 5:6-21 and in various other places throughout both the Injeel and the Qur'an.

## FORGIVENESS FROM ALLAH

This concern may be frequently on our heart and minds: "What if a man sins? Is there forgiveness with Allah?" The answer is unreservedly "Yes." If any man sins and then asks for forgiveness, Allah has promised to forgive. But we must ask, sincere in our repentance, and also be willing to turn from (forsake) the evil. Allah will give us repentance; He will give us a sorrowful heart to the point where we no longer will want to be involved with sin. Notice the words in the Injeel, in Acts 5:31: "Him [Isa al-Masih] hath God exalted with his right hand to be a Prince and a Saviour [al-fida], for to give repentance … and forgiveness of sins." It is through Isa al-Masih, whom Allah sent down, that He gives us repentance and forgiveness of sins. Isa became the ransom for sin on behalf of the human race. He is the great gift of Allah! May we take hold of that gift and not reject what was sent down to us! We must not miss this point! It is through Isa al-Masih that we are forgiven! Receive Him!

## Isa al-Masih Gives Power

We again turn to that ancient prophet, the one from the East whom the record says "eschewed [turned from] evil." Job 1:1 (Taurat). How was Job (Ayub) able to do that? How can anyone turn from evil? Does man in himself have the power to do that? Can a man in his own strength fight effectively against Iblis (Satan), the originator and perpetuator of sin? The Taurat records the following in Jeremiah 17:5 NLT: "This is what the LORD says: 'Cursed are those who put their trust in mere humans, **who rely on human strength** and turn their hearts away from the LORD.'"

With man there is only failure. There is no hope in trusting in ourselves or in another man to recover us from our fallen condition. We can have hope only as we look to Allah and to Him Who was sent down as our helper, Isa al-Masih! Injeel John 1:12 states, "But as many as received him [Isa al-Masih], to them gave he **power** to become the sons of God, even to them that believe on his name."

Isn't that what we all need? Power to resist evil? Power over our sinful habits? Power to do right?Listen, dear friend of Allah. It is through Isa al-Masih that we receive this power from Allah. Injeel 1 John 1:9 says, "If we confess our sins, he [Isa al-Masih] is faithful and just to forgive us our sins, and to cleanse us from all unrighteousness."

"And O my people! Ask forgiveness of your Lord, and turn to Him (in repentance): He will send you the skies pouring abundant rain, and add strength to your strength: so **turn ye not back in sin!**" Sura 11.52 Hud.

# Allah's Guide to Health

## ALLAH'S WAY TO HEALTH

Beloved friends of Allah, this topic of discussion you will find very interesting and beneficial. This is vital information which affects the lives of every living soul on earth: **health**! Someone has said that health is not everything, but without it, everything is nothing! You may be the richest man, but if you have lost your health, even if you had gold as plentiful as sand, you could not enjoy life! Our aim, therefore, should be to find out how to retain or regain our God-given health and be a blessing to humanity!

Allah is most compassionate and kind to the family of man. His care for us is far greater than the care of our earthly parents for us. As our parents gave us counsel in our childhoods, even so will Allah give us careful instruction, that we may preserve or restore our bodies' health. Following His instructions will also protect our minds from the sinful pollutions of this world!

The ancient Zabur given to the prophet Daud, contains a promise from Allah which all should know. Zabur Psalm 67:2: "That thy way may be known upon earth, **thy saving health among all nations**." It is to be no secret that Allah wishes for all nations to experience health! He wants the saving health message to be brought to all. Allah wishes only the best health for all His human creations. He has made known to the sons of men how to have the best health possible while we are here on planet earth. But will we pay attention to this sacred counsel?

## ALCOHOL AND GAMBLING

We need to be much in prayer (*du'a*) concerning what constitutes "saving health." To enjoy health, we must heed the counsel sent down to us. Notice the words recorded in the Honored Qur'an that have to do with retaining health: "They ask thee concerning wine and gambling. Say: 'In them is great sin, and some profit, for men; but the sin is greater than the profit....'" Sura 2.219 Al-Baqara.

Allah knows both the health-destroying effects of wine (alcohol) as well as the soul-destroying effects of gambling. He informs us of these dangers, so that we can be educated to avoid them. Notice the words of the ancient prophet Solomon in Proverbs.

"It is not for kings, O Lemuel,[Solomon] it is not for kings to drink wine; nor for princes strong drink: Lest they drink, and forget the law, and pervert the judgment of any of the afflicted." Proverbs 31:4-5

The prophet Isaiah gave the same counsel. Taurat Isaiah 5:11 says, "Woe unto them that rise up early in the morning, that they may follow strong drink; that continue until night, till wine inflame them!"

We can clearly see that alcoholic beverages are forbidden (*haram*) to the followers of Allah. If we wish to be among the *Mutaqeen* (the Righteous), we will avoid all use of alcohol for drink.

## Allah's "Saving Health"

Are there other items which many use as food which are clearly forbidden by Allah? Yes! Why would not Allah give us clear instruction as to what is *halal* (lawful or clean) and what is *haram* (unlawful or unclean)? He is the Creator of our bodies and minds, so surely Allah would not leave us ignorant regarding how to maintain the bodies He has given us in the best condition. He wants us to enjoy good health, long life.

Everyone who has ever purchased an automobile and wishes to make it function well for many years will take time to study the owner's manual provided by the manufacturer. How much more important are our bodies? Perhaps we can readily purchase new auto parts to replace malfunctioning ones, but this is not so easy with our bodies! To say it another way, we would not put dirty fuel into our cars, neither should we place into our body, but only that which is pure and healthful. Indeed, the bodies given to us by Allah were made for service that would bring us health, and glory and honor to Him. Should it not be very important to learn what constitutes "saving health"?

People will devote years to gaining an education to become skillful in a trade or occupation. They will spend tens of thousands of dollars to become a doctor, lawyer, pharmacist, etc., but they are often very uneducated as to how to preserve their own health! Are there harmful foods, drink, and eating habits that they—and we—are unaware of?

## The *Halal* and *Haram*

In the Taurat given to Musa, Allah has carefully outlined for us the clean and unclean animals. The unclean (*haram*) animals were not to be used as food. Leviticus Chapter 11 clearly outlines both the clean and unclean animals. Leviticus 11:3: "Whatsoever parteth the hoof, and is clovenfooted, and cheweth the cud, among the beasts, that shall ye eat." A "cloven-footed" animal has a split hoof, such as have cattle, deer, goats, sheep, etc. Those animals also "chew the cud." Therefore, they were considered by Allah to be animals which are clean for food.

In Taurat Leviticus 11 are named the animals which are unclean (*haram*). The first one on the list is the **camel**, and Allah gives us the reason. Leviticus 11:4 reads, "Nevertheless these shall ye not eat of them that chew the cud, or of them that divide the hoof: as the camel, **because he cheweth the cud, but divideth not the hoof; he is unclean [*haram*] unto you**." In fact, although the camel chews the cud, it has no hoof; it has toes, instead. Therefore, the camel is considered unclean (*haram*) for food. The camel was created as a beast to carry the burdens of man, but not for food.

Leviticus 11 continues the list of the unclean ((*haram*): The coney (rock badger or hyrax), the rabbit, the swine (hogs or pigs), even all creeping things such as the mouse, rat, lizard, snake-- except those like the locust and grasshopper. Unclean animals such as camels, horses, donkeys, etc., were made as beasts of burden, to carry man and transport his goods, but were never meant for food. The swine is among the most unclean! Since the swine's nature has not changed since this counsel in Leviticus was recorded, swine (pigs) are still unclean for food.

The counsel in the Qur'an is likewise to totally avoid the use of swine's flesh…

"Forbidden to you (for food) are: dead meat, blood, the flesh of swine…that which hath been killed by strangling, or by a violent blow, or by a headlong fall, or by being gored to death; that which hath been (partly) eaten by a wild animal; unless ye are able to slaughter it (in due form)…" Sura 5.3 Al-Maeda

Leviticus 11:9-25 lists the sea creatures and the fowl that Allah considers safe (*halal*) and those that are unclean (*haram*) for food. Clean (*halal*) fish are those having **both fins and scales**. Sea creatures without both fins and scales, such as eels, shrimp, lobster, clams, oysters, squids, octopus, and all shell fish, are considered unclean and are forbidden as food. Most of these forbidden creatures are the water's cleaning agents; they are the bottom- feeders and scavengers of the sea.

Among the fowl, birds of prey such as eagles, ospreys, hawks, owls, etc., are considered unclean (*haram*). Other forbidden fowl are scavenger birds such as ravens, buzzards, crows, vultures, etc.

Remember the "saving health" of Allah is for all nations. He does not pick one particular group of people as the only ones to enjoy good health. He wishes only the best for us; therefore, He wants all people in all nations to enjoy health. Allah wishes all to be among the *Mutaqeen*. Therefore, He is making known His saving health among all nations. Dear reader, Allah has your best interest in mind.

## SAVING HEALTH FOR THE *MUTAQEEN*

As we are now living in the last days of earth's history, it is even more important that we pay close attention to our health. Though the reason is very simple, it is critical that you understand it. Our health is of primary importance because it is only through our minds that Allah can communicate with us. He does so through the Holy Spirit (*Ruh Allah*) and through His written Word. If our bodies are taking in unclean or otherwise unhealthy foods, the result is only unclean, unhealthy blood. This blood circulates throughout the body, even into the brain cells. If impurities enter those cells via the blood—if our minds become dulled and disordered by eating foods that are forbidden by Allah— then we cannot receive or understand Allah's messages to us. That is a most serious matter! Those messages can make the difference between our receiving eternal life and eternal death! Therefore, as Allah reveals His wishes to us regarding proper food to eat and harmful food to refuse, we would be most wise to submit to His wisdom and will. Our Creator knows best.

## ALLAH'S DIET FOR MANKIND

If it is your desire to obtain **the best health**, it is wise to stop consuming animal flesh (meat), even from among the clean animals. Why? Because our Creator, our bodies' Designer, intended for us to have a better diet, for optimal health! In the original Garden of Eden home, the first human couple did not use flesh (meat) as food. Only fruits, grains, nuts and seeds were eaten. In Taurat Genesis 1:29, we read Allah's specific dietary wisdom: "And God said, Behold, I have given you **every herb bearing seed** [grains and seeds], which is upon the face of all the earth, and **every tree, in the which is the fruit of a tree yielding seed** [fruits, nuts, seeds]; **to you it shall be for meat** [food]."

After man sinned, Allah added root and other vegetables—"herbs of the field"—to the human diet. Genesis 3:18 reads, "…**Thou shalt eat the herb of the field."**

It was not until after the earth had been destroyed by the Flood that animal flesh was permitted for food. Since it would take years for trees to bear fruit and nuts again, that additional food source was granted—but only from the clean animals. However, we have no grounds to conclude that the emergency diet permitted by Allah is now the best diet for mankind. In fact, to obtain the best health—"saving health"—it is far better to entirely abstain from the use of flesh for food, and to return to the ideal diet of Eden. Indeed, all manner of weaknesses and disease comes from eating animal flesh. The Taurat reveals that human lifespans became much shorter after the Flood.

However, if we still choose to use animal flesh (meat) for food, it remains our duty "to make a difference between the unclean and clean.…" Taurat Leviticus 11:47. It is our solemn obligation to please Allah and submit to His way. All who strive to be among the *Hanif* and be listed among the *Mutaqeen* will gladly yield to Allah's will.

God wishes you to be healthy! "Beloved, I wish above all things that thou mayest prosper and be in health, even as thy soul prospereth." Injeel 3 John 1:2. Dear reader, is that your choice today? This is our only wish for all. May the Eternal Peace of Allah rest with you this day!

For a complete guide to Saving Health to those living in these last days, the reader is directed to write to the author to obtain the book entitled: *Allah's Healing Way*

# Allah Revealed!

Dear reader, we have often dwelt upon the Divine greatness of Allah. It is only true and proper to speak of His unlimited creative power, His universal strength, His presence everywhere simultaneously, His awareness of all things at all times, His sustaining the universe. But could it be there is a dimension of Allah we may have overlooked?

In other words, does Allah have human characteristics? Could there be human features to His Divine aspect? According to the Honored Qur'an and the Holy Books (Bible Scriptures), this appears to be true. But does this detract from Him being Divine? May Allah bless you as you seek Him in reverent prayer (*du'a*) for guidance, direction, and wisdom.

Consider the following ayat: "…Whoever rejects evil and believes in Allah hath grasped **the most trustworthy hand-hold, that never breaks. And Allah heareth and knoweth all things.**" Sura 2.256 Al-Baqara.

Allah has hands, it says. How else could we take hold of the most trustworthy **hand-hold**?

Also notice the words in the Taurat from one of the wisest men of ancient times, a prophet of the East. Job (Ayub) 12:9-10 says, "Who knoweth not in all these that **the hand** of the LORD [Allah] hath wrought this? In whose hand is the soul of every living thing, and the breath of all mankind." Thus according to both the Honored Qur'an and the Holy Books, Allah has hands! Isn't that amazing? We can trust our lives safely into His Hands.

Allah also has ears! "Allah heareth…." Sura 2.256 Al-Baqara. How else could He hear?

This same fact is brought out in the Holy Books, in the Zabur given by Allah to Daud. Psalms 18:6: "In my distress I called upon the LORD [Allah], and cried unto my God: he heard my voice out of his temple, and my cry came before him, even into his **ears**."

Allah, the most compassionate and merciful, has ears that are open unto your cry! Are these not portraying a "human side" of Allah? It gives us confidence to come to Him as we would approach a close friend of ours.

Allah has eyes, also, for He told Noah to "construct an ark under our eyes." Sura 11.37. The Zabur in the Holy Books agree, this time from Psalms 34:15: "The eyes of the LORD [Allah] are upon the righteous, and his ears are open unto their cry."

Solomon, among the wisest of men who ever lived, wrote in Proverbs 15:3: "The **eyes of the LORD** [Allah] are in every place, beholding the evil and the good."

In continuing our study about Allah's features, we learn from the sacred record that Allah has a nose.

"...I [Allah] despise your feast days, and **I [Allah] will not smell** in your solemn assemblies...." Amos 5:21-22. Amos, one of the ancient prophets, recorded those words of Allah. In Amos' time, God's people had departed from Him. Although they still attended the feast days and came together to worship God, their day-to-day lives told a different story— one of forgetting God and His holy Law. Therefore, God (Allah) would not accept their worship or feast days.

Not only does God smell, but He also laughs—particularly at the foolishness of the wicked, whose plans He will ultimately defeat. Zabur Psalms 2:2-4 says, "The kings of the earth set themselves, and the rulers take counsel together, against the LORD, and against his anointed.... He that sitteth in the heavens shall laugh: the Lord shall have them in derision."

## Allah's Human Form?

Has anyone from among the human family seen a human form of Allah? Yes! Exodus 24:9-11 states, "Then went up Moses, and Aaron, Nadab, and Abihu, and seventy of the elders of Israel: And **they saw the God** of Israel: and there was under his **feet** as it were a paved work of a sapphire stone.... **They saw God**...." They saw Him in His human form, for they saw that He had feet.

Then there is Jacob's experience of seeing God. Genesis 32:30 tells us, "And Jacob called the name of the place Peniel: **for I have seen God face to face**, and my life is preserved." Jacob saw the face of Allah!

Did Allah come down to someone else, too --close enough to be seen in His human form? Yes. The first recorded person to see Allah was Hagar, the mother of the Children of the East, the origin of the Arab people. She had fled in distress from the camp of Ibrahim into the desert, when she was being treated harshly. She was feeling unloved and forsaken, until Someone cared enough to come near to her. Listen to her testimony from Taurat Genesis 16:13 TNIV: "She gave this name to the LORD who spoke to her: 'You are the God who sees me,' for she said, **'I have now seen the One who sees me.'"**

Moses also saw Allah. Exodus 3:6 records their meeting: "Moreover he said, I am the God of thy father, the God of Abraham, the God of Isaac, and the God of Jacob. And Moses hid his face; for he was afraid to look upon God."

Do these words from both the Honored Qur'an and the Holy Books (Bible) firmly establish that God at times has revealed Himself to humans in human form? Dear reader, there are so many verses from the Holy Books that we cannot be mistaken.

As we continue, we read that Allah also has arms. Again the prophet Job (Ayub) speaks to us. Taurat Job 40:9 says, "Hast thou an **arm** like God? or canst thou thunder with a **voice** like him?"

Thus God has a mouth and from it, His voice is heard. "God's voice is glorious in the thunder. We can't even imagine the greatness of His power." Job 37:5 NLT. "We have heard the voice of the living God. We've heard him speaking out of the fire. Has any other human being ever heard him speak like that and stayed alive?" Taurat Deuteronomy 5:26.

The verses just quoted mention that, at times, Allah speaks to mankind in a voice. The Holy Qur'an tells us: "Allah **speaketh** the truth." Sura 3.95 Aal-E-Imran. How could the truth be spoken and how could Allah's voice be heard, if He did not have a mouth?

The Qur'an reveals that the ancient prophet Moses not only heard Allah's voice, but he also saw a form.

"But when he came to the (Fire), a voice was heard from the right bank of the valley, from a tree in hallowed ground: 'O Moses! Verily **I am Allah**, the Lord of the Worlds....'" Sura 28.30 Al-Oasas. What Moses saw as he listened was a burning tree that the fire did not consume, from which came Allah's voice. To converse with Moses, Allah had taken on the form of a tree on fire. Imagine that! What an awesome privilege He gave to Moses. It is apparent that Allah has no limitations as we humans have.

## Whom Did the Prophet Daniel See?

The Taurat tells us that the ancient prophet Daniel was taken off in vision. In that vision, Daniel saw an unusual person, whom he called a "man," and whom he described: "Then I lifted up mine eyes, and looked, and behold a certain man clothed in linen, whose loins [waist] were girded [wrapped] with fine gold of Uphaz: His body also was like the beryl, and his face as the appearance of lightning, and his eyes as lamps of fire, and his arms and his feet like in colour to polished brass, and the voice of his words like the voice of a multitude." Taurat Daniel 10:5-6.

Notice the distinct human characteristics of the One whom the prophet Daniel saw in vision:

1. This "man" was clothed in linen.
2. His "loins" (waist) were wrapped in fine gold.
3. His "body" had the color of a precious stone.
4. His "face" shone like lightning.
5. His "eyes" resembled lamps of fire.
6. His "arms" and "feet" shone like brass.
7. His "voice" sounded like many voices.

In the Injeel, in Revelation Chapter 1, Yahya (John the Revelator) saw the same man. Yahya saw Him as the "Alpha and Omega." This same being was "like unto the Son of man." Here are John's details:

1. A "man" in a garment and golden girdle.
2. "Head" and "hair" white, like wool or snow.
3. His "eyes" like a flame of fire.
4. His "feet" like fine brass.
5. His "voice" like the sound of many waters.
6. Out of His "mouth" went a sharp sword.
7. His "face" shone as the sun in its strength.
8. Yahya says in verse 18 that this **man** "liveth, was dead and now is alive forever more."

Here in Revelation Chapter 1 (Injeel) the "man" seen by Yahya (John) is the same Person the prophet Daniel had seen. Allah reveals even more to us in Revelation 2:18. There we read, "These things saith the Son of God, who hath his eyes like unto a flame of fire, and his feet are like fine brass." Yahya calls this important man seen in vision "the Son of Allah."

Yahya continues to unfold more clearly who this is. In Revelation 19:11-16 he describes the very same person, who is called "Faithful and True," having "eyes as a flame of fire" and many crowns upon His head. He is clothed with a "vesture [garment] dipped in blood," and his name is "**The Word** of God" (*Kalimatu Allah*)—the same as in Suras 3.39, 45 Aal-E-Imran. His name is "King of Kings, and Lord of Lords," and again it is said that "out of his mouth goeth a sharp sword." Thus once more we see:

1. Eyes like flames
2. Mouth with sword
3. Clothed in a garment of blood (crucifixion)
4. Called the Word of God (Allah)
5. His name: "King of Kings and Lord of Lords"

Isa al-Masih ibyn Maryam, **the Word** from Allah!

"Behold! the angels said: 'O Mary! Allah giveth thee glad tidings of **a Word from Him: his name will be Christ Jesus**, the son of Mary, held in honour in this world and the hereafter and of (the company of) those nearest to Allah.'" Sura 3.45 Aal-E-Imran. He is the straight path (*siratun mistaqueem*). Sura 3.51 Aal-E-Imran and Sura 43.61 Az-Zukhruf.

Injeel John 1:14 bears record: "And **the Word** [Isa al-Masih] was made flesh [human] and dwelt among us." Dear friend of Allah, here in the most concise language, Allah has revealed to us that there can be—indeed, there has been--an appearance of Allah as a human like us. His name is called "Isa al-Masih."

The Holy Scriptures tell us that "no man hath seen God [the Father] at any time; [but] the only begotten Son [the Word], ... he hath declared [revealed] him" by literally coming to dwell among us. Alhumdillah!

What better way could Allah communicate with us, than for Him to come in human form, so that humanity could experience, understand, and tell others what Allah is really like. In the life of Isa al-Masih we see the character of Allah fully displayed. Isa came to pay the ransom (*ul-Fida*) for the fallen sons of Adam. Sura 37.107 As-Saaffat. He came to purchase back, to redeem, men from Iblis's (Satan's) strong hold. Isa came to reveal both the Divine character of Allah and the human side of Allah! Truly in the life of Isa al-Masih ibn Maryam, we see the clearest demonstration to mankind what the character of Allah is really like. Be blest by inviting Him into your life.

# "Allah...created the heavens and the earth in six days."

Dear reader, we take up a subject that is among the most dear to my heart: Creation. In our world today we see the sinful effects of the most deplorable teaching of the doctrine of "evolution," also known as "**evil**ution." It teaches that all living things, including mankind, "evolved" from a lower, very primitive form of life through a random process taking billions of years. It denies the Creator Allah as the One who created all things fully formed in six days. Allah is ignored— left out! Men's reasoning has clearly been heavily influenced by Iblis (Satan).

Even among those claiming to believe the Holy Books, misleading ideas are being embraced. Some claim, for example, that it took Allah millions of years to create what we now see upon planet earth! However, both the Holy Books and the Honored Qur'an tell us that Allah created the world in which we live-- including our sun, moon and stars-- **in six literal days**-- not millions or billions of years. Whom do you believe, dear reader? Even high ranking leaders of religion have recently said:

Pope Francis the leader of the Roman Catholic church has declared: "evolution and Big Bang theory are real and God is not 'a magician with a magic wand'". The news article mentioned:

"Speaking at the Pontifical Academy of Sciences, the Pope made comments which experts said put an end to the "pseudo theories" of creationism and intelligent design that some argue were encouraged by his predecessor, Benedict XVI." He further mentions: "The Big Bang, which today we hold to be the origin of the world, does not contradict the intervention of the divine creator but, rather, requires it."

This message should cause us alarm, that a leader of a religious group claiming to be God's representative on earth is totally against what has been revealed in the Holy Books and in the Qur'an. Dear friends of Allah, creation was and is never a "pseudo theory"

## Seven Golden Verses

Seven golden verses from the Honored Qur'an teach us that the world was created in six days-- not millions of years. Here they are, for your very own to read in Yusef Ali's English translation of the Qur'an:

1. "Your Guardian-Lord is Allah, Who created the heavens and the earth **in six Days**, and is firmly established on the Throne (of authority): He draweth the night as a veil o'er the day, each seeking the other in rapid succession: **He created the sun, the moon, and the stars,** (all) governed by laws under His Command. Is it not His to create and to govern? Blessed be Allah, the Cherisher and Sustainer of the Worlds!" Sura 7.54 Al-Araf.

2. "Verily your Lord is **Allah, who created the heavens and the earth in six Days**, and is firmly established on the Throne (of authority), regulating and governing all things. No intercessor (can plead with Him) except after His leave (Hath been obtained). This is Allah your Lord; Him therefore serve ye: will ye not receive admonition?" Sura 10.3 Yunus.

3. "He it is Who created the heavens and the earth **in six Days**-- and His Throne was over the Waters-- that He might try you, which of you is best in conduct. But if thou wert to say to them, 'Ye shall indeed be raised up after death,' the Unbelievers would be sure to say, 'This is nothing but obvious sorcery!'" Sura 11.7 Hud.

4. "He Who created the heavens and the earth and all that is between, **in six days**, and is firmly established on the Throne (of Authority): Allah Most Gracious: ask thou, then, about Him of any acquainted (with such things)." Sura 25.59 Al-Furqan.

5. "It is Allah Who has created the heavens and the earth, and all between them, **in six Days**, and is firmly established on the Throne (of Authority): ye have none, besides Him, to protect or intercede (for you): will ye not then receive admonition?" Sura 32.4 As-Sajda.

6. "We created the heavens and the earth and all between them **in Six Days**, nor did any sense of weariness touch Us." Sura 50.38 Qaf.

7. "He it is who created the heavens and the earth in six Days, and is moreover firmly established on the Throne (of Authority)...." Sura 57.4 Al-Hadid.

These seven verses or ayats reveal how Allah created the world in exactly six days. Each of these days were twenty-four hours in length. It was not at all impossible for Allah to do this; He alone is all-powerful. He needs only to speak a word and it is done. Who among men can do that? From the Zabur Psalms, many of which Daud wrote, we have this text: "For **he [Allah] spake**, and it was done; he commanded, and it stood fast." Psalms 33:9. Allah needs only to speak and it appears.

Regarding how man was created, the Holy Books and the Qur'an are very clear. Man did not evolve for periods of millions of years, but rather it happened instantaneously as the Word of Allah has power to create. Here is the testimony of these books.

From the Qur'an:

Sura 15.26 Al-Hijr "We created man from sounding clay, from mud moulded into shape:"

Sura 15.29 Al-Hijr "When I have fashioned him (in due proportion) and breathed into him of My spirit…"

Sura 32.7-9 As-Sajda "He who has made everything which He created most good: He began the creation of man with (nothing more than) clay…But He fashioned him in due proportion, and breathed into him something of His spirit. And He gave you (the faculties of) hearing and sight and feeling (and understanding):"

There is no indication from the Qur'an that it took long periods of time to create man…but rather that the creation of man and of all else was instant.

"When He decides upon an affair, He says to it, "Be", and it is." Sura 40.68

"Verily, when He intends a thing, His command is, "Be", and it is. Sura 36.82 Ya-Seen

From the Taurat:

Genesis 2:7 "And the Lord God formed man of the dust of the ground, and breathed into his nostrils the breath of life; and man became a living soul."

The ancient prophet Isaiah records the same account:

Isaiah 64:8 "But now O Lord, thou art our father; [maker] we are the clay, and thou the potter; and we all are the work of thy hand."

Ayub or Job an ancient wise man from the East has testified: "Job 10:8-9 "Thine [Allah's] hand have made me and fashioned me together round about…thou has made me as the clay…"

Job 33:4 "The Spirit of God hath made me, and the breath of the Almighty hath given me life."

Allah simply formed man from clay and breathed into his nostrils and man became a living being. It was instant work with our Creator. Not millions of years for man to evolve from lesser forms of life. Dear friends let no man deceive you with vain philosophy and false teachings.

Now here is the account from the Taurat how the first week of time came about. This is the story of the creation week.

### The Holy Books Tell the Story of Creation Week

The entire account of the creation of Earth is carefully recorded for us in the Holy Books of the Bible, primarily in the first chapter of Taurat Genesis. In fact, the very first verse in the Bible is about creation: "**In the beginning God [Allah] created the heaven and the earth**." Genesis 1:1.

Taurat Genesis 1:3-5 names the first thing created: "And God said, Let there be light: and there was light. And God saw the light, that it was good: and God divided the light from the darkness. And God called the light Day, and the darkness he called Night. **And the evening and the morning were the first day**."

Thus ended the first day of creation. That "day" the Taurat calls "the evening and the morning." According to Allah's time-reckoning, a day begins in the evening at sunset (night) and continues the next day until sunset, when the next 24-hour day begins.

More creation was to come: Genesis 1:6-8 states, "And God [Allah] said, Let there be a firmament [expanse or dome] in the midst of the waters, and let it divide the waters from the waters. And God made the firmament, and divided the waters which were under the firmament from the waters which were above the firmament: and it was so. And God called the firmament Heaven. **And the evening and the morning were the second day**."

Genesis 1:9-13 records the third day's creation: "And God said, Let the waters under the heaven be gathered together unto one place, and let the dry land appear: and it was so. And God called the dry land Earth; and the gathering together of the waters called he Seas: and God saw that it was good. And God said, Let the earth bring forth grass, the herb yielding seed, and the fruit tree yielding fruit after his kind, whose seed is in itself, upon the earth: and it was so. And the earth brought forth grass, and herb yielding seed after his kind, and the tree yielding fruit, whose seed was in itself, after his kind: and God saw that it was good. **And the evening and the morning were the third day."**

The fourth day is covered in Genesis 1:14-19: "And God said, Let there be lights in the firmament of the heaven to divide the day from the night; and let them be for signs, and for seasons, and for days, and years: And let them be for lights in the firmament of the heaven to give light upon the earth: and it was so. And God made two great lights; the greater light to rule the day, and the lesser light to rule the night: he made the stars also. And God set them in the firmament of the heaven to give light upon the earth, And to rule over the day and over the night, and to divide the light from the darkness: and God saw that it was good. **And the evening and the morning were the fourth day."** So upon the completion of the fourth day, Allah had made the sun, moon and stars to give light by day and by night.

Genesis 1:20-23 records the fifth day: "And God said, Let the waters bring forth abundantly the moving creature that hath life, and fowl that may fly above the earth in the open firmament of heaven. And God created great whales, and every living creature that moveth, which the waters brought forth abundantly, after their kind, and every winged fowl after his kind: and God saw that it was good.... God blessed them, saying, Be fruitful, and multiply, and fill the waters in the seas, and let fowl multiply in the earth. **And the evening and the morning were the fifth day."**

On the sixth and final day of creating, Allah did something very unique. He created man **in His own image.** Genesis 1:24-31 says, "And God said, Let the earth bring forth the living creature after his kind, cattle, and creeping thing, and beast of the earth after his kind: and it was so. And God made the beast of the earth after his kind, and cattle after their kind, and every thing that creepeth upon the earth after his kind: and God saw that it was good. And God said, Let us make man in our image, after our likeness: and let them have dominion over the fish of the sea, and over the fowl of the air, and over the cattle, and over all the earth, and over every creeping thing that creepeth upon the earth. **So God created man in his own image, in the image of God created he him; male and female created he them**. And God blessed them, and God said unto them, Be fruitful, and multiply, and replenish the earth, and subdue it: and have dominion over the fish of the sea, and over the fowl of the air, and over every living thing that moveth upon the earth…. And God saw every thing that he had made, and, behold, it was very good. **And the evening and the morning were the sixth day.**"

## How Allah Ended His Creation Week

Allah ended His Creation week by "resting" from creating— but in no way was He weary and needing rest. Although He did not bring any more physical things into existence, He did do something with time. He blessed a certain time period! Taurat Genesis 2:1-3 explains: "Thus the heavens and the earth were finished, and all the host of them. And on the seventh day [Saturday or *Sabt*] God [Allah] ended his work which he had made; and he rested on the seventh day from all his work which he had made. And God [Allah] blessed the seventh day, and sanctified it: because that in it he had rested from all his work which God [Allah] created and made."

Allah, by His own example, set the seventh day apart from other days by resting on it and blessing it. Starting with Adam and Eve, that special day was to become a day upon which all creation would come together to honor and cherish the Creator. By observing this day each week, man would always remember that His Creator created him within the first six days; he did not evolve over millions of years.

Had man always remembered the seventh-day Sabbath (al-*Sabt*) by honoring it, he would never have embraced the idea of evolution. However, as man has forgotten that day, he has gone far astray from the right course. Today most of mankind is out of harmony with Allah. Even among those who profess to believe, this sacred day that Allah has set aside for Holy use is **totally ignored.**

In Moses' lifetime, Allah spoke from the towering heights of Sinai to all, admonishing us to "**remember**" and observe the Sabbath (al-Sabt or Saturday), which was to be a blessing for all mankind forever. He said, "Remember the sabbath day [al-Sabt], to keep it holy. Six days shalt thou labour, and do all thy work: But the seventh day is the sabbath of the LORD thy God: in it thou shalt not do any work, thou, nor thy son, nor thy daughter, thy manservant, nor thy maidservant, nor thy cattle, nor thy stranger that is within thy gates: For **in six days the LORD made heaven and earth**, the sea, and all that in them is, and rested the seventh day: wherefore the LORD blessed the sabbath day, and hallowed it." Taurat Exodus 20:8-11.

Any attempt to confuse mankind into thinking that it took millions of years for Allah to create man and all that which is around us, also does away with the truth regarding the Sabbath, the last day in the Creation week. That special day which Allah designed for mankind to weekly remember the Creation account.

That day was blessed by Allah, no one can alter God's blessing.

"…For when you grant a blessing, O Lord, it is an eternal blessing." Taurat I Chronicles 17:27 NLT

You too will be blessed by keeping it holy and sacred.

.

# Who is the "Comforter"?

Thinking men and women all over the world are asking, "Who is the Comforter?" Could it be that the Prophet Mohammed (PBUH) is the "Comforter" about whom the Injeel (Gospel) of the Bible Scriptures speaks? Certain intelligent scholars today are teaching so, but is that what the Injeel truly says?

We wish to explore this important question by going into the teachings of the Injeel itself. Before we do this, it is necessary that we spend time asking Allah for guidance in prayer (*du'a*) concerning this and every other issue which has to do with our eternal salvation. Dear reader, I encourage you to send your prayer (*du'a*) to the Creator who knows the truth in every issue! He will give us guidance.

"Allah gives guidance towards truth..." Sura 10.35 Yunus. "Allah doth advance in guidance those who seek guidance..." Sura 19.76 Maryam

Ibrahim was the intimate friend (*Khalil*) of Allah. Have you ever had a close friend who will tell you what he knows in order to help you in time of need? In the same way, it is important to have Allah as a *Khalil*, a close friend to whom one can go for answers. To Him we can present our petitions without fear. Every honest heart who seeks guidance from Allah will never be turned away. Go, dear reader. Go to Allah, and present your requests in earnest.

Most answers will be found in the Holy Books that were sent down from Allah. They were given to mankind to inform us of the teachings and will of Allah. Some may venture to ask, "Can we trust the Taurat (Books of Moses) and the Injeel (Gospel of Isa al-Masih) as the authority on any topic?" The answer is "Yes." The Honored Qur'an tells us that the Taurat and Injeel were sent down from Allah as a **guide for mankind**! Read Sura 3.3.

"It is He Who sent down to thee (step by step), in truth, the Book, confirming what went before it; and He sent down the Law (of Moses) and **the Gospel (of Jesus)** before this, as **a guide to mankind**, and He sent down the criterion (of judgment between right and wrong). Sura 3.3 Aal-E-Imran

"And in their footsteps We sent Jesus the son of Mary, confirming the Law that had come before him: **We sent him the Gospel: therein**

**was guidance and light**, and confirmation of the Law that had come before him: a guidance and an admonition to those who fear Allah." Sura 5.46 Al-Maeda

"...Say: "Who then sent down **the Book which Moses brought?- a light and guidance to man**: But ye make it into (separate) sheets for show, while ye conceal much (of its contents): therein were ye taught that which ye knew not- neither ye nor your fathers." Say: "Allah (sent it down)..." Sura 6.91 Al-Anaam

Dear friend of Allah, never fear. The promise is that you will be guided aright! Trust Allah! He well knows how to protect and keep His words intact from evil minds. No matter what other voices may sound in your ears regarding the books of the Taurat and Injeel, the Honored Qur'an makes it very clear that these books were sent previously to mankind for guidance and direction: "And remember We gave Moses the Scripture and the Criterion (between right and wrong): there was a chance for you to be guided aright." Sura 2.53 Al-Baqara. "It is He [Allah] Who sent down to thee (step by step), in truth, the Book, confirming what went before it; and He sent down **the Law (of Moses)** and **the Gospel (of Jesus)** before this, as a guide to mankind, and He sent down the Criterion (of judgment between right and wrong)." Sura 3.3 Aal-E-Imran. "In the past We granted to Moses [Taurat] and Aaron the Criterion (for judgment), and a Light and a Message for those who would do right...." Sura 21.48 Al-Anbiya.

From just these few texts of the Honored Qur'an and more like them, we find that the desert prophet was told that these sources were for light, guidance, and the criterion between right and wrong. Dear reader, we may safely turn to these sources for guidance.

## Is It Mohammed (PBUH)?

Intelligent scholars sometimes freely quote from these sources to try to say that the prophet Mohammed was indeed the "Comforter" promised by Isa al-Masih Ibn Maryam. But where is this implied or recorded in the Injeel or the Taurat? Nowhere! That is why we need to be in earnest prayer [*du'a*] for wisdom and discernment. Allah will give understanding if we sincerely ask for it: "If you need wisdom, ask our generous God, and He will give it to you. He will not rebuke you for asking." Injeel James 1:5 NLT. Allah is longing to help us, but we must ask.

Some well meaning scholars will quote from the Injeel, claiming that the following verse refers to the prophet Mohammed. (Injeel) John 14:16 reads, "And I [Isa al-Masih] will pray the Father, and he shall give you another **Comforter**, that he may abide with you for ever." However, those same scholars will not quote the other verses before and after this single sentence of Isa's, to get a full and honest answer as to who He says the Comforter really is! You, dear reader, be the judge as to the identity of the Comforter, based upon what is written in the Injeel. John 14:16 tells us that the Comforter would "abide with us forever." This cannot be true of the Prophet Mohammed, because he is not physically present! Every thinking Muslim knows that Mohammed has died and is buried, like all others who have gone before us. They now rest in their graves, awaiting the resurrection. The desert prophet is not with us today! He therefore cannot be the Comforter, as he is not abiding with us today.

## THE TRUE COMFORTER

In fact, after Isa's recorded promise to send the Comforter, the very next verse tells us who the Comforter is. Injeel John 14:17 states, "Even **the Spirit of truth**; whom the world cannot receive, because it seeth him not, neither knoweth him: but ye know him; for **he dwelleth with you, and shall be in you.**

Isa calls the Comforter the "Spirit of Truth." Indeed, this Spirit of Truth would dwell in us! Here we see that the Comforter is the Spirit of Truth or the *Ruh* of Allah. He will be present with us forever. My dear reader, this presence Mohammed could never maintain!

If one is yet in doubt as to who the Comforter is, John 14:26 clarifies: "But **the Comforter, which is the Holy Ghost [*Ruh*],** whom the Father will send in my name, he shall teach you all things, and bring all things to your remembrance, whatsoever I have said unto you." Here in unmistakable language the Injeel tells us the Comforter is the "**Holy Spirit,**" the *Ruh* of Allah! This is crystal clear, directly from the Injeel!

Ten distinct points inform us who the Comforter is and what His functions are. Each point is based on the words of Isa al-Masih Ibn Maryam, as found in the Injeel in John 14:16-26, 15:26, 16:7-14:

1. The Comforter **is "the Holy Ghost."** (*Ruh*)
2. "He will teach you **all** things...." Can someone who is dead teach us **all** things?
3. He will "**bring all things to your remembrance.**"

4. He would **teach what Isa al-Masih Ibn Maryam taught and would testify of Him.**
5. He would **abide** (dwell) **in you and with you forever!**
6. He **reproves the world of sin, righteousness, and judgment.**
7. He **cannot be <u>seen</u> nor known by the world.**
8. He **guides into all truth.**
9. The Comforter will **show you things to come.** (He knows the future.)
10. He will **glorify Isa al-Masih Ibn Maryam!**

Dear friend, you be the judge. Do these ten points of description from the Injeel fit the Honored Prophet Mohammed?

## How Long Should They Wait?

When Isa al-Masih was upon earth, He had much to say concerning the Holy Spirit-- the *Ruh* of Allah or the Comforter. In John 16:7 He said, "Nevertheless I tell you the truth; It is expedient for you that I go away: for if I go not away, the Comforter will not come unto you; but **if I depart, I will send him unto you.**"

Isa al-Masih assured His followers that it was expedient (profitable or necessary) for Him to leave this earth, so that He could send the Comforter from the Father. Now another question: Were the followers of Isa al-Masih to wait another 500 years, till the time of Prophet Mohammed, for the Comforter to arrive? Did not the followers of Isa al-Masih need help from heaven right away to assist them in the important work and severe trials they faced? They were in dire need of Someone who could give them strength, guidance and encouragement for the task ahead. If they were to wait until another **500 years** passed, they would long be rotted in their graves, making the promises of Isa al-Masih of no effect. But, dear reader, we know that the Comforter came sooner than that. He was sent down from Allah just as Isa al-Masih said He would be.

## Not 500 Years, but 50 Days

The timing of the Comforter's coming is found in Injeel Acts 2:1: "And when the day of Pentecost was fully come, they were all with one accord in one place…." Fifty days after the Passover (when Isa al-Masih was crucified) would come Pentecost, known as "the fiftieth" [day].

On that specific day, just fifty days after Isa al-Masih had returned to heaven, the Holy Spirit (*Ruh*) descended from heaven upon the gathered group of Isa's closest followers. Fifty days later-- the same span of time as when God's children fled from Egypt and were delivered through the Red Sea, escaping Pharaoh's pursuing army. They fled (*Hijra*) into Paran (Arabia). There, fifty days later, the Law (Ten Commandments of Allah) was given from Mount Sinai. Just fifty days later!

### The Comforter's Arrival

The manner of the Comforter's arrival is recorded in the Book of Acts: "And suddenly there came a sound from heaven as of a rushing mighty wind, and it filled all the house where they were sitting. And there appeared unto them cloven tongues like as of fire, and it sat upon each of them. And **they were all filled with the Holy Ghost [*Ruh* of Allah],** and began to speak with other tongues [languages], as the Spirit [*Ruh*] gave them utterance." Acts 2:1-4. This happened fifty days after Isa al-Masih had returned to Heaven. The promised Holy Spirit or Comforter came upon those who had been preparing for Him. He empowered the early believers to bear witness regarding Isa al-Masih, testifying that He was the true Messiah and the sacrifice for mankind's sins.

This same Comforter is promised again in these last days of earth's history, in order to prepare us to stand through the final crisis hours that are foretold in the Scriptures. Again, it is those who are waiting and preparing for the return of Isa al-Masih who will be asking for this same gift, and who alone will receive it. Through them, under the power of the Holy Spirit, the world will be enlightened with the truths of God, so that humans can make intelligent decisions regarding the things that matter regarding eternity. John 16:8 NLT explains the work of the Holy Spirit: "And when He comes, He will convict the world of its sin, and of God's righteousness, and of the coming judgment." If we are willing, our lives will then be brought into harmony with Heaven. Thus The Holy Spirit will prepare us to stand through the Judgment of God.

Isa al-Masih reassures us: "I have told you all this so that you may have peace in Me. Here on earth you will have many trials and sorrows. But take heart, because I have overcome the world." John 16:33 NLT. Dear friend, today Allah wants you to receive this precious gift of the Comforter from Heaven. Are you willing and ready? May Allah grant unto you His Eternal Peace.

# Wise Men from the East

**The wise men from the East were descendants of Isma'il.
What was their purpose in coming to Israel?
Whom did they come to worship?**

Dear reader, in every age Allah has had His *Mutaqeen* (pious and righteous ones) whom He used-to do His bidding. Most often He chooses the common people who submit to Him in trusting faith, but at times He uses those of elevated rank or influence. Throughout the history of Allah's people, we often find descendants of Isma'il being the ones used by Allah for special tasks. The story we're about to study is an example. In it, we find that ancient "wise men" from the East were the ones chosen by Allah for a special work.

We must remember how in mercy Allah spared Hagar and Isma'il so long ago, when they were dying of thirst in the wilderness after being driven from Ibrahim's home. The Angel of the Lord came to Hagar to sustain her and her son Isma'il. Henceforth, Allah had a purpose and mission for the faithful ones from the offspring of Isma'il.

This story of the wise men is taken from the Holy Books (Injeel); it tells how they were chosen for the special task of announcing to the Jews in Jerusalem the arrival of the King, the Anointed One. They also brought gifts of special importance for Maryam and her husband Yusef and Maryam's newborn son Isa al-Masih Ibn Maryam (Christ the Messiah).

Our story today is taken from the Injeel, Matthew chapter two. I invite the reader to begin with a private prayer (*du'a*) to Allah for guidance, for without the presence and guidance of Allah, all our seeking is vain. We need Heaven's wisdom and the aid of the Spirit (*Ruh*) of Allah before opening the Holy Books, that we may discern truth.

### Wise Men from the East

There came a time when Allah was about to send Isa al-Masih into this world to be the ransom and sacrifice for sin. While most of the Jews in Israel were totally unaware of what Allah was about to do, some of the "children of the East," had been studying the writings of the ancient prophets. The Scriptures call them "wise men." One whose writings they read was also descendant of the children of the East; his name was Balaam. He was the son of Beor, a king of Edom; Allah had chosen him to be a prophet. Taurat Numbers chapters 22-24, and especially Numbers 24:17, are a record of Balaam's prophecies. Those wise 'children of the East' read one of his prophecies with particular interest: "I shall see him, but not now: I shall behold him, but not nigh: there shall come **a Star out of Jacob**, and a Sceptre shall rise out of Israel…."

The Injeel doesn't give many details about these wise men from the East; it doesn't name which country they were from nor how many there were. However, the account does indicate they were men of intelligence, for as they studied foreign prophecies and astronomy, they realized something of great significance was occurring. Being men of integrity, they acted on their convictions. They endured the hardships of long travel westward because, unknown to them, they had a mission to complete for Allah.

Allah used them to proclaim Jesus' birth to Israel. Injeel Matthew 2 tells the complete story: "Now when Jesus was born in Bethlehem of Judaea in the days of Herod the king, behold, there came **wise men from the east** to Jerusalem, Saying, Where is he that is born King of the Jews? for **we have seen his star in the east**, and **are come to worship him**." Matthew 2:1-2.

These men were also wealthy, and the rich gifts they brought to Isa al-Masih of gold, frankincense and myrrh give us a good idea as to where they came from. We know that frankincense grows in present-day Saudi Arabian peninsula, the country of Yemen. Gold and myrrh are also both present there.

## THE PROPHECY OF DANIEL CHAPTER 9

There can be no doubt that the prophecy of Daniel chapter 9 was at least somewhat understood by these men of the East. And in Israel there were those awaiting the arrival of the Messiah, the "Anointed One," based upon Daniel's prophecy. But because of the Jews' negligence to search and know the Holy Books, most of them failed to know **when** He, the Saviour of men, would be sent into the world. Occupied with their own plans, they were unmindful of Allah's revealed plans. Most were unaware of the Person (Isa al-Masih Ibn Maryam) being sent down right on time, just as prophesied.

Here is that time prophecy of Daniel, from chapter 9:24-27: (A day equals a year in prophetic passages.)

"Seventy weeks [490 days/years] are determined upon thy people [Jews] and upon thy holy city [Jerusalem], to finish the transgression, and to make an end of sins, and to make reconciliation for iniquity, and to bring in everlasting righteousness, and to seal up the vision and prophecy, and to anoint the most Holy [Isa al-Masih]. ***Know therefore and understand, that from the going forth of the commandment to restore and to build Jerusalem [given in 457 BC: Ezra 7:11-26] unto the Messiah the Prince [Isa] shall be seven weeks, and threescore and two weeks:*** the street shall be built again, and the wall, even in troublous times. And after threescore and two weeks [62 weeks] shall Messiah be cut off, but not for himself: and the people of the prince that shall come shall destroy the city and the sanctuary; and the end thereof shall be with a flood, and unto the end of the war desolations are determined. And ***he [Isa the Messiah] shall confirm the covenant with many for one week [7 years in prophecy]: and in the midst of the week [3.5 years] he [Isa] shall cause the sacrifice and the oblation to cease [by His own sacrifice]....***"

## THE GIFTS

This prophesied "Star out of Jacob" that would come to Palestine and be the sin offering for this world was Isa al-Masih Ibn Maryam. The time prophesied in the book of Taurat Daniel chapter 9 had finally come. All Israel should have been anxiously waiting and longing for the coming of Messiah the "Anointed," but except for some lowly shepherds and a few others, most were actually unconcerned. However, from among the "children of the East," among the descendants of Isma'il, were believers in the coming of Messiah.

They had been studying and praying for light, and Allah directed these special praying ones to the land of Judah (Israel). As they went in search of this "Anointed One," the Messiah, they were led by a mysterious star to Jerusalem. However, upon arriving there, they were perplexed because no one knew of the coming of this special Person. Finally, someone told them the Holy Books said the "Anointed One" would be born in a small village of Judea called Bethlehem. As they departed Jerusalem for Bethlehem, the star again guided them until they arrived in Bethlehem and found the home where the young child (Isa al-Masih Ibn Maryam) was.

The Holy Books tell us the wise men brought to the child Isa gifts fit for a King, for truly He was a king, and yet much more than a king. He was the "Saviour," the One who would die as a ransom for man. Wicked King Herod, ruler in Jerusalem at that time, was the first to seek to take His life. The gifts of gold, frankincense, and myrrh that Allah had moved upon the wise men to bring became the means needed by the family of Isa al-Masih to make their escape, their Hijra (flight), into Egypt, until after Herod's death. The descendants of Isma'il, not someone from the Jews of Israel, provided this necessary favor to Isa al-Masih and his family. Allah also warned the wise men in a dream to avoid that same jealous king. Matthew 2:12.

The Holy Books reveal that in the time of the last days of earth, kings of the East again will provide special assistance to the cause of Allah. See Isaiah 60.

## Promises

Allah's promise to Isma'il still holds true today. All those who believe, those whose ears are open to Allah to receive truth, will be blessed of Allah. Taurat Genesis 17:20. These wise men were among those who believed, because the account says they came to worship Isa al-Masih. Tragically, what those in Israel failed to see was that the One whom these "children of the East" came to Israel to worship was the long-awaited "Anointed One," the Messiah of the world. Injeel Matthew 2.

Only Allah is to be worshipped. How is it that these men worshipped the young child? Were they misled? The Honored Qur'an says that Isa al-Masih is to be obeyed and followed: "When Jesus came with Clear Signs, he said: 'Now have I come to you with Wisdom, and in order to make clear to you some of the (points) on which ye dispute: therefore fear Allah and **obey me**.'" Sura 43.63 Az-Zukhruf.

Did these wise men also read and understand that about thirty-three years later, this "Anointed One," the Messiah, would voluntarily lay down His life for the sins of the entire world? Isa al-Masih said, "The Father loves Me because I sacrifice My life so I may take it back again. **No one can take My life from Me. I sacrifice it voluntarily**. For I have the authority to lay it down when I want to and also to take it up again. For this is what My Father has commanded." Injeel John 10:17-18 NLT.

All who believe and follow Isa al-Masih Ibn Maryam will be eternally blessed. "Behold! Allah said: 'O Jesus! I will take thee and raise thee to Myself and clear thee (of the falsehoods) of those who blaspheme; **I will make those who follow thee superior to those who reject faith**, to the Day of Resurrection….'" Sura 3.55 Aal-E-Imran.

The Holy Books say that all who wish to may come and find, in Isa al-Masih, deliverance from sin. What would it take for someone to lay down his life for someone else? It would take love and compassion--supreme love and compassion. That is what Allah is all about: Love so supreme that He would provide a sacrifice for our sins. All the sacrificed animals mentioned in the Holy Books and the Qur'an pointed towards this great sacrifice for mankind. Sura 5.2; 22.32; 37.107. This is the forgiveness of Allah, so that the fallen sons and daughters of Adam could live eternally and not die eternally. Today, this book you hold brings to you glad tidings of deliverance from sin, if you believe. Allah of Heaven is interested in all His people whom He created. He longs to bring salvation to you! Dear friend of Allah, will you accept the sacrifice (ransom) made for you in the life of Isa al-Masih?

# *Ibrahim, friend of Allah*
## Khalil (Intimate Friend) of Allah!

Dear reader, today we consider a topic which greatly warms our hearts. Just imagine being called a "friend" [*Khalil*] of Allah! Can anything be more significant in this world than that? Nothing could possibly bring more hope to the soul than to be called "Allah's friend [*Khalil*]"! It is the highest honor, and yet so very humbling, to think that the Creator of the universe, He who keeps galaxies in orbit and the unnumbered stars in their circuit, is One who seeks our friendship! Please read the following: "Who can be better in religion than one who submits his whole self to Allah, does good, and follows the way of Abraham the true in Faith? For Allah did take Abraham for a friend." Sura 4.125 An-Nisa.

In the Holy Books of the Bible Scriptures, the same sentiments about true faith are expressed. Injeel James 2:23 reveals why (Ibrahim) Abraham had such a close relationship with Allah: "And the scripture was fulfilled which saith, Abraham believed God [Allah], and it was imputed unto him for righteousness: and **he was called the Friend [Khalil] of God [Allah].**" It is evident that Abraham's belief in God (Allah)—his faith in God and His revealed Word-- brought about his "doing good" spoken of in the previous sura.

The Honored Qur'an expresses the importance of the revelations given to Moses: "It was We who revealed the law (to Moses): therein was guidance and light…. If any do fail to judge by (the light of) what Allah hath revealed, they are (no better than) Unbelievers." Sura 5.44 Al-Maeda.

Please note the honor given to Abraham in the Taurat of the Bible Scriptures, in 2 Chronicles 20:7: "Art not thou our God [Allah], who didst drive out the inhabitants of this land before thy people Israel, and gavest it to the seed of **Abraham [Ibrahim] thy friend *[Khalil]*** forever?" What a high honor for Ibrahim to be an intimate friend of Allah!

## OTHER INTIMATE FRIENDS OF ALLAH

Did others also have a close relationship with Allah? Yes, indeed. Musa (Moses) was a man who suffered great trials in life, yet he remained faithful to Allah. Not only was Musa a friend of Allah; he actually was permitted to come close enough to Allah to behold his form! In fact, the sacred record says he was blessed enough to see Allah "face to face." Taurat Exodus 33:11 tells us: "And the LORD [Allah] spake unto Moses face to face, as a man speaketh unto his **friend [Khalil]**...."

Another man who was a *Khalil* of Allah was Daniel the Prophet. Three times the Holy Scriptures say of Daniel that heaven considered him "greatly beloved"! Taurat Daniel 10:11: "And he said unto me, O Daniel, a man **greatly beloved**, understand the words that I speak unto thee...." See also Daniel 9:23; 10:19.

Anciently, before the flood of Noah's time, there was a man named Enoch. Taurat Genesis 5:24 tells of him: "And Enoch walked with God [Allah]: and he *was* not; for God [Allah] took him." So closely did Enoch draw near to Allah that Allah finally took him to Himself. Enoch never experienced death. Before Allah took him, though, He rewarded Enoch's faithfulness by giving him a revelation of the last days, and of the return of Isa al-Masih Ibn Maryam to this earth. Some sobering details of that revelation can be read in Injeel Jude 1:14. The ungodly attitude of sinners was thus rebuked; they were warned of the great judgment.

## HOW TO BECOME A FRIEND OF ALLAH

Can we also become close friends of Allah, as Ibrahim and others were? Yes! If it were impossible, heaven would never have titled any human as "friend" or "greatly beloved." Therefore, we may strive to also be among the friends (*Khalil*) of Allah. But how?

We can learn more about how to become Allah's friend by simply reading in the Holy Books about the lives and actions of those who have gone before who were called the friends of Allah. The Honored Qur'an points to the same source: "And in their footsteps We sent Jesus the son of Mary, confirming the Law [Taurat] that had come before him: We sent him the **Gospel** [**Injeel**]: therein was **guidance** and **light**, and **confirmation of the Law** that had come before him: a **guidance** and an **admonition** to those who fear Allah." Sura 5.46 Al-Maeda.

In the Holy Scriptures we find that Ibrahim was submitted to Allah in his daily life. This was not just something which Ibrahim did in theory. Submission was a vital part of his life. Whatever Allah spoke, Ibrahim believed, yielding his own thoughts and will. Not only that, but he carried out God's wishes in the acts of his life. To Ibrahim, belief was only the beginning! Belief evidenced itself by **action!** Taurat Genesis chapter 12 tells us that when Ibrahim was called by God to leave his country, to pack up and go, he listened to the voice of Allah and obeyed, leaving his country. He carried out the wishes of Allah, whatever they were-- even when Allah asked of him something that seemed very foolish to others. Imagine Abraham, beginning to pack his considerable belongings. His friends likely went to him and asked, "Ibrahim, what are you doing"?

Ibrahim probably said, "I am packing up my camp."

"Where are you going?"

"I don't know. Allah has called me, and He will show me the way."

Some of Ibrahim's friends may well have thought him insane. "Why would you leave your community (*ummah*), family and friends and your security, Ibrahim? You don't even have a destination yet!"

Nevertheless, Ibrahim obeyed from the heart. His obedient actions gave evidence of his trust in Allah, and so it must be with us, if we would be among the *Kahlil*, the intimate friends of Allah. If Allah has spoken, we must be willing not only to listen, but to carry out in action what Allah has spoken.

## #1: Voluntary Submission

At least two changes must take place for one to be a *Khalil*, or intimate friend, of Allah. First, there must be a willingness to become completely submissive to the will of Allah. Anyone who is not willing to become submissive to Allah cannot become an intimate friend. This submission must be completely voluntary, as Allah will never force the will of any human. "Let there be no compulsion in religion...." Sura 2.256 Al-Baqara. Allah wants your heart-willingness; therefore He wins our submission, rather than compels it, even though He has power to compel. It must and will come from within one's heart and mind.

This unconditional submission is not only to Allah, but to the Word sent down, which includes the Taurat and Injeel of the Bible

Scriptures, the Law (the Ten Commandments), the Prophets, and Isa al-Masih Ibn Maryam (Christ the Messiah, the Word from Allah). "It is He Who sent down to thee (step by step), in truth, the Book, confirming what went before it; and He sent down the Law (of Moses) and the Gospel (of Jesus) before this, **as a guide to mankind**, and He sent down **the criterion (of judgment between right and wrong)**." Sura 3.3 Aal-E-Imran.

The Taurat gives us another example of one who submitted to the Word from Allah. She was Hagar, the servant woman, the second wife of Ibrahim. Because of the abuse she was receiving from Sarai, Ibrahim's first wife, conditions became unbearable for her in Ibrahim's household, and she fled to the desert. The Angel of the Lord met her there and asked her (Taurat Genesis 16:8-9): "And he said, Hagar, Sarai's maid, whence camest thou? and whither [where] wilt thou go? And she said, I flee from the face of my mistress Sarai." Then the angel of the Lord (Allah) told her to "Return to thy mistress, and submit thyself under her hands." She faithfully obeyed the voice of the angel of the Lord; she returned and submitted.

This is precisely the attitude we must have. We must be willing to listen to the voice of Allah and submit faithfully to Him in all things. The question remains, Will we be true? What will happen if the command from Allah comes in a manner we do not expect, or asks what is unexpected? Will we still be among the *Muttaqeen*? It is the righteous or pious (*Mutaqeen*) who faithfully follow wherever Allah leads. Remember, Allah has only our best interests in mind. Trusting and obeying Him is for our eternal security.

### #2: Learn Allah's Will

The second change in us if we would be *Kahlil* of Allah must be that we seek to learn what Allah's will is! Where does one learn that? The Honored Qur'an says: "Say: 'We believe in Allah, and in what has been revealed to us and what was revealed to Abraham, Isma'il, Isaac, Jacob, and the Tribes, and in (the Books) [The Bible Scriptures] given to Moses, Jesus, and the Prophets, from their Lord: We make no distinction between one and another among them, and to Allah do we bow our will....'" Sura 3.84 Aal-E-Imran. The ancient prophets made clear what the will of Allah is! In the Taurat we indisputably can find what the wishes of Allah are for the family of man.

The people back in the days of Isa al-Masih were much like the people of today. They did not search into what had been revealed to the prophets of old time. Luke 24:25-7 recounts Isa's reproof of the people of His day for their unbelief: "How foolish you are, and how slow to believe all that the prophets have spoken! Did not the Messiah have to suffer these things and then enter his glory? And beginning at Moses and all the prophets, he expounded unto them in all the scriptures the things concerning himself."

We find Allah's will revealed so very clearly in the Injeel which came to us from Isa al-Masih (Christ the Messiah). I Thessalonians 4:3 says, "For this is the will of God [Allah], even your sanctification, that ye should abstain from fornication." Sanctification is holiness to Allah; it is holiness of heart and life! It is allowing Allah to write His Law of the Ten Commandments in our hearts.

Notice how clear the directions are that we are given to follow: Taurat Ecclesiastes 12:13 says, "Let us hear the conclusion of the whole matter: **Fear God [Allah], and keep his commandments: for this is the whole [entire] duty of man.**" Isa al-Masih, sent from Allah, said in John 15:14: "Ye are my friends, if ye do whatsoever I command you." So we see in the Holy Books that the duty and obligation of complete and willing submission to Allah, of following His commandments, and of obeying the Words sent down through Isa al-Masih is how we become the friends of Allah. May you become a close friend of Allah. May Allah grant unto you His eternal peace!

# *How Job (Ayub) Lost His Health and His Wealth*

### Two Mysteries

Perhaps you know the story of Ayub (Job), who was among the greatest men of the East long ago. This man, in quick succession, lost all of his possessions, all of his servants, and all ten of his children. Then even his health was severely affected (Sura 38.41 Sad). Ayub was in a most painful, discouraging situation.

What villain was responsible for Ayub's (Job's) pain, sorrow and loss? And how would such an evil person as that come into existence? The answers to those questions will solve two mysteries.

For this and other topics of study, we need to be much in private prayer (*du'a*), as Allah will certainly guide and direct those who seek Him earnestly. May Allah, who is oft-forgiving and full of loving-kindness (Sura 85.14 Al-Burooj), be near you, dear reader, as you read.

Would Allah, who is most Merciful and most Gracious (Sura 1.1 Al-Fatiha ), create Iblis (Satan)?  Would the Holy One, who is the source of Peace (and Perfection), the Supreme, the Exalted in Might and Guardian of Faith, as well as the Preserver of Safety (Sura 59.23 Al-Hashr)-- would He create sin and Satan, the devil? Would He who has the most beautiful names (Sura 7.180 Al-Araf) be involved with creating such a vile thing as sin and evil?

Or was it the choices that Iblis made, that made him into Satan the devil, as Allah simply granted Him the freedom to choose?

Allah is not responsible for the existence of sin and suffering and evil. Instead, He provides the remedy for them. Some who do not understand this actually blame Allah, who is holy, just and pure, for creating evil, but Allah did not bring sin into existence. No, never should we think such thoughts. It should not enter our minds that Allah is responsible for the existence of evil, or that He delights in seeing people suffer. But all can plainly see that there is indeed terrible corruption in the earth. Evil is everywhere we look. So how or where or when did this thing called sin and evil come into existence?

## How It First Happened

The Holy Books give us insight into how Iblis or Satan came into existence. The Taurat tells us that initially, that person who now is called Satan had the name of Lucifer (Taurat Isaiah 14:12). Lucifer means "Light Bearer." The Holy Books reveal that he was at one time an exalted angel. Taurat Ezekiel 28:14-15 says, "Thou art the anointed cherub [angel] that covereth; and I [Allah] have set thee so: thou wast upon the holy mountain of God; thou hast walked up and down in the midst of the stones of fire. **Thou wast perfect in thy ways from the day that thou wast created, till iniquity was found in thee**."

Allah created Lucifer a pure, holy, perfect, and very beautiful being. Gradually over time, Lucifer began to look to himself and exalt himself instead of his Creator. He admired his own beauty and power, and began to think more highly of himself than any created being ought to think. Harboring such thoughts finally led to the point where Lucifer became jealous of Allah and plotted to take over the throne of Allah! Taurat Isaiah 14:12-14 provides some details: "How art thou **fallen from heaven**, O Lucifer, son of the morning! how art thou cut down to the ground, which didst weaken the nations! For thou hast said in thine heart, **I will** ascend into heaven, **I will** exalt my throne above the stars of God: **I will** sit also upon the mount of the congregation, in the sides of the north: **I will** ascend above the heights of the clouds; **I will be like the most High**."

Sad but true, Lucifer the Light Bearer, abused his holy privileges and perverted his ways through his own corrupt thinking. He became unhappy with his exalted position near to the throne of Allah, and selfishness set in. Especially was he jealous of Isa al-Masih Ibn Maryam, who was nearest to Allah (Sura 3.45 Aal-E-Imran). Over time Lucifer, privileged by Allah to be the covering angel, developed a hatred for Isa al-Masih Why? Because Lucifer was only a created being, and as such, he was not included in the councils of the High Chiefs when they discussed matters among themselves (Sura 38.69 Sad). It appears that in the far distant past, during a council of the High Chiefs, the creation of man was being discussed. Isa al-Masih was in that council, but Lucifer was excluded. His animosity against Isa al-Masih finally developed into open rebellion in Heaven.

Lucifer began this rebellion by expressing his jealous discontent to the other angels. He hoped to make them discontented, also. The results of that work spread like a contagious and dreaded disease.

Many of those who listened to Lucifer were deceived and misled due to Lucifer's trickery, and they chose to side with him against Isa al-Masih! In mercy, the High Chiefs reasoned with those angels, warning them that if they insisted on sympathizing with these perverted ideas of Lucifer, they would have to leave Heaven, but for many of the angels, they had already transferred their loyalty to Lucifer.

## War in Heaven

It finally led to war in Heaven! Imagine Heaven, a place of peace and tranquility, becoming a scene of war! Injeel Revelation 12:7-9 gives this important history: "And there was war in heaven: Michael [Isa al-Masih] and his angels fought against the dragon [Satan]; and the dragon fought and his angels, And prevailed not; neither was their place found any more in heaven. And **the great dragon** was cast out, that old serpent, **called the Devil, and Satan**, which deceiveth the whole world: **he was cast out into the earth, and his angels were cast out with him.**"

Once an exalted being, Satan was forced to leave Heaven. Isa al-Masih said, "I beheld Satan as lightning **fall** from heaven." Injeel Luke 10:18.

Lucifer's new name, "Satan," means "accuser." Satan had questioned—rather, challenged—the holy will of Allah, and his very first work was to transgress Allah's law [the ten commandments]. Later he came to Eve in the garden of Eden, and through his temptations, he caused both Eve then Adam to disbelieve Allah's word. Their disbelief led them to break the commandments, as he had done.

Allah has a kingdom, a constitution, and laws to govern those whom He has created. It was and is Satan's plan to war against the God of heaven and His Holy laws, first in heaven and then on earth. It would be a dreadful mistake to side with Satan and be found on the wrong side, warring against the government of Heaven and against Allah's holy and just laws, the ten commandments.

After Satan was cast out of Heaven, he set up his headquarters here on this earth. Ever since, he has continued to practice his deceptive arts on others. He sows the seeds of evil, lawlessness, and discontent among mankind, just as he did in heaven. Now, however, after millennia of experience, his ability to deceive is much greater. He is behind all the hatred, crime, wars, and bloodshed we see upon earth today, yet Allah in His abundant mercy and compassion does not leave us without help.

Allah, the Lord of truth, still gives the *Ruh* of Allah (Holy Spirit) to strengthen the believers (Sura 16.102 An-Nahl) in the warfare against Satan. Today we can claim a promise that all who come to Allah through His chosen instrument Isa al-Masih can also be filled with the *Ruh* of Allah (Holy Spirit) and be able to contend with this wily foe (Satan), "for I [Allah] will contend with him that contendeth with thee...." Taurat Isaiah 49:25.

## Who Troubled Ayub with Grief?

Now to answer the first question from the beginning of our discourse: Who caused the distress and evil in Ayub's life? Taurat Ayub (Job 1:8-21) gives us insight: "The LORD said unto Satan, Hast thou considered my servant Job [Ayub], that there is none like him in the earth, a perfect and an upright man, one that feareth God, and escheweth [avoids] evil?" Allah was speaking to none other than Satan, the one who fell from heaven.

The account continues: "Then Satan answered the LORD, and said, Doth Job [Ayub] fear God for nought [nothing]? Hast not thou made a hedge [of protection] about him, and about his house, and about all that he hath on every side? thou hast blessed the work of his hands, and his substance is increased in the land. But put forth thine hand now, and touch all that he hath, and he will curse thee to thy face. **And the LORD said unto Satan, Behold, all that he hath is in thy power; only upon himself put not forth thine hand.** So Satan went forth from the presence of the LORD. And there was a day when his sons and his daughters were eating and drinking wine in their eldest brother's house: And there came a messenger unto Job, and said, The oxen were plowing, and the asses feeding beside them: And the Sabeans fell upon them, and took them away; yea, they have slain the servants with the edge of the sword; and I only am escaped alone to tell thee. While he was yet speaking, there came also another, and said, The fire of God is fallen from heaven, and hath burned up the sheep, and the servants, and consumed them; I only am escaped alone to tell thee. While he was yet speaking, there came also another, and said, The Chaldeans made out three bands, and fell upon the camels, and have carried them away, yea, and slain the servants with the edge of the sword; and I only am escaped alone to tell thee. While he was yet speaking, there came also another, and said, Thy sons and thy daughters were eating and drinking wine in their eldest brother's house: And, behold, there came a great wind from the wilderness, and smote the four corners of the house, and it fell upon the young men, and they are dead; and I only am escaped alone to tell thee. Then Job arose, and rent his mantle, and shaved his head, and fell down upon the ground, and worshipped, And said, Naked came I out of my mother's womb, and naked shall I return thither: the LORD gave, and the LORD hath taken away; blessed be the name of the LORD."

From this account in the Holy Books of what happened long ago, we can see that it is Satan who afflicts all who choose to follow Allah. However, Satan's power is limited. He cannot touch us beyond Allah's permission. Someday soon, according to the Holy Books, Satan's power will be completely broken. When Isa al-Masih returns, He will bind Satan so that he can no longer tempt and destroy lives.

Now you know how Satan came into existence, and how evil and sin came into this world. Stay close to Allah and the Ones whom He sends to help us: the Holy Spirit (*Ruh*) and Isa al-Masih. Spend time each day thanking Allah for His goodness, mercy, and power, given freely to those who desire these blessings in the jihad against sin and evil. May Allah grant unto you His eternal Peace.

# *Can those hear, who are buried in the grave?*

I greet you in the name of Allah, the most merciful and most gracious (Sura 1.1 Al-Fatiha). May His blessings overshadow you this day!

Our topic in this trifold is one about which many are confused. Even among believers, a lack of certainty exists as to the answers to these two critical questions: What happens to a person after death? Can I still communicate with him or her?

This subject is of greatest importance. It is extremely vital that we know the truth, because Iblis (Satan) well knows that if we are confused or uncertain upon this point, then he will be able to mislead us.

Only as we are guarded and guided by the Holy Books and by the Spirit [*Ruh*] of Allah can we stand against the deceptions of Iblis in these last days. Today, therefore, we wish to research **the Holy Books, the Taurat and Injeel** to find the answers to this most important issue with eternal consequences. What is Allah's wisdom and truth regarding the dead? Is the traditional teaching true that after death, a person lives on in some type of spirit world, sometimes communicating with loved ones alive on earth?

We need to always be in earnest prayer (*du'a*) before we begin our search. Allah will always inform those who are submissive to His will. He will reveal His truth to those who are humble and earnest to learn what is right and true.

Allah has sent down Holy Books for us to study, that we may understand truth. The Honored Qur'an plainly teaches that the **Taurat** given to Moses and the **Injeel (Gospel)** given to Isa al-Masih (Christ the Messiah) were for our admonition, for guidance and light. They are the criterion of the judgment. See Sura 2.53 Al-Baqara; Sura 3.3 Aal-E-Imran; Sura 21.48 Al-Aniva. Upon Jesus the son of Mary was bestowed the Injeel, or Gospel. Sura 57.27 Al-Hadid.

## Learning from Allah's Servant Job

Sura 38.41 Sad tells us to "commemorate our servant Job...." Why? Job was one of the ancient men of the East who walked with Allah.

He went through grievous trials yet maintained his hold upon Allah, even though Iblis (Satan) tried him sorely. This servant of Allah had much to say in respect to the dead. He has given us valuable counsel that we need today in order to avoid the trickery of Iblis, for Iblis is seeking to deceive many, even the entire world. Will we heed the inspired counsel given by this great servant of Allah of ancient times? Was not knowledge given to him from Allah? It rests with us to heed the counsel and be submissive learners.

Can the dead communicate with the living? Taurat Job 14:7-14 gives wisdom: "For there is hope of a tree, if it be cut down, that it will sprout again, and that the tender branch thereof will not cease. Though the root thereof wax [grow] old in the earth, and the stock thereof die in the ground; yet through the scent of water it will bud, and bring forth boughs like a plant. **But man dieth, and wasteth away**: yea, man giveth up the ghost, and where is he? *As* the waters fail from the sea, and the flood decayeth and drieth up: **So man lieth down, and riseth not: till the heavens be no more, they shall not awake, nor be raised out of their sleep**. O that thou would hide me in the grave, that thou would keep me secret, until thy wrath be past, that thou would appoint me a set time, and remember me! If a man die, shall he live again? All the days of my appointed time will I wait, till my change come."

Allah's servant Job assures us that after a man dies, he will not rise or be "awake" again until "awakened" in the resurrection. He remains "asleep" in the grave, until the time appointed by Allah when his "change" will come. This "change" refers to the resurrection, when Isa al-Masih Ibn Maryam returns to earth to call Allah's faithful ones back to life and take them to the heavenly gardens.

## What Iblis Does Not Want You to Know

Why is this topic so crucial to understand? In these final days of earth, Iblis wants us to believe that the dead are not really dead, but continue to live on somewhere else. This is a deception whereby millions are fooled. The truth is that **when a man dies, he is laid to rest in the grave and never has anything to do with anything more done here on earth**.

The Honored Qur'an also tells us: "Nor are alike those that are living and those that are dead. Allah can make any that He wills to hear; but **thou canst not make those to hear who are (buried) in graves**." Sura 35.22 Fātir. It clearly states they cannot hear us now!

The prophet Daud likewise confirms that when a man dies, "his breath goes forth; he returns to the earth; **in that very day his thoughts perish.**" Zaboor Psalms 146:4.

Isa al-Masih Ibn Maryam taught the same thing-- that when a man dies, he sleeps the sleep of death until he is awakened in the resurrection. "Marvel not at this: for the hour is coming, in the which all that are in the graves shall hear his [Allah's] voice." Injeel John 5:28. This is a clear issue. Where are they when Isa al-Masih calls for them? Resting in their graves.

Finally, notice these inspired words from the Taurat. Ecclesiastes 9:5-6 teaches us: "For the living know that they shall die: **but the dead know not any thing,** neither have they any more a reward; for the memory of them is forgotten. Also their love, and their hatred, and their envy, is now perished; neither have they any more a portion for ever in any thing that is done under the sun." Their lives are over; they have nothing to do anymore with anyone or anything done under the sun until the resurrection.

### The First Lie

Iblis hates these verses from the Taurat, because he is not able to deceive those who understand this truth. The Taurat reveals more that is very important that we know. Satan (Iblis), since his fall from Heaven, has used unnumbered lies to deceive humans. He is the "father of lies," so we should not expect anything different than lies. "...He [Satan] was a murderer from the beginning. He has always hated the truth, because there is no truth in him. When he lies, it is consistent with his character; for he is a liar and the father of lies." Injeel John 8:44 NLT.

The first lie ever told (and believed) upon this earth was told in the beautiful garden of Eden to Eve, the first woman, helpmate of Adam. Taurat Genesis 3:1-19 tells us how "by deceit he [Iblis] brought about their [man's] fall." Sura 7.22 Al-Baqara.

Allah had clearly and positively stated to Eve that neither she or her husband Adam were to eat of the one "forbidden tree in the midst of the garden." (Sura 2.35 Al-Baqara; Suras 7.19-20, 22 Al-Araf; and Sura 20.121 Ta-Ha.) Thus Allah spoke and warned them that if they should violate this command, they would die: "But of the tree of the knowledge of good and evil, thou shalt not eat of it: for in the day that thou eatest thereof thou shalt surely die." Taurat Genesis 2:17.

Iblis, or Satan, almost always uses a medium through whom he works in disguise, so that the unwary soul does not see the potential danger. In Eden, Iblis used the serpent as a medium. As he spoke to Eve through the serpent, he denied what Allah had so clearly stated. Although Allah had plainly stated they would "surely die" if they ate of the forbidden fruit, "the serpent said unto the woman, ye shall not surely die." Taurat Genesis 3:4. Iblis directly contradicted what Allah had said—in effect, accusing Allah of lying! The deception was successful. Eve believed the serpent and ignored Allah's warning. Adam also ate of the fruit, and mankind has suffered and sinned ever since.

## Deceptions of Iblis in the Last Days

Believing that first lie today makes one very vulnerable to Satan's deceptions. As Iblis did in Eden, he continues to work through various mediums to carry out his evil plans against us. Iblis will come supernaturally to many in the form of departed loved ones, impersonating their appearances, tones of voice, and even their personalities. In this way millions will be fooled into thinking that the dead are not really dead, but are in another state of existence. In those fascinating supernatural disguises, he (Iblis) will tell those to whom he appears that the dead aren't really dead, so they can still communicate with the living.

Often Iblis, through those mediums, will say things regarding the listeners' private lives—perhaps things known only to themselves. And thus many are led to believe that since so much is known by these supposedly dead ones, then whatever else they say must be true, also. Once the first lie is accepted, additional lies will likely also be accepted as truth by those seeing the supernatural images. Thus Satan (Iblis) can deceive the multitudes of earth with more lies which, if listened to and accepted as truth, will lead souls to eternal destruction. It is as he would have it.

## Allah's Warning Today

Today many are going to places where the dead are supposedly contacted for counsel. Since the dead are "asleep" and "know nothing," this type of activity is nothing less than communication with devils (*Jinns*), which impersonate the dead ones. Since ancient times, Allah has strictly forbidden any such attempt to communicate with deceased ones. Iblis, the fallen foe, stands ready to deceive all who will not heed the careful instructions sent from Allah. Taurat Leviticus 19:31 NLT commands: "Do not defile yourselves by turning to mediums, or to those who consult the spirits of the dead. I am the LORD your God."

An ancient prophet named Isaiah reproves (rebukes) us: "Some will tell you to ask for advice from people who get messages from those who have died. Others will tell you to ask for advice from people who talk to the spirits of the dead…. Shouldn't you ask for advice from your God? **Why should you get advice from dead people to help those who are alive?**"

## The Second Creation

Beloved friend of Allah, as you accept these truths of Allah's Word, you will understand and have peace concerning those who pass to the grave. They now await the Second Creation, or the raising of the dead, that takes place when Isa al-Masih returns. Sura 53.47 An-Najm states: "…He hath promised a Second Creation (Raising of the Dead)…."

When does this Second Creation take place? The Injeel tells us that "in a moment, in the twinkling of an eye, **at the last trump**: for the trumpet shall sound, and the dead shall be raised incorruptible, and we shall be changed." 1 Corinthians 15:52. It happens when the trumpet of Allah sounds. You need not worry that you miss it, for all will hear that trumpet. Allah will see to it that none miss out on this world-wide event.

Today may Allah grant you His Eternal Peace.

# "A Prophet like Musa"

May the peace of Allah be upon you, and may He guide your life.

Much discussion has revolved around the phrase found in the Bible Scriptures which is the title of this paper. Many scholars state that the verse in the Bible that contains that phrase points forward to the desert prophet Mohammed!

Here is that verse, spoken by Musa many millennia ago, in its context: Taurat Deuteronomy 18:15,18 says, "The LORD thy God [Allah] will raise up unto thee a Prophet from the midst of thee, of thy brethren, like unto me; unto him ye shall hearken...." Moses next repeats what Allah said to him: "I [Allah] will raise them up a Prophet from among their brethren, like unto thee, and will put my words in his mouth; and he shall speak unto them all that I shall command him."

## CONFUSION AND CLARIFICATION

Intelligent Muslim scholars freely quote the verses above and confidently say, "These verses in Taurat Deuteronomy of the Old Testament Scriptures refer to the desert prophet." To casual readers, this may seem to be true. However, we need to further investigate these claims, to verify them. Indeed, we might readily believe those scholars, were it not for the fact that there are also many scholars in Islam that claim that the Bible Scriptures have been corrupted! They say that they have been falsified, so that we cannot trust them. Then why do Muslim scholars quote from a source that they feel has been corrupted? How do they know that the very verses they quote are not themselves among the corrupted? It can be quite confusing, unless we search out the facts from fiction for ourselves.

The Honored Qur'an clearly states, "To thee We sent the Scripture in truth, **confirming the scripture that came before it, and guarding it in safety**: so judge between them by what Allah hath revealed, and follow not their vain desires, diverging from the Truth that hath come to thee...." Sura 5.48 Al-Maeda. This statement in the Qur'an tells us that the Scriptures or Holy Books have been confirmed by the Qur'an. Allah, who sent His messages to the prophets of old, is also guarding them from wicked minds. He had sent the Taurat through Musa, the Zabur (Psalms) through Daud (David), and the Injeel through

Isa al-Masih Ibn Maryam. So how can it be that man claims that the Scriptures sent by Allah are now corrupted or falsified? Who is there that is above Allah, who would be able to do such a thing?

## Spiritually Discerned

There are perhaps many verses in the Holy Books which appear to the casual reader to be misleading, but upon earnest prayer (*du'a*) and even with fasting (*saum*), these words can be understood. Remember that spiritual things are spiritually discerned. We therefore need the mind of heaven in order to understand spiritual themes. Precious truths are often hidden to those who would misuse them, but to those who are earnest in heart and to those who are seeking truth, Allah will reveal His will.

Injeel Matthew 11:25 says, "At that time Jesus [Isa al-Masih] answered and said, I thank thee, O Father, Lord of heaven and earth, because **thou [Allah] hast hid these things from the wise and prudent**, and hast **revealed them unto babes [humble learners]**." If we are wise in our own eyes, we will miss the things heaven is trying to reveal to us. It is therefore necessary that we pray for humility and to receive the spirit of a learner. After all, who among us can teach Allah? Who can know more than He? Only one who is spiritual can understand that which is spiritual. First Corinthians 2:14 NLT explains, "But people who aren't spiritual can't receive these truths from God's Spirit. It all sounds foolish to them and they can't understand it, for only those who are spiritual can understand what the Spirit means."

It would certainly be a terrible insult to Allah, Who has without question sent down words for mankind, to even suggest that He, Allah, cannot keep His previous words from being corrupted. Is not Allah stronger than Iblis and the Jinn (fallen spirits), or those affected by them? Therefore, we must be among those who believe and not doubt, for a confirmed doubter will receive nothing from Allah except eternal loss.

Remember, Allah can be trusted to keep His word: "…**Allah never fails in His promise**." Sura 3.9 Aal-E-Imran. One of Allah's promises is that what He sends down, He will guard from corruption: "We have, without doubt, sent down the Message; and We will assuredly guard it (from corruption)." Sura 15.9 Al-Hijr.

There are nevertheless those who doubt as to what Allah has revealed. The Qur'an instructs us that if we are in doubt, then we are to ask those who were given the Book (Bible Scriptures) beforehand: "If thou wert in doubt as to what We have revealed unto thee, **then ask those who have been reading the Book from before thee: the Truth hath indeed come to thee from thy Lord**: so be in no wise of those in doubt." Sura 10.94 Yunus.

## Prophet's Identity Revealed and Confirmed

Today we wish to ask those who have been reading the Book, the Bible Scriptures, the truth regarding the identity of the person spoken about in the Taurat Deuteronomy 18:18, which says: "I [Allah] will raise them up a Prophet from among their brethren, like unto thee...."

Injeel Acts 3:20-22 gives the clear answers we need as to who that person is: "And he [Allah] shall send Jesus Christ [Isa al-Masih Ibn Maryam], which before was preached unto you: Whom the heavens must receive until the times of restitution of all things, which God [Allah] hath spoken by the mouth of all his holy prophets since the world began. For Moses truly said unto the fathers, A prophet shall the Lord your God raise up unto you of your brethren, like unto me; him shall ye hear in all things whatsoever he shall say unto you." Acts 3:20-23.

Those verses in the biblical book Acts of the Apostles makes it very clear that Isa al-Masih Ibn Maryam would be sent; He would be like the prophet Musa. Those verses in Deuteronomy 18, then, were plainly referring to Isa al-Masih, and not someone else.

How can we be sure? Just in case we did not understand correctly the first time, Allah in mercy caused the information to be repeated. This additional statement in Acts 7:37-38 confirms the identity of the One who was raised up to be like unto Musa. The repetition reads thus: "This is that Moses, which said unto the children of Israel, **A prophet shall the Lord your God [Allah] raise up unto you of your brethren, like unto me [Musa]; him shall ye hear**. This is he [Isa], that was in the church [*ummah* of believers] in the wilderness with the angel which spake to him in the mount Sinai, and with our fathers: who received the lively [living] oracles to give unto us."

In Acts 7:52 the messenger Stephen said to the Jews of old, "Which of the prophets have not your fathers persecuted? and they have slain them which shewed before of the coming of the Just One [Isa al-Masih]; **of whom ye have been now the betrayers and murderers**." Stephen's words tell us that this special person that would be sent would be *like* the prophet Moses (Musa). He would be the same person that was with those who came out of Egypt, and that was with those in the wilderness when Allah's voice was heard from Mount Sinai. It was Isa al-Masih whom Allah sent to be in the cloud protecting the Hebrews during the day, and He was also in the fire which gave light to their camp during the night. (Taurat Exodus 13:21, 22; Numbers 9:16, 21; Numbers 14:14; Deuteronomy 1:33; Nehemiah 9:19.) It was not the desert prophet Mohammed who was there in the wilderness, but Isa al-Masih Ibn Maryam. If we are patient and inquiring, we will find that Scripture will always interpret or explain itself. So now we understand that Isa al-Masih is the One to whom this text of Taurat Deuteronomy 18:15, 18 refers, and not Mohammed.

## Like Unto Musa...

It was Isa al-Masih who was appointed to lead believers out from bondage of sin, as the prophet Moses was appointed by Allah to lead Israel out from the slavery of Egypt to freedom! As they journeyed from Egypt, they passed through the Red Sea which Allah opened for them. Then they passed through the wilderness deserts. Moses endured many struggles. At times the ones he had led to freedom became weary and impatient, even to the point that they wanted to take his life.

Even so, Isa al-Masih, in the same way, is leading a people (those who believe) out from the wilderness of sin and darkness into the glorious liberty of truth. As with Moses, He was not appreciated by all, and in the end, those who plotted to take His life succeeded.

## Our Prophet Today

Today we have a leader like Moses of old—Isa al-Masih Ibn Maryam—who is leading His people to a heavenly promised land. Isa, however, is a far greater leader than was Moses, for Isa will deliver from the bondage of sin and sorrow, so that we may have peace and joy. Will we allow Him to lead us? If we accept Him, He promises to lead us and grant us eternal life through His sacrifice.

The prophet Moses died in the wilderness, was buried and was resurrected and taken to Heaven, in the same way Isa al-Masih died and also was resurrected and taken to Heaven. However, a careful and prayerful study of both the Quran and the Bible reveals that Isa al-Masih was much more than a prophet.

Now Isa ministers before God in our behalf. Soon—no one knows how soon--Isa is returning to earth to take the faithful and true back to heaven. Now is preparation time to get ready. When Allah is speaking to you through the *Ruh* Allah, or Spirit of Allah, it is time to pay careful attention. Allah wishes to connect with you. Are you listening when He speaks to your heart?

For those who are blessed, a goodly land awaits them where peace forever reigns. A joyous, peaceful people who love truth will be there--people whose lives have been changed by the One who has been leading them all along.

Today is the day to allow Him to have His will in our lives. Now is the time to say "Yes" to Him as He is earnestly wanting to lead you in straight paths. Are you listening? May you and I be among the *Mutaqeen* (Righteous) as we allow the Prophet like Moses, Isa al-Masih, to lead us to the heavenly Canaan. My heart-felt prayer this day is that Allah will grant that you be among them.

# "The Law and the Gospel"
## ...as Revealed in the Honored Qur'an!

Asalamu 'aliekum! Greetings in the name of Allah, the most compassionate and merciful! May you enjoy His peace in your life.

This tract concerns the Law (Taurat) and the Gospel (Injeel) as they are revealed in the Honored Qur'an. Intelligent scholars are often heard denouncing the Law and the Gospel, yet we find no such negativity in the Honored Qur'an. Indeed, today we will look at specific verses in the Honored Qur'an that talk about the very Law and the Gospel that some scholars are so quick to condemn. We need to be in earnest prayer (*du'a*) over any topic of study, asking for guidance, and the *Ruh* of Allah, the Holy Spirit (Sura 16.102 An-Nahl), will guide us into all the understandings we need as we journey to the eternal city.

We cannot afford to be on the wrong side! If the scholars' claims are true that the Law and the Gospel are outdated, or were falsified or corrupted, then why would the Honored Qur'an have so much to say about them? (Sura 7.157 Al-Araf). Would not one or two ayats suffice to explain that they are no longer valid? But no, there is silence in that respect. Therefore, dear reader, we ask that you, after *du'a* for guidance, evaluate for yourself the following verses that contain the words "Law" and "Gospel."

### SURAS WITH "THE LAW" AND "THE GOSPEL"

Sura 3.3 Aal-E-Imran: "It is He Who sent down to thee (step by step), in truth, the Book, confirming what went before it, and He sent down **the Law (of Moses) and the Gospel (of Jesus)** before this, as a **guide to mankind,** and He sent down the criterion of judgment between right and wrong."

Sura 3.48 Aal-E-Imran: "And **Allah will teach** him the Book and Wisdom, **the Law and the Gospel....**"

Sura 3.65 Aal-E-Imran: "Ye People of the Book! Why dispute ye about Abraham, when **the Law and the Gospel** were not revealed Till after him? Have ye no understanding?"

Sura 5.46 Al-Maeda: "And in their footsteps We sent Jesus the son of Mary, **confirming the Law** that had come before him: We sent him the **Gospel**: therein was **guidance and light**, and **confirmation** of the Law that had come before him: a guidance and an admonition to those who fear Allah."

Sura 5.47 Al-Maeda: "Let the people of **the Gospel** judge by what Allah hath revealed therein. If any do fail to judge by the **light** of what Allah hath revealed, they are no better than those who rebel."

Sura 5.66 Al-Maeda: "If only they [Christians] had stood fast by the **Law, the Gospel,** and all the revelation that was sent to them from their Lord, they would have enjoyed happiness from every side. There is from among them a party of the right course: but many of them follow a course that is evil."

Sura 5.68 Al-Maeda: "Say: 'O People of the Book! **ye have no ground to stand upon unless ye stand fast by the Law, the Gospel,** and all the revelation that has come to you from your Lord.' It is the revelation that cometh to thee from thy Lord, that increaseth in most of them their obstinate rebellion and blasphemy. But sorrow thou not over these people without Faith."

Sura 5.110 Al-Maeda: "Then will Allah say: 'O Jesus the son of Mary! Recount My favour to thee and to thy mother. Behold! I strengthened thee with the holy spirit, so that thou didst speak to the people in childhood and in maturity. Behold! I [Allah] taught thee the Book and Wisdom, **the Law and the Gospel**....'"

Sura 9.111 At-Tawba: Allah hath purchased of the believers their persons and their goods, for theirs in return is the garden of Paradise: they fight in His cause, and slay and are slain: **a promise binding on Him in truth, through the Law and the Gospel,** and

the Qur'an: and who is more faithful to his covenant than Allah...?"

Sura 48.29 Al-Fath: "Muhammad is the messenger of Allah; and those who are with him are strong against Unbelievers, (but) compassionate amongst each other. Thou wilt see them bow and prostrate themselves (in prayer), seeking Grace from Allah and (His) good Pleasure. On their faces are their marks, being the traces of their prostration. This is their similitude in **the Taurat;** and their similitude **in the Gospel** is: like a seed which sends forth its blade, then makes it strong; it then becomes thick, and it stands on its own stem, (filling) the sowers with wonder and delight. As a result, it fills the Unbelievers with rage at them. Allah has promised those among them who believe and do righteous deeds forgiveness, and a great Reward."

Sura 57.27 Al-Hadid: "Then, in their wake, We followed them up with others of Our messengers. We sent after them Jesus the son of Mary, and bestowed on him **the Gospel**; and We ordained in the hearts of those who followed him Compassion and Mercy...."

## The Law and the Gospel Upheld

Now, dear reader, please consider what you have just read. From the sources quoted above, one can easily see that in no instance is the Law or the Gospel criticized. Why would the Law and the Gospel be mentioned as "**a guide to mankind**", and the "**criterion of judgment between right and wrong**" (Sura 3.3 Aal-E-Imran), if they are to be replaced or if they had been corrupted in Mohammed's day?

Think, dear reader, and pray that we do not listen to those who make light of the Law and the Gospel.

If someone determines to follow what Allah teaches, then that person is on a right course. Sura 3.48 Aal-E-Imran clearly says "**Allah will teach ... the Law and the Gospel.**" Where are those who will dare discredit these suras? They will surely meet with scorn on the Day of Judgment for violating these words and teaching men to have a disregard for the Taurat and the Injeel, the Law and the Gospel.

Next, dear friend, we see in Sura 5.46 Al-Maeda that through Jesus (Isa al-Masih Ibn Maryam) the Gospel was sent. "...We sent Jesus the son of Mary, **confirming the Law** that had come before him: **We sent him the Gospel**...." The Law and the Gospel came from Allah. Was that which was previously sent now to be obsolete? Does Allah make mistakes? Does He later have to make corrections or alter His course? Who can "extinguish **Allah's Light** (by blowing) with their mouths"? Sura 61.8 As-Saff.

Allah has sent these blessings, so why should anyone listen to words denouncing the Law (Taurat) and the Gospel (Injeel)? The Honoured Qur'an continues to testify that in the Law and the Gospel is "guidance and **light**, and confirmation of the law ... and an admonition to those who fear Allah." Sura 5.46 Al-Maeda.

## Encouragement for the Judgment

Friend, do you fear Allah? Then these words are for you. These people (scholars) are indeed blowing against Allah's light with their mouths, but in vain. **Allah's Light, the Law and the Gospel,** will shine, though a thousand tongues attempt to darken it. Such men who do so will face Allah's judgment, in which they must answer for their words and actions. Imagine having to face the Judgment of Allah, and there find that you are charged with speaking against the Law and the Gospel of Allah! Perhaps you are one who kept thousands from hearing and believing the truth of Allah through the Taurat, Injeel and the Zabur.

Dear reader, where do you stand? Sura 5.66 Al-Maeda states these tragic words: "**If only they had stood fast by the Law, the Gospel....**" That is where I have chosen to stand. Who can fault one who abides by these words? When Allah impresses you with the truth of these last days upon earth, take note. It is time to stop and listen carefully. The Law and the Gospel are indeed "...the light of what Allah has revealed...." Sura 5.44, 45, 47 Al-Maeda.

"Let the people of **the Gospel** judge by what Allah hath revealed therein. If any do fail to judge by **the light of what Allah hath revealed,** they are no better than those who rebel." Sura 5.47 Al-Maeda.

The Taurat and Injeel are light. Long ago the prophet Daud wrote, "**Thy word** is a lamp unto my feet, and **a light** unto my path." Zabur Psalms 119:105. A careful study of the Scriptures sent down before reveals that "all scripture is given by inspiration of God, and is profitable for doctrine, for reproof, for correction, for instruction in righteousness: That the man of God may be perfect, thoroughly furnished unto all good works." 2 Timothy 3:16-17.

When Isa al-Masih Ibn Maryam came from Allah, He wisely counseled those who were not giving attention to the Prophets previously sent. Notice the rebuke: "Then he said unto them, O fools, and slow of heart to believe all that the prophets have spoken." Injeel Luke 24:25.

Allah has taken great pains to reveal to us His holy and sacred will, always for mankind's benefit. His will was revealed to special persons we call "prophets of Allah," or "seers," because they were able to "see" what we cannot, and they revealed to us the sacred will of Allah in the Taurat and Injeel, "the Law and the Gospel." In the Taurat, Zabur and the Injeel God has revealed His plans for this sinful world.

Soon will be our last day. Tomorrow we may draw our last breaths. Now is a very critical time—time to pay careful attention to what God is revealing to us through the ancient prophets. There is no time to sleep or delay, but with much private prayer (*du'a*), we need to appeal to Allah to have mercy and show us His Will. Wise men today will pay attention when Allah is seeking to speak with them. Will you be among the wise?

Sura 5.110 Al-Maeda says **"I [Allah] taught thee ... the Law and the Gospel."** If Allah teaches the Law and the Gospel, then who are the scholars that say they are to be discarded?

I encourage **every thinking Muslim** to obtain a copy of the Law (Taurat) and the Gospel (Injeel) as quickly as possible, for therein, says the Honoured Qur'an, is Allah's Light revealed. Dear reader, make no mistake. Do not delay another minute, but search for the Taurat and the Injeel. To delay is dangerous. We know not how long our lives may last. Search for a copy today. They are also available in various languages free on this website:

**www.e-sword.org**

Enjoy reading these words and allow Allah to speak to you. Peace will come.

# How Hagar Prefigured Maryam

In the Honored Qur'an we find that the Taurat (Law of Moses) and Injeel (Gospel of Isa al-Masih) are highly spoken of. The Taurat--known often as the Book, or the Law of Moses-- is mentioned sixty-five times, and the Injeel—the Gospel of Isa al-Masih-- is mentioned forty-four times. These Holy Books need to be respected and honored, as they were given to mankind by Allah. (See Sura 3.3 Aal-E-Imran.)

In these Holy Books are found many similarities between two women and their sons: Hagar, the second wife of Ibrahim, and her son Isma'il, and Maryam (the virgin Mary) and her son Isa al-Masih Ibn Maryam (Christ the Messiah, the son of Mary). The Honored Qur'an speaks highly of Isa al-Masih (Christ the Messiah) in over ninety ayats (verses) and in fifteen suras (chapters). Therefore, we must take serious note of this important topic.

What follows is a brief comparison of how Isma'il (Ishmael), the firstborn of Ibrahim (Abraham), and Hagar, his mother, prefigured or foreshadowed Maryam (the virgin Mary) and Isa al-Masih Ibn Maryam (Christ the Messiah, the son of Mary).

1. **BOTH WOMEN IN THIS ACCOUNT WERE UNMARRIED WHEN THEY WERE CHOSEN FOR A SPECIAL ROLE.**

Hagar, the servant handmaid in Abraham and Sarai's home. Genesis 16:1: "Now Sarai Abram's wife bare him no children: and she had an [unmarried] handmaid, an Egyptian, whose name was Hagar.... And Sarai ... gave [Hagar] to her husband Abram to be his wife," and "she conceived." Hagar foreshadowed Maryam the virgin, who would bear a Son in her virginity.

Maryam the virgin: Isaiah 7:14: "Therefore the Lord himself shall give you a sign; Behold, a virgin shall conceive, and bear a son, and shall call his name Immanuel." This reference to Maryam in Bible prophecy came hundreds of years before she lived.

2. **BOTH WERE VISITED BY A HEAVENLY MESSENGER.**

Hagar: Genesis 16:7: "And the angel of the LORD found her by a fountain of water in the wilderness, by the fountain in the way to Shur."

Maryam: Luke 1:26-27: "And in the sixth month the angel Gabriel was sent from God unto a city of Galilee, named Nazareth, to a virgin espoused to a man whose name was Joseph, of the house of David; and the virgin's name was Mary [Maryam]."

### 3. BOTH SUBMITTED TO HEAVEN'S MESSAGE.

Hagar: Genesis 16:9: "And the angel of the LORD said unto her [Hagar], Return to thy mistress, and **submit thyself under her hands**."

Maryam: Luke 1:38: "And Mary said, Behold the

handmaid of the Lord; **be it unto me according to thy word**. And the angel departed from her."

### 4. BOTH WERE HANDMAIDS (SLAVES, OR SERVANTS).

Hagar: Handmaid of Sarai. Genesis 16:1: "Now Sarai Abram's wife bare him no children: and she had an handmaid, an Egyptian, whose name was Hagar."

Maryam: Handmaid of Allah. Luke 1:38: "And Mary said, Behold the handmaid of the Lord; be it unto me according to thy word...."

### 5. BOTH FLED INTO THE DESERT TOWARDS EGYPT.

Hagar: When Hagar was severely oppressed by Sarai because Hagar was with child by Abram, she fled towards Egypt, her former home. Genesis 16:6-7: "But Abram said unto Sarai, Behold, thy maid is in thy hand; do to her as it pleaseth thee. And when Sarai dealt hardly with her, she fled from her face. And the angel of the LORD found her by a fountain of water in the wilderness, by the fountain in the way to Shur." (Shur was located on the northeastern border of Egypt.)

Maryam, after Isa al-Masih was born: Matthew 2:13: "And when they were departed, behold, the angel of the Lord appeareth to Joseph [Yusef] in a dream, saying, Arise, and take the young child [Isa al-Masih] and his mother [Maryam], and flee [Hijra] into Egypt, and be thou there until I bring thee word: for Herod will seek the young child to destroy him." Hagar's flight toward Egypt foreshadowed this later Hijra (flight) of Maryam with her baby Isa al-Masih to Egypt.

### 6. Both women were chosen to bear offspring.

Hagar: Genesis 16:2: "And Sarai said unto Abram…I pray thee, go in unto my maid; it may be that I may obtain children by her." Genesis 16:11: "And the angel of the LORD said unto her [Hagar], Behold, thou art with child, and shalt bear a son…."

Maryam: Luke 1:28: "And the angel came in unto her [Maryam], and said, Hail, thou that art highly favoured, the Lord is with thee: blessed art thou among women." Luke 1:31: "And, behold, thou [Maryam] shalt conceive in thy womb, and bring forth a son, and shalt call his name JESUS [Isa al-Masih]."

### 7. Both were told their sons' names prior to birth.

Hagar's son: Genesis 16:11: "And the angel of the LORD said unto her … thou … shalt call his name Ishmael"… [Isma'il, meaning Allah shall hear].This naming of her son foreshadowed the coming of a Son whom Allah again would name: Isa al-Masih (Christ the Messiah):

Maryam's Son: Matthew 1:21: "…Thou shalt call his name JESUS [Isa]: for he shall save his people from their sins."

### 8. Both sons were first-born.

Hagar, Abraham's second wife: Isma'il was her first-born. Genesis 16:15: "And Hagar … bare Abram a son…."

Maryam: Psalm 89:27: "Also I [Allah] will make him [Isa al-Masih son of Maryam] my firstborn" Luke 2:7: "And she [Maryam] brought forth her firstborn son…."

### 9. Both of the sons were blessed by Allah.

Hagar: Genesis 17:20: "And as for Ishmael, I [Allah] have heard thee: Behold, I have blessed him, and will make him fruitful, and will multiply him exceedingly; twelve princes shall he beget, and I will make him a great nation."

Maryam: Luke 1:30-32: And the angel said unto her … behold, thou shalt conceive in thy womb, and bring forth a son, and shalt call his name JESUS. He shall be great, … and of his kingdom there shall be no end." Only Allah could give such a blessing.

### 10. Both women agonized over their sons' anguish.

Hagar: Genesis 21:15-16: "And the water was spent in the bottle, and she cast the child under one of the shrubs. And she went, and sat her down over against him a good way off, as it were a bowshot: for she said, Let me not see the death of the child. And she sat over against him, and lifted up her voice, and wept." This foreshadowed the suffering of Maryam over the Son of her virginity, Isa al-Masih.

Maryam at Golgotha witnessed her Son suffering upon the cross: John 19:25, 28: "Now there stood by the cross of Jesus his mother...: After this, Jesus knowing that all things were now accomplished, that the scripture might be fulfilled, saith, I thirst."

### 11. Both sons were rejected.

Hagar's son was rejected by Sarah, the first wife of

Ibrahim. Genesis 21:10: "Wherefore she said unto Abraham [Ibrahim], Cast out this bondwoman and her son: for the son of this bondwoman shall not be heir with my son, even with Isaac." This foreshadowed the rejection of Isa al-Masih by Israel (Jews).

Maryam's Son: Isa al-Masih (Christ the Messiah) was rejected by the Jews (daughter of Zion-Israel). That nation had been Allah's chosen religious community (*ummah*) of that day. John 19:15: "But they [Jews and the Jewish leaders] cried out, Away with him, away with him, crucify him. Pilate saith unto them, Shall I crucify your King? The chief priests answered, We have no king but Caesar."

### 12. Both sons left the comforts of home.

Isma'il: The honored firstborn son of Abraham was sent away without an inheritance, or honor, or security, or the comforts of home. Genesis 21:10: "…Cast out this bondwoman and her son: for the son of this bondwoman shall not be heir with my son, even with Isaac." This foreshadowed Isa al-Masih leaving the comforts of Heaven to come to this fallen and wicked planet.

There is a contrast here, though. Jesus willingly left the glory, honor, comforts, and security of Heaven to submit to Heaven's will. Isa al-Masih: Psalms 89:44: "Thou [Allah] hast made his [Isa's] glory to cease, and cast his throne down to the ground [earth]."

### 13. Both were protected by Allah as they grew.

Isma'il: Genesis 21:20: "And God [Allah] was with the lad; and he grew, and dwelt in the wilderness, and became an archer."

Isa al-Masih: Luke 2:40: "And the child grew, and waxed strong in spirit, filled with wisdom: and the grace of God was upon him."

### 14. Both sons were separated from their Fathers, which caused deep anguish.

Isma'il: Allah directed Abraham to "hearken unto" Sarah's voice, to "cast out" his beloved Isma'il and his mother Hagar from his home, in order to gain peace in his family. Doing so caused Abraham great grief. Genesis 21:11: "And the thing was very grievous in Abraham's sight because of his son." This foreshadowed the anguish which the Heavenly Father would experience when He had to separate from His Son Isa al-Masih on the cross of Calvary.

Isa al-Masih: His coming to this fallen world and voluntarily taking upon Himself the sin and penalty of the human race caused a separation from His Heavenly Father. Matthew 27:46: "And about the ninth hour Jesus [Isa al-Masih] cried with a loud voice, saying, Eli, Eli, lama sabachthani? that is to say, My God, my God, why hast thou forsaken me?"

### 15. Both spent time in the wilderness (desert).

Isma'il: Genesis 21:14: "And Abraham rose up early in the morning, and took bread, and a bottle of water, and gave it unto Hagar, putting it on her shoulder, and the child, and sent her away: and she departed, and wandered in the wilderness of Beersheba."

Isa al-Masih: Matthew 4:1: "Then was Jesus led up of the Spirit into the wilderness to be tempted of the devil."

Notice the many close comparisons between Isma'il and Isa al-Masih! What should be our response to these numerous parallels? Allah has spoken to the seed of Ibrahim from the line of Isma'il and Hagar. So many experiences of Isma'il were but foreshadowing the experiences of Isa al-Masih. Allah, in His compassion and love for the souls of all men, wants the truth of Isa al-Masih, the Saviour of mankind, to be understood by all. Allah has not left anyone destitute but has come near to us again. A fountain has been opened in the desert of this world for all. Why remain thirsty? Drink and be filled. Believe in your heart that Allah sent Isa al-Masih, the Holy One as your Saviour, Intercessor, *Shafi*, *Wali*, Protector and Redeemer from sin.

# Why Allah Rejected Ancient Israel

There is a question that must be asked by all thinking Muslims. It is quite clear from the Honored Qur'an and from the Holy Books that ancient Israel-- the Jewish nation—was at one time the chosen people of Allah. Indeed, they had been preferred above all others (Sura 2.40, 47 Al-Baqara) and with them God had established His covenant. But then something went terribly wrong, and Allah rejected them as His chosen people!

Yet were they not the people whom Allah had delivered from cruel slavery in Egypt? Both the Holy Books of Scripture and the Qur'an state clearly that ancient Israel had been the people whom Allah had blessed with truth and knowledge from heaven for well over a thousand years. They had been given manifold blessings which were to be shared with the world. But what failed? Why were they rejected?

For answers we look to the sacred Books that Allah has sent down for our guidance and admonition. But first, our priority is to invite the reader to send a prayer (*du'a*) to Allah, for we must not only be in submission to Him, but also look to Him for understanding. Without the Spirit (*Ruh*) of Allah to guide us we will surely end up in error. We have not wisdom in and of ourselves to help us; thus we look heavenward. Help will be given us if we humbly seek heavenly wisdom.

## Isa al-Masih's Arrival and Work Foretold

Some say that ancient Israel forfeited its status as God's special people because the Jews refused to acknowledge Isa al-Masih, as pointed out to them in the Old Testament Scriptures. Sura 5.44 Al-Maeda reads, "It was We who revealed the law (to Moses): therein was guidance and light. By its standard have been judged the Jews, by the prophets who bowed (as in Islam) to Allah's will, by the rabbis and the doctors of law: for to them was entrusted the protection of Allah's book, and they were witnesses thereto: therefore fear not men, but fear me, and sell not my signs for a miserable price. If any do fail to judge by (the light of) what Allah hath revealed, they are (no better than) Unbelievers."

Allah did not wish to reject the Jews. Neither did He want the Jews to reject Isa al-Masih when He was sent down to them. Allah plainly foretold in the Hebrew Scriptures how al-Masih (the Messiah) would come. Ancient prophets were sent with numerous messages, so that the Jews needed not to fail in receiving Him with gladness. Below are just a few of those messages regarding Isa, along with their prophetic fulfillment:

In the Taurat, Moses (Musa) wrote prophetically about 1451 BC that Isa al-Masih would be a prophet like himself: "...The Lord thy God will raise up unto thee a prophet like unto me; unto him ye shall hearken." Deuteronomy 18:15

This prophecy was fulfilled in the life of Isa al-Masih. The Injeel, in Acts 3:20-22, written around 33 AD (1484 years later), says of Isa, "...And he [Allah] shall send Jesus Christ, for Moses truly said a prophet shall the Lord our God raise up like unto me."

The prophet Isaiah, writing in approximately 742 BC, foretold that Isa al-Masih would be born of a virgin: "Behold, a virgin shall conceive and bear a son, and shall call his name Emanuel." Isaiah 7:14.

This prophecy's fulfillment came more than 700 years later, in 4 BC, and was recorded in the Injeel in Matthew 1:18, 21: "When ... Mary [Maryam] was espoused to Joseph, before they came together, she was found with child of the Holy Ghost [*Ruh* of Allah]."

Even the exact village where Isa al-Masih was to be born was clearly foretold. The prophet Micah of the Taurat wrote this in 742 BC: "But thou, Bethlehem Ephratah, though you be little among the thousands of Judah, yet out of thee shall he come forth unto me that is to be ruler in Israel, whose going forth have been from of old, from everlasting." Micah 5:2.

In the Injeel we read of the fulfillment of this ancient prophecy, in 4 BC: "Now Jesus [Isa] was born in Bethlehem of Judea...." Matthew 2:1.

The prophet Daud (David) foretold that kings from the East would come to adore Isa and to present rare gifts to Him. Zabur Psalms 72:10 states: "The Kings of Tarshish and of the Isles shall bring presents: the kings of Sheba and Seba shall offer gifts."

The fulfillment of this ancient prophecy was recorded in Matthew 2:1, 2, 11: "There came wise men from the east to Jerusalem ... to worship him.... They presented unto him gifts: gold and frankincense and myrrh."

Ancient prophets also foretold the manner of the Messiah's work. For example, Taurat Isaiah 35:5, 6, recorded in 713 BC, has this prophecy: "Then the eyes of the blind shall be opened and the ears of the deaf shall be unstopped. Then shall the lame man leap as an hart, and the tongue of the dumb sing...."

This prophecy was fulfilled in 31 AD: "Jesus [Isa] answered and said ... the blind receive their sight and the lame walk, the lepers are cleansed, and the deaf hear, the dead are raised up, and the poor have the gospel preached unto them." Injeel Matthew 11:4-6.

## Isa's Rejection Also Foretold

Despite these recorded prophecies and their fulfillment, and more like them, Daud recorded something very strange in the Zabur. He wrote that Isa al-Masih would be rejected by the Jews! Yes, the unthinkable would happen. Although Allah had favored the ancient Jews with unnumbered blessings, to prepare them to proclaim and receive the coming Messiah, the ancient prophets clearly stated that Isa al-Masih would be rejected. Zabur Psalms 118:22 says, "The stone [referring to Isa al-Masih] which the builders refused is become the head of the corner."

The fulfillment of that prophecy is found in Matthew 21:42: "Jesus saith unto them, did ye never read in the scriptures, the stone which the builders rejected, the same is become the head of the corner: This is the Lord's doing, and it is marvelous in our eyes."

To the prophet Daud was revealed the startling fact that one of Isa's disciples would betray Him into the hands of ungodly men who would severely abuse Him. Zabur Psalms 41:9 says, "Yea, mine own familiar friend, in whom I trusted, who did eat of my bread, hath lifted up his heel against me."

Isa applied this prophecy to Himself in Injeel John 13:18, 21. "I speak not of you all: ...but that the scriptures may be fulfilled, He that eateth bread with me hath lifted up his heel against me.... Verily, verily, I say unto you, that one of you shall betray me." He was referring to Judas Iscariot, who that same night betrayed Isa to the Jewish priests and Roman soldiers." The details of that betrayal were recorded in Injeel John 18:1-13.

The prophet Isaiah foretold that the Jews and the Romans would treat Isa cruelly. Written in 712 BC, Taurat Isaiah 50:6 reads, "I gave my back to the smiters, and my cheeks to them that plucked off the hair: I hid not my face from shame, and spitting."

Over seven centuries later, a brief record of Isa's abuse was written in Injeel Mark 14:65: "And some began to spit on him, and to cover his face, and to buffet him." John 19:1 added some details: "Pilate took Jesus and scourged him" (had him whipped).

The ancient prophet Zechariah in 487 BC foretold that Isa would be smitten and his followers scattered. Taurat Zechariah 13:7: "Smite the shepherd and

the sheep shall be scattered." Prophetic fulfillment came in 33 A.D: "Then all the disciples forsook him,

and fled." Matthew 26:56.

The prophet Zechariah even foretold the sum the Jews would pay Judas for betraying Isa: "If ye think good, give me my price: so they weighed for my price thirty pieces of silver." Taurat Zechariah 11:12. The Injeel bears record of fulfillment in 33 AD: "And

they [the chief priests] covenanted with him [Judas] for thirty pieces of silver." Matthew 26:15. Matthew 27:3-5 confirms that fact: "[Judas] brought again the thirty pieces of silver to the chief priests and elders, saying, ...I have betrayed the innocent blood ... and he cast down the pieces of silver in the temple...."

### THE REJECTION OF ANCIENT ISRAEL RECORDED

After all this evidence, it seems strange that the Jews would have rejected Him whom was sent down. But we must realize that Isa did not come as the Jews expected Him. They wanted a powerful ruler who would drive the hated Romans from their land. When Isa did not fulfill their expectations, they refused to recognize Him. They failed to comprehend that He was sent with a different mission. He was to be the sacrifice for the sins of humanity. The prophet Isaiah foretold in 712 AD that Isa would bear the sin of all:

"Surely he hath borne our griefs and carried our sorrows.... He was wounded for our transgressions. He was bruised for our iniquities [sin]. The Lord hath laid on him the iniquity [sin] of us all." Taurat Isaiah 53:4-6. The Injeel confirms Isa's true purpose in Isa's own words: "...The Son of man came ... to give his life a ransom for many." Matthew 20:28.

But the ancient Jews rejected all this evidence, and finally Isa told them: "…**The kingdom of God will be taken away from you,** and given to a people who will produce its fruit." Injeel Matthew 21:43 TNIV.

Centuries earlier, the Shekinah (glory of Allah) over the ark of the covenant in the temple had been withdrawn. But when Allah, in the form of Isa al-Masih, was repeatedly rejected by the Jews, He could no longer be the Protector of Israel and of the temple. Both the temple and the nation were finally forsaken by Allah.

Isa knew of the terrible consequences to come from the decisions the Jews were making. The pleading voice of heaven was heard in the voice of Isa al-Masih: "Jerusalem, Jerusalem, you who kill the prophets and stone those sent to you, how often I have longed to gather your children together, as a hen gathers her chicks under her wings, and you were not willing. Look, **your house is left to you desolate**." Injeel Matthew 23:37-38 TNIV. He fearfully told them, "Daughters of Jerusalem, weep not for me, but weep for yourselves, and for your children." Injeel Luke 23:28. In 70 AD Titus, the Roman general, came with his fierce military and destroyed not only Jerusalem but also the glorious temple, and over a million Jews. Thousands more were sold into slavery.

This lesson stands in history. Are we paying attention? Might we not also reject Him who was sent down? Rather, accept the offer of mercy from Allah, which is the righteousness of Isa al-Masih for us. When Allah calls, be listening and do not stall His intentions. Isa was the most powerful representation of Himself that Allah could send to mankind, but the majority of the Jews rejected Him. We cannot do the same without suffering the same eternal loss. Today may we make intelligent decisions and be wise. Today may Allah grant you His eternal peace. -

# Blazing Fire

May Allah, by His Abounding Grace, lead you to escape the "blazing fire" that is reserved for all who persist in sin and refuse to submit and surrender to the love of Allah. May we be among the *Mutaqeen* (pious ones) and receive the righteousness of Allah, rather than this tragic fate!

"Verily Satan is an enemy to you: so treat him as an enemy. He only invites his adherents, that they may become Companions of the blazing fire". Sura 35.6 Fatir.

It is Satan and his fallen agents for whom the "blazing fire" is prepared. So shun him by the Grace of Allah.

Just what exactly is "blazing fire"? For whom was it created? Does this judgment of Allah, 'blazing fire' last for eternity? How can one avoid this torment? We need to be much in private prayer (*du'a*) over this issue, for truly it involves our eternal destiny.

It is only by humbly submitting to Allah and asking Him to reveal truth to us that we can find the needed answers to these questions. How often the Honored Qur'an points souls to the Scriptures which Allah, in mercy, sent down to mankind. The Qur'an says that in the Holy Books-- in the Taurat, Zabur and the Injeel—"light" is revealed to us (Sura 21.48 Al-Anbiya). It says therein is a "guide to mankind" (Sura 3.3 Aal-E-Imran). These books are called "Allah's Book" (Sura 5.44 Al-Maeda).

"…Allah sent Messengers [prophets of the past] with glad tidings and warnings; and with them He sent **the Book** in truth [Taurat, Zabur, and Injeel]…. Allah by His Grace Guided the believers to the Truth…. Allah guides whom He will to a path that is straight." Sura 2.213 Al-Baqara.

Many in Islam today seem to have some mistaken idea that the Taurat and Injeel are corrupted or altered. However, the Qur'an continually points to these sources for us to study and use as the "message" (Sura 21.48 Al-Anbiya) to those who do right! Now this important question! Would Allah direct the "unlettered" prophet to a corrupted source? No, never. Then how dare anyone disregard His admonition?

Allah knows what He is doing and we need to pay special attention to what has been sent down to Musa, Daud, Isa al-Masih and many prophets of the past. We will turn to these sacred revelations of the past prophets of Allah for our study today.

## For Whom Intended?

Was the "blazing fire" designed for men that Allah Himself made? No, not for men. Injeel Matthew 25:41 Isa al-Masih, Messenger from Allah tells us: "Then shall he say also unto them on the left hand, Depart from me, ye cursed, into everlasting fire, prepared for the devil and his angels." It was never the intention of Allah to destroy man's life in the fires of hell. Allah is not at all pleased that any should perish in the fires of hell.

The Injeel clearly states that the fire was prepared for the "devil and his angels," and not for mankind. However, God (Allah) will soon and with finality deal with the sin problem that originated with Iblis (Satan), and which has been continued by much of mankind. Those who insist on continuing in sin— those who prefer to hold onto their sins and do not seek the forgiveness so freely offered by Allah through Isa al-Masih-- such will finally perish in the same flames intended only for the devil and his angels.

Mercifully, Allah has prepared a way of escape for all who choose to escape, in the same way that many apartment buildings have fire escapes attached to their exteriors in the event of fires. God in mercy has prepared a way to avoid the fires of the last day by giving us a "fire escape"—namely, Isa al-Masih Ibn Maryam.

## Allah's Question for Mankind Today

It is a terrible misunderstanding of the character of Allah to think that it will bring Him pleasure to see those created in His image suffering in the flames of fire! Rather, He is seeking through all measures to encourage mankind to seek Him, confess their wrongs, and find forgiveness. It pains His Holy Heart to see mankind make unwise choices. Taurat Ezekiel 33:11 reveals His heart toward man: "Say unto them, As I live, saith the Lord GOD, **I have no pleasure in the death of the wicked**; but that the wicked turn from his way and live: turn ye, turn ye from your evil ways; for why will ye die…?"

## Lessons from Sodom and Gomorrah

Will the fire be the "Eternal Home" (Sura 41:28 Fussilat) of unbelievers and unrepentant sinners, as well as the devil and his angels? Will this Hell-fire have no end? It would be well for us to "explain … what Hell-fire is" (Sura 74.27 Al-Muddaththir), and we have an excellent example of it in the story of Lud [Lot] and the city of Sodom: "Even as Sodom and Gomorrah, and the cities about them in like manner, giving themselves over to [sexual] fornication, and going after strange flesh, are set forth for an example, **suffering the vengeance of eternal fire.**" Jude 1:7.

The Holy Books give a distinct picture of this "eternal fire." It will clearly do its work, without the interference or aid of anyone. It is a fire from which no lost person or fallen angel can escape, nor is anyone able to extinguish these flames. However, if you should travel today to the area where once stood those beautiful cities of the plain-- Sodom, Gomorrah and others-- you would clearly see that this area is no longer on fire! The "eternal" fire has gone out! It has done its work and has gone out. There is nothing more to burn. Those immoral cities, which were so corrupt as to have called down the vengeance of an offended God, forever vanished in the flames. There remains not even a coal to warm the hands.

Such will be the eternal fire at the end of the world. Then the wrath of Allah will be poured out upon all who have remained unbelievers-- those who have refused to receive the love of Allah and rejected "His Abounding Grace" (Sura 11:3 Hud) so mercifully provided for all. The fire also will descend in full measure upon the fallen angels [*Jinn*] and the devil himself [*Shatan*], who has plagued this world for so many years. In the Revelation given to Isa al-Masih from Allah, it very clearly states the end of the wicked…

"And they [all the wicked of earth] went up on the breadth of the earth, and compassed the camp of the saints about, and the beloved city: and **fire came down from God out of heaven, and devoured them.**" Injeel Revelation 20:9.

Allah in mercy will finally and completely destroy and eradicate all sin and its work. Never shall Iblis the devil (Shatan) be anymore. "All they that know thee among the people shall be astonished at thee: thou shalt be a terror, and never shalt thou be any more." Ezekiel 28:19. The process of burning will end, but the results of this fire are eternal.

This fire cannot be put out until it has completed the work that Allah has intended it should do. It burns away all the wicked, including Shatan/Iblis the devil and all the Jinn. If any person holds onto his sins, preferring them to obedience to Allah, he must perish forever along with those cherished sins when they are destroyed in the "eternal fire." Even cherishing just one sin of disobedience is rebellion against Allah and His way. But when all sin is at last devoured by the flames, the fire will have finished its divine purpose, and it will go out. Now in this our hour of probation given to us, is the time to earnestly request the cleansing of our lives from the stain of sin.

Dear friend of Allah, a way of escape has been made for all the descendants of Adam to escape this "blazing fire" that will come at the end of this world. Allah never intended anyone in the human family to suffer in what the Holy Book says is "the second death." Revelation 2:11, 20:6, 20:14, 21:8. It was designed only for Shatan/the devil and his angels. Allah, in great mercy and love for the family of Adam, has sent down Someone to take the punishment which was due unto us for sinning. That Someone is Isa al-Masih Ibn Maryam. He became the Messiah not only for the Jews, but for all the descendants of Adam—for all whosoever will accept this offer of mercy from the throne of Allah!

"…And whosoever will, let him take the water of life freely." Revelation 22:17. That water of life is Isa al-Masih, who is the Saviour of men! Even now, if the *Ruh* (Spirit) of Allah is moving upon your heart and mind, accept that which Heaven sent down. Do not disappoint Allah, who made such a rich provision for us! With gratefulness, accept Allah's mercy.

## Nuh (Noah) and the Flood of Water

Many years ago, the wicked purposes of man led Allah to urge upon Nuh a special project. Nuh was to build an ark (large boat) in which to save himself and his family and all the animals abroad, along with anyone who chose to be saved, from the watery grave that was coming upon the whole earth. Through Nuh and his building project, Allah sent a warning of impending judgment; He told the world that their wickedness would bring about a Flood. Sura 21.76 Al Anbiya. He wanted the wicked to have time to reflect on this warning, and repent and turn from their wicked ways, and be healed. Tragically, they refused to yield themselves to Allah and give up their wickedness. In fact, so extreme were their selfish ways that the Taurat says, "And GOD saw that the wickedness of man was great in the earth, and that every imagination of the thoughts of his heart was only evil continually." Taurat Genesis 6:5.

"Only evil continually." That was what was in their darkened minds. And so, all the world was washed clean of its wicked inhabitants, just as Allah had warned. Only faithful Nuh and his family survived the Flood, safe in the ark.

Today we have rich underground coal and oil fields scattered around the world. Those "fossil fuels" of today are the trees, plants and animals from the days before the Flood. These vast oil fields, located deep within our earth, stand as a witness of what happens when men no longer fear Allah, nor find pleasure in following His ways. Sadly, however, the water could not clean the sinfulness from the hearts of those who were born afterward. As generations rose up after Nuh, they again turned away from Allah.

Now we are once again at the final stages of earth's history. The time is near when Allah will finally, once and for all, deal with the sin issue and with those who choose to cling to their sin rather than allow Allah, through Isa al-Masih, to put away that sin.

The Revelation from Allah states that this fire will have eternal results. In this time before that fire, when a man dies, he will once again appear alive upon the earth, on the day of resurrection, in order to receive his eternal reward of life or death. However, from the "second death" in this "eternal fire" that comes upon the unbeliever and the unrepentant, there will be no resurrection. Never again will they appear anywhere. Satan/Iblis the devil, the Jinn (fallen angels) and all the incurably wicked will be brought to ashes upon this earth. The prophet Malachi carefully wrote for us,

"And ye shall tread down the wicked; for they shall be ashes under the soles of your feet in the day that I shall do this, saith the LORD of hosts." Malachi 4:3.

There will remain nothing but ashes of what was once Iblis the deceiver, and all his agents, and all those from earth who refused the love of God to cleanse and purify them from sin. Then the universe shall be clean forevermore.

It is time now to listen carefully as the Spirit of God speaks to you. Hinder not His will for your life. Plead with Him today to escape the blazing fire. He will hear your plea. "Allah is Oft-forgiving, Most Merciful". Sura 2.173 Al-Baqara

His Mercy is expressed through Isa al-Masih, accept this Gracious offer today!

# The Throne of Allah

"His Throne doth extend over the heavens and the earth, and He feeleth no fatigue in guarding and preserving them for He is the Most High, the Supreme in glory." Sura 2.255 Al-Baqara

In the name of Allah, the Most Merciful, and He who has compassion on mankind. May the sweet peace of Allah be with you. May you have a knowledge of His Word, as well as have His Word abiding in you!

An earthly king has a throne and a territory, and the subjects of his kingdom know the extent of his kingdom. But what about Allah's throne and kingdom? How far does it extend? The Honored Qur'an gives us the answer: "His Throne doth extend over the heavens and the earth…. He is the Most High, the Supreme in glory." Sura 2:255 Al-Baqara.

In the Zabor the prophet Dawd (David) tells us, ""The LORD hath prepared his throne in the heavens; and his kingdom ruleth over all." Psalms 103:19.

Isa Himself described His kingdom as not being an earthly kingdom: "Jesus answered, My kingdom is not of this world: if my kingdom were of this world, then would my servants fight, that I should not be delivered to the Jews: but now is my kingdom not from hence." Injeel John 18:36.

Clearly it is revealed that Allah's dominion extends over the entire created universe. Yet in all that immensity, there is one place where He is not able to plant His banner-- one place where He is not able to rule. Where is that domain? It is none other than the unwilling human heart.

An ancient prophet of Allah tells us that the human "heart is deceitful above all things and desperately wicked: who can know it?" Jeremiah 17:9. That inborn condition of the heart is why it has no place for Allah; there, His benevolent rule is resisted or refused.

Nor will Allah force His will upon anyone. We are free to choose who will be our Master. Force is never used in Allah's kingdom.

## Words from the Honored Qur'an

"Let there be no compulsion in religion: Truth stands out clear from Error: whoever rejects evil and believes in Allah hath grasped the most trustworthy hand–hold, that never breaks." Sura 2.256 Al-Baqara.

The kingdom of Allah neither needs nor wants human hands to force it upon its subjects. Those who become subjects in this kingdom do so willingly, without any external force.

The question is, Who rules on the throne of your heart? Is Allah there, or is selfish "self" presiding there? This is an honest question that each of us ought to ask ourselves often. Who is really in charge of my life? Have I fully surrendered to Allah, or does "self" still want to be in charge? Often the members of your own family can tell you what kind of person you are to live with. Are you kind and compassionate? Or do you often lose your temper, get angry at the children and throw things around in a fury? Is there peace in your heart consistently? What kind of words are spoken daily? Are they harsh words, or are they peaceful and helpful words? What spirit rules in your heart?

## Can the Human Heart Be Changed?

To change the human heart from evil to goodness requires submission to Allah. Only He can change the human heart from one of wickedness to that of kindness and love. An ancient wise prophet wrote of our inability to change ourselves: "Can the Ethiopian change his skin, or the leopard his spots? then may ye also do good, that are accustomed to do evil." Taurat Jeremiah 13:23. The truth is, apart from Allah, try as we will with our human effort, we can neither change our hearts nor work our way to heaven through good works. There must be a supernatural intervention from Allah for the human heart to turn and live right.

It takes a miracle to change the human heart, and fortunately, Allah is in the business of miracles—but for this to happen to us, we must first desire a change. We need to give Allah permission to rule in our hearts. Without our consent, Allah cannot change our corrupt hearts, for He will not force us to change.

From the time of the fall of Adam in the garden of bliss, all human hearts and thoughts have been impure and deceitful, and we cannot trust them. Iblis has corrupted our hearts with evil and sin, and our very nature is in rebellion against Allah and His Law. But whosoever will turn to Him can have his heart and nature cleansed and renewed.

## How Is the Human Heart Changed?

The Taurat tells us plainly that our human hearts cannot be trusted. They are "deceitful above all things and desperately wicked...." Taurat Jeremiah 17:9. Yet there is a promise in the Injeel-- a blessing for those who are "pure in heart"-- that "they shall see God." Injeel Matthew 5:8. How can we become "pure in heart"? The answer lies in trusting and accepting the promises of Allah. To Ezekiel, another ancient prophet, sheds much light on this subject of how the human heart receives cleansing. Here is what Allah has said, and we know that what Allah has promised to one, He will give to all, for He loves all:

"For I will take you out of the nations; I will gather you from all the countries.... I will sprinkle clean water on you, and you will be clean; I will cleanse you from all your impurities and from all your idols. **I will give you a new heart and put a new spirit in you**; I will remove from you your heart of stone and give you a heart of flesh. And **I will put my Spirit** [*Ruh* Allah] **in you** and move you to follow my decrees and be careful to keep my laws." Ezekiel 36:24-27 TNIV.

Our fallen natures have selfish inclinations to live unlawfully, contrary to the sacred laws of Allah, the ten commandments. We separate ourselves from God. But by the Grace of Allah, if He is allowed entrance into our lives, He gives us a desire to live above the strong pulls of the fallen natures we possess. A heavenly desire to do righteousness can be born within us. How does Allah do this in us and how can we obtain His Spirit (*Ruh* Allah)?

Many years ago, Allah sent someone who was like Him in character. He was the One who was sent down from all eternity. Isa al-Masih (Christ), who is the **Word of Allah** (Sura 3.45 Aal-E-Imran) was always united with God. He, the Word of Allah, came to this earth; He took upon Himself human nature, yet He was still one with God. He is the One and only necessary link or connection which unites Allah with humanity.

"Because God's children are human beings--made of flesh and blood--the Son [the Word] also became flesh and blood. For only as a human being could He die, and only by dying could He break the power of the devil, who had the power of death. Only in this way could He set free all who have lived their lives as slaves to the fear of dying.

We also know that the Son did not come to help angels; He came to help the descendants of Abraham. Therefore, **it was necessary for Him to be made in every respect like us,** His brothers and sisters, so that He could be our merciful and faithful High Priest before God. **Then He could offer a sacrifice [Himself] that would take away the sins of the people."** Hebrews 2:14-17 NLT.

It is only through Isa al-Masih that we can receive new natures and His Righteousness to become children of God. To all who believe on Him, He gives power to become the sons and daughters of Allah. (Injeel John 1:12). Thus through this One and only transforming "link" named Isa al-Masih, the human heart becomes the temple of the living God. It is because Isa al-Masih took our human nature that men and women may become partakers of the divine nature. He brings life and immortality to light through His life. Thus by receiving Him (Isa al-Masih) who was sent down, by accepting this gift from heaven, a transformation will take place in our hearts and Allah will rule upon the throne in each willing heart.

"Let God transform you into a new person by changing the way you think. Then you will know God's will for you." Romans 12:2 NLT. Our entire lives can then change, from one of selfishness and sinfulness to one of wanting to do good deeds and unselfish acts of kindness to all around us.

Dear friend, do you desire Allah to be seated upon the throne of your heart? Do you wish to put an end to the evil and sinful acts that you do in your life? Do you want wicked thoughts to no longer control your life? Yes, it all can be done. Today accept Christ the Sin-bearer [*al-fida*] into your heart. Ask Isa al-Masih to come into your heart and give you a new life-- a new life in Christ.

## Ancient Israel Chose Another Master

Years ago, ancient Israel chose another master. They turned away from Allah, the source of peace, and chose Iblis [Satan] instead of Allah. The Lord declares, "O Israel, thou hast destroyed thyself." "Hear, O earth: behold, I will bring evil upon this people, even the fruit of their thoughts, because they have not hearkened [listened] unto My words, nor to My law, but rejected it." Taurat Hosea 13:9; Jeremiah 6:19. When Isa al-Masih came to ancient Israel, they turned away from Him and thus destroyed themselves. Yet even today, Isa still seeks to restore peace in troubled minds.

Isa is the One who will bring new consciences into the lives of those who gratefully submit to Him. We will then reproduce His purity and loveliness. These new hearts come as a result of committing our lives to Isa al-Masih, Who was given to us from Allah.

Today, dear friend, let nothing hinder you from accepting this precious gift from heaven. Appeal to Allah, for He longs for us to come to Him, claiming His promises! God has promised: "I will give you a new heart, and put a new spirit in you; I will remove from you your heart of stone and give you a heart of flesh. And I will put my spirit in you and move you to follow my decrees ... and **to keep My laws**." Ezekiel 36:26-27.

### How do I begin?

Find a quiet place-- one where you will not soon be disturbed. Then offer a personal prayer (*du'a*) to Allah, asking Him through Isa al-Masih whom was sent, to reveal Himself to you in a special way. Ask Him to give you peace and a new heart, new thoughts and new actions. Ask Him to rule in the throne of your heart. Allah loves to answer such a prayer of faith. Day by day, keep asking until His promise of a new heart finds fulfillment in your life. Some may ask, "But I am afraid; what should I do?" Often in the Holy Books [the Taurat and Injeel], we read that when Allah sent an angel to those upon earth, the first words the angel spoke were "fear not" or "do not be afraid." He speaks those same comforting words today to those who fear to talk directly to Him. Fear not; Allah will give you a new heart and new motives if that is your heart's desire. You can approach Him with confidence. He loves to have you draw near. Experience His peace and joy today. Experience His love and goodness. Ask, then trust that He will fulfill His promises. Seek Him! Move forward without fear!

# How Hagar Found Allah to be Gracious

May the Grace of Allah be upon thee, for He is "the Lord of Grace abounding." Sura 57.29-30 Al-Hadid. As we open the Holy Books, we ask in humbleness that Allah will hear our prayer (*du'a*) that He will help us understand more of the grace He gives to mankind. Sura 27.73 An-Nami. May we be among those who are grateful for grace.

The topic of grace is found throughout the Honored Qur'an, as well as in the Taurat and Injeel. The Qur'an mentions "grace" seventy-four times! Should this not tell us that the grace of Allah is something we need to study deeply? Just what is grace? How is it defined? We need to know before we can begin to understand what Allah is trying to give us in His gift of grace.

A dictionary defines "grace" as "**the free unmerited love and favor of God,** the spring and source of all the benefits men receive from him." Therefore, if grace is "unmerited love and favor of God," that means it is freely given, because we can have no merit or action sufficient enough to acquire it. If we could somehow earn or deserve it, then it would no longer be grace, but due recompense. Indeed, it must be freely given, because it is of such immeasurable value that it is impossible in any way for mortal man to gain it by his own efforts. Is it then any wonder that the prophet of the desert spoke so often of grace?

Dear reader, seventy-four times grace is spoken of in the Qur'an. We are all sinners, and sinners deserve death, but God freely gives His wonderful grace. Are you, dear reader, a seeker of Allah's grace? "… Seek ye the Grace of Allah…." (Sura 73.20 Al-Muzzammil) and you will surely find it.

## THE STORY OF HAGAR

In the Taurat is found one of the most moving examples ever given to mankind of the grace of Allah.

It is a story from olden times—from the desert-- of someone who personally experienced Allah's grace. The Qur'an states that we need to "mention in the Book (the story of) Isma'il..." (Sura 19.54 Maryam).

In order to get the entire account, though, we need to go to the Bible (Taurat), to Genesis chapter 16, because the story is not found in the Qur'an-- yet the Qur'an instructs the reader to know the story of Isma'il. Muslims therefore need the Bible, for only in the Bible is this story given. In fact, the Qur'an often refers to stories not revealed in the Qur'an, but which are fully described in the Bible. This story of Isma'il is no exception.

In this story, God had promised the wealthy patriarch Abraham [Ibrahim] and his barren wife Sarai (Sarah) a son. "And, behold, the word of the LORD came unto him [Abraham], saying, … he that shall come forth out of thine own bowels shall be thine heir. And he brought him forth abroad, and said, Look now toward heaven, and tell the stars, if thou be able to number them: and he said unto him, So shall thy seed be. And he [Abraham] believed in the LORD; and he counted it to him for righteousness." Genesis 15:4-6.

Years passed, yet no son was born to them. Had God forgotten? Had He failed in His promise of a son to Abraham? It seemed impossible for God to now keep His promise, yet how they longed for a son upon whom to bestow their love, affections, and blessings. Nor was there an heir to the riches that Abraham possessed. Above all, there was no one in Abraham's line to continue to promote the cause of Allah in that heathen land.

Often they remembered that precious promise of an heir which God had years past promised to them. In their impatience with the apparent delay, they devised a plan to assist God in accomplishing His purpose to give them a son. (Does Allah need assistance to carry out His designs?)

Their plan is detailed in the Taurat Genesis 16:1, and repeated here. One day Sarai, the wife of Abraham, suggested a way whereby Abraham could have a child. "Now Sarai Abram's wife bare him no children: and she had an handmaid, an Egyptian, whose name was Hagar. And Sarai said unto Abram, Behold now, the LORD hath restrained me from bearing: I pray thee, go in unto my maid; it may be that I may obtain children by her. And Abram hearkened to the voice of Sarai. And Sarai Abram's wife took Hagar her maid the Egyptian, after Abram had dwelt ten years in the land of Canaan, and gave her to her husband Abram to be his wife. And he went in unto Hagar, and she conceived: and when she saw that she had conceived, her mistress was despised in her eyes." Taurat Genesis 16:1-4.

"And Sarai said unto Abram, My wrong be upon thee: I have given my maid into thy bosom; and when she saw that she had conceived, I was despised in her eyes: the LORD judge between me and thee. But Abram said unto Sarai, Behold, thy maid is in thy hand; do to her as it pleaseth thee. And when Sarai dealt hardly with her, she fled from her face. And the angel of the LORD found her by a fountain of water in the wilderness, by the fountain in the way to Shur. And he said, Hagar, Sarai's maid, whence camest thou? and whither wilt thou go? And she said, I flee from the face of my mistress Sarai. And the angel of the LORD said unto her**, Return to thy mistress, and submit thyself under her hands**. And the angel of the LORD said unto her, I will multiply thy seed exceedingly, that it shall not be numbered for multitude. And the angel of the LORD said unto her, **Behold, thou art with child, and shalt bear a son, and shalt call his name Ishmael; because the LORD hath heard thy affliction**. And he will be a wild man; his hand will be against every man, and every man's hand against him; and he shall dwell in the presence of all his brethren. And she called the name of the LORD that spake unto her, Thou God seest me: for she said, Have I also here looked after him that seeth me? Wherefore the well was called Beerlahairoi; behold, it is between Kadesh and Bered. And Hagar bare Abram a son: and Abram called his son's name, which Hagar bare, **Ishmael**. And Abram was fourscore and six years old, when Hagar bare Ishmael to Abram." Taurat Genesis 16:4-16.

This is how humans sought to fulfill God's promise of a son to them. Their plan was not God's plan, but even so, God did not abandon them; He still worked with them. God's plan was for Sarai, the wife of Abraham, to give birth to a son herself, and this she eventually did. After many more years—long after Sarah had passed child-bearing age—she conceived and bore a son to Abraham in their old ages. Isaac's conception and birth were miracles that came only by the grace of God. Abraham and Sarah rejoiced. God's promises know neither haste nor delay. The wheels of divine providence sometimes seem to turn slowly, but still they keep turning.

Then severe contention developed between Sarah and Hagar, the two wives of Abraham: "And the child [Isaac] grew, and was weaned: and Abraham made a great feast the same day that Isaac was weaned. And Sarah saw the son of Hagar the Egyptian, which she had born unto Abraham, mocking. Wherefore she said unto Abraham, Cast out this bondwoman and her son: for the son of this bondwoman shall not be heir with my son, even with Isaac. And the thing was very grievous in Abraham's sight because of his son. And God said unto Abraham, Let it not be grievous in thy sight because of the lad, and because of thy bondwoman; in all that Sarah hath said unto thee, hearken unto her voice; for in Isaac shall thy seed be called. And also of the son of the bondwoman will I make a nation, because he is thy seed. And Abraham rose up early in the morning, and took bread, and a bottle of water, and gave it unto Hagar, putting it on her shoulder, and the child, and sent her away: and she departed, and wandered in the wilderness of Beersheba. And the water was spent in the bottle, and she cast the child under one of the shrubs. And she went, and sat her down over against him a good way off, as it were a bowshot: for she said, Let me not see the death of the child. And she sat over against him, and lift up her voice, and wept." Genesis 21:1-16.

At this point, all looked hopeless. Hagar and Isma'il, having been sent out of Abraham's camp, wandered in the inescapable heat of the desert. It wasn't long before the water that Abraham had provided them was consumed, as well as the food. Isma'il could endure no more, and lay dying. Hagar placed him under a bush and began weeping.

It is then, when death seemed inevitable, that the grace of Allah appeared, for it says in Genesis, "And God heard the voice of the lad; and the angel of God called to Hagar out of heaven, and said unto her, What aileth thee, Hagar? fear not; for God hath heard the voice of the lad where he is. Arise, lift up the lad, and hold him in thine hand; for I will make him a great nation. And God opened her eyes, and she saw a well of water; and she went, and filled the bottle with water, and gave the lad drink. And God was with the lad [grace]; and he grew, and dwelt in the wilderness, and became an archer. And he dwelt in the wilderness of Paran...." Taurat Genesis 21:17-21.

Allah fulfilled His promises to Isma'il, for this son of Hagar was cared for by Allah throughout his youth and into manhood. The Taurat tells us Allah gave him twelve sons-- "twelve princes" as the foundation of a "great nation"-- as promised (Genesis 17:20):

"Now these are the generations of Ishmael, Abraham's son, whom Hagar the Egyptian, Sarah's handmaid, bare unto Abraham: And these are the names of the sons of Ishmael, by their names, according to their generations: the firstborn of Ishmael, Nebajoth; and Kedar, and Adbeel, and Mibsam, And Mishma, and Dumah, and Massa, Hadar, and Tema, Jetur, Naphish, and Kedemah: These are the sons of Ishmael, and these are their names, by their towns, and by their castles; twelve princes according to their nations. And these are the years of the life of Ishmael, an hundred and thirty and seven years: and he gave up the ghost and died; and was gathered unto his people." Genesis 25:12-17. Thus we see the grace of Allah in the lives of Hagar and Isma'il.

Dear reader, are you troubled? Is your life in turmoil, as was Hagar's out in the desert? Perhaps you are in a situation from which you can see no relief. Trust Allah to hold your hand in whatever experience you are going through. Trust fully in Him and cease not to present your cares and perplexities to Him. He cares for you, just as He cared for Hagar in her distress. Whoever you are, Allah is near. His grace is abounding for even the chief of sinners. If we will only turn to Him with the whole heart and seek His grace, He will hear our cries for help. Dear reader, today seek His grace. Make no delay. Allah is very near, and ready to hear the cry of the weakest sinner, just as He heard the cry of Isma'il dying in the wilderness and came to his aid.

# Healing the disease of the Human Heart!

Our world today seems on the verge of destruction. Everywhere you look you find that mankind has grown to the point where selfishness reigns. Wars rage, strife everywhere abounds, the evils of humanity are seen in every nation, none are exempt. How to obtain money at all costs is on the minds of millions. Selfishness has deepened to the point that few care for each other. Will it ever end? Who knows the cure for the selfish human heart? Only Allah knows!

The Quran often speaks of the disease of the human heart. Numerous times this is pointed out and this is the reason that mankind is in the condition it is in. It is because of the disease of sin which man has allowed to take deep root in our hearts (minds). Sura 2.10 Al-Baqara, Sura 5.52 Al-Maeda.

Our natural thoughts are so foreign to Allah that even He must feel ashamed of mankind as He views what is taking place on this planet. This earth with its teeming billions of souls are on this massive ball which is hurling through space at such tremendous speeds, it is only Allah who through His mercy and compassion is keeping it all together and in motion.

Yet most of mankind is unmindful that it is Allah who is sustaining and maintaining it all. While men daily eat from the bounties of earth provided by Him, yet how few consider and appreciate all which Allah has done? How few realize that this world is fast drawing to a close and that life on planet earth as we know it will soon end. Our probationary time is so soon to close. The Last Day is soon to be upon us. "Those who believe (in the Qur'an), and those who follow the Jewish (scriptures), and the Christians and the Sabians,- any who believe in Allah and the Last Day, and work righteousness, shall have their reward with their Lord; on them shall be no fear, nor shall they grieve." Sura 2:62 Al-Baqara.

A prophet of old times from the Holy Books spoke for our day… Zephaniah 1:14 "The great day of the LORD is near, it is near, and hasteth greatly, even the voice of the day of the LORD: the mighty man shall cry there bitterly." As we near the final days of earth, we find that wickedness will only grow worse and worse. "But evil men and seducers shall wax worse and worse, deceiving, and being deceived." 2 Timothy 3:13

### Make use of the probationary time...

Meanwhile, Allah is giving us precious probationary time to help us become acquainted with Him.

It is Allah's will that the human heart be cleansed from the wickedness of the disease called sin. This disease has entered every human heart, yet who knows the cure, who has gone to Allah for cleansing? Who has experienced and understands what Allah wants to do. Even the most sinful and wicked, if he turns to Allah with all the heart will find relief from this disease. The Honored Qur'an mentions sin well over 60 times. Yet how do we deal with this disease? There is but One Hope...

### Seeking the Physician, Allah's Plan

There is healing for the disease which is called sin in the human heart. Sin is mentioned numerous times in both the Quran and the Holy Books of scripture. The Quran associates sin with crime. (Sura 7:84 Al-Araf) It mentions that the flood of Nuh's (Noah's) day deluged those who 'persisted in sin'. (Sura 29.14 Al-Ankaboot). It also states that men ought to 'eschew' or avoid all sin, whether open or secret. (Sura 6.120 Al-Anaam) and finally it reassures us that sin can be forgiven by Allah. (Sura 40.3 Al-Ghafir). It all began with the sin of Adam and Eve that we now continue living in this world of evil and wickedness.

So how can we define sin? There are some would not know what is mean by the word 'sin'! So what is the definition? Quite simply, sin is being out of harmony with Heaven. It is **transgressing or violating Allah's Holy and just Laws, the Ten Commandments.**

Sin is breaking God's Law. (I John 3:4 NLT) It states the same in (1 Samuel 15:24) where the ancients sinned by transgressing or violating God's commandment Laws.

The prophet Daniel realized that sin occurred when the ancient Israel of God turned away from God's Laws and commands. (Daniel 9:5)

Sin brings guilt and shame to us. Sin also comes with a penalty... eternal death. However man is not left without hope in his sinful condition. Allah has promised pardon for the disease called sin and cleansing from it. (Jeremiah 33:8)

God is the Great Physician who alone can cure the disease of sin. Allah has a plan and it is effective. Millions have sought His help and have found relief from the pain and sorrow of sin. Allah is all-powerful, He is not caught short in knowing how to deal with the sin problem in the human heart. Ever since the days of our first parents Adam and his wife Eve, after they partook of the forbidden tree with it's fruit and became the first sinners. It was then they lost their innocence and from then on mankind needed the cure which only Allah can provide. All through the ages, men and women have sought Allah and have found peace in their hearts as well as relief in their lives over the problem of sin. Whether the problem was stealing, lying, cheating, hatred, strife, adultery, murder, pride, violating the Seventh Day Sabbath, slander, bowing to idols, harboring evil thoughts, the list goes on and on. These and many more is what makes up sin which is the disease of the human heart.

Try as men would, the defiled human heart has found no cure apart from Allah. He alone has the cure. You too can find that cure. It clearly states, with Him is forgiveness. Sura 40.3 Al-Ghafir. We need not wait any longer which you know was wrong? There is forgiveness with Allah. He welcomes repentance. Repentance is simply having an inward sorrow for sin which leads one to want to cease continuing in sin. "But those who do wrong but repent thereafter and (truly) believe,- verily thy Lord is thereafter Oft-Forgiving, Most Merciful." Sura 7:153 Al-Araf

Through the providence of God, He is the one who is leading you to repent: "Or despisest thou the riches of his goodness and forbearance and longsuffering; not knowing that **the goodness of God leadeth thee to repentance?**" Romans 2:4

...'He [God] does not want anyone to be destroyed, but wants everyone to repent.' 2 Peter 3:9 NLT

An ancient prophet saw the mercy of Allah when he wrote these words...

'Say unto them, As I live, saith the Lord GOD, I have no pleasure in the death of the wicked; **but that the wicked turn from his way and live**: turn ye, turn ye from your evil ways; for **why will ye die**...?' Ezekiel 33:11

We must go to Allah in prayer du'a, and confess that we have sinned, and in sorrow of heart we repent of the wicked deeds in our hearts. We are promised that Allah will forgive. But how can Allah forgive our sins? Who bears the penalty for our sin? Someone always has to pay!

## THE STOLEN GOAT...

Just suppose a man has committed a crime against his neighbor. He may have stolen a goat from his herd when the owner was not watching, but someone else saw the man commit the act. The neighbor confronts the man and says why did you steal my goat? The man now in sorrow says please forgive me, but I have eaten it already. I cannot repay. The owner of the stolen goat can now do one of several things. He can go to the police and then the police will make the thief pay for his crime or the owner can say…"I forgive you this crime" "I will myself will suffer the cost". Sin always has a cost, someone must always pay. In this case either the thief can pay for his crime or the owner can say I will bear this cost myself and endure the loss. In the same way sin always has a cost and the price is high. In order for Allah to forgive sin, He then must pay the price for our sin. The price for sin is very high… it is death, eternal death to the offender! A wise writer has written, Romans 6:23 "For the wages [price] of sin is death, but the gracious gift of God is eternal life in Christ Jesus our Lord!"

It was through Isa al-Masih that Allah was able to forgive our sins. He became the Great Sin Bearer for us! It is now through Isa al-Masih Ibn Maryam, that Allah will forgive our sin and also to write the law of love upon our human hearts. It is up to us to receive Isa al-Masih as our personal Saviour from sin and it's result, eternal death! Remember someone has to pay for your sin. Allah's Justice cannot overlook the crime of sin no more than a judge of earthly courts can overlook a crime here. Justice demands a penalty. Isa al-Masih was sent to pay that penalty for all the world, but how few accept this payment for sin. Today dear reader Isa invites you to receive Him and His payment for your sin. But what is to keep us from continuing in sin? What will make us stop or can we? Is there a remedy that we cease from sin? Can the human heart actually change?

## It takes a miracle

What was written with the finger of Allah upon tables of stone, is to be written upon human hearts so that we now seek to obey Allah. It was no less than a miracle years ago when Musa went to the towering heights of Sinai, to receive tables of stone upon which Allah wrote the sacred Law of Allah with His own finger upon stone. It is also no less a miracle today for Him to write upon the fleshly tables of the human heart His sacred Law. This requires unquestioning submission, this requires an acknowledgement from the human being to allow Allah to do just that. Unless we give Him our complete consent, He cannot do this. We will still continue our lives as before and continue to violate that Sacred and Holy Law the Ten Commandments given to Musa on Sinai. Thus the question is before each of us, will I allow Allah to change my heart, my mind to obedience to Him and His Law? It is again through Isa al-Masih Ibn Maryam, that this miracle happens. When we allow Him to perform this miracle then it produces the peace and joy of heaven.

Allow Allah to have your heart today! Time now to be wide awake listening to His voice speaking to us.

# *Allah, the Holy One; Isa, the Holy Son*

May Heaven's sweet peace be upon thee. May you be blessed to be among those who are dressed in green garments of silk and recline on green cushions in the hereafter (Sura 55.76 Ar-Rahman, Sura 76.21 Al-Insan). May the blessing of Allah the Most Merciful and the One Most Compassionate be upon you today!

The Honored Qur'an mentions Isa al-Masih in fifteen suras (chapters). He is referred to in over ninety ayats (verses)! There must be something very special about Him to be mentioned so frequently. It is quite clear from the Honored Qur'an that Isa is termed "Holy," but who was He? For this question and several others, we seek answers. Since Allah knows all things, we must seek Him in private prayer (*du'a*), that He teach us.

Who was Isa? In the Honored Qur'an, Sura 19.19 Maryam tells us he is Allah's "gift of a holy son" to humanity. Any gift from Allah is to be greatly treasured, but now another question: Whose son was He? Allah's Son or man's son? And how did this "holy son" come into existence as a man?

The Honored Qur'an states and explains very openly that Isa was born of a woman (Maryam) who had had no intimate male relationship: "She [Maryam (Mary)] said: 'How shall I have a son, seeing that **no man has touched me**, and **I am not unchaste**?' He said: 'So (it will be): Thy Lord saith, "That is easy for Me: and (We wish) to appoint him as a Sign unto men and a Mercy from Us": It is a matter (so) decreed.' So she conceived him....." Sura 19.20-22 Maryam (Mary).

Thus we are told definitively that Isa came forth from Allah. In fact, Allah said it was an "easy" thing for Him to carry out His own will in this matter. Now consider, please. Everyone knows that begetting an offspring requires both male and female persons. We know that it is impossible for a woman to conceive a child by herself. Yet Isa is someone who came into existence without the union of male and female; Maryam was a virgin when she gave birth. These things were possible only because Isa came forth from Allah. This makes Him Allah's Son. Assuredly, God's purity and majesty is far, far above His creatures, so we do not mean that in the sense of a sexual relationship, but because the Honored Qur'an says clearly that He was born through the *Ruh* of Allah (Spirit of Allah):

"And Mary ... guarded her chastity; and **We [Allah] breathed into (her body) of Our spirit**; and she testified to the truth of the words of her Lord and of His Revelations, and was one of the devout (servants)." Sura 66.12 At-Tahrīm.

## REFUSING THE GIFT OF ALLAH

Has there ever been another like Isa? No, never. Isa al-Masih came forth from Allah, dear ones, so we must honor and accept what Allah has sent down to us. However, many scholars today struggle greatly, unable or unwilling to believe that Isa was sent from Allah, as Allah's Son. Yet why should this be so difficult for us to understand? Simply put, Allah's love for this world caused Him to reveal Himself to us in a most magnificent way-- a way in which He had never before been revealed. The greatest manifestation of Allah came in the person of Isa al-Masih Ibn Maryam. May His name be blessed forever. Never before in human history had mankind been privileged to see for themselves what Allah is really like in holy character.

The prophet Daud instructs us that Isa's purpose was to benefit and bless mankind. Zabur Psalms 107:20 says that "He [Allah] sent his word, and healed them, and delivered them from their destructions."

Isa, the Holy Son, was able to defuse any previous misrepresentations of Allah. Even the Jews, as pious as they thought themselves to be, had seriously distorted views of Allah. They grossly misunderstood Allah, though they could have known Him, and should have known Him, because of the Holy Books previously sent down, as well as all the prophets of old sent to them. And so when Isa came in a manner different from their misled expectations, they rejected Him completely. Ultimately, their rejection of Him led to their holy city Jerusalem being destroyed by the Romans in AD 70. All means of reaching out to the Jews were encompassed in the great gift of Isa. If we reject Him also, our fate must surely be the same.

Isa is called "Holy," even from birth. After Adam's sin, which of the sons of men have ever been born holy or righteous? "As it is written, there is none righteous, no, not one." Injeel Romans 3:10. In addition, no other person in the Honored Qur'an is called "Holy," not even the desert prophet. This makes Isa al-Masih a very unique, special person, indeed. The same term "Holy" was used by the ancient prophet Isaiah when he wrote about Isa:

Is it not strange that this great person whom Allah would send would be "despised" and "abhorred" by much of mankind, but especially by His own nation to whom He came? Other nations (man, rulers) also have turned from Him, as the sacred account stated. Yet Isa al-Masih was and is truly a miracle from heaven.

### Isa's Birth and Special Work

Indeed, Isa's miracle birth is much greater than the miracle birth of a son to Ibrahim in his old age. Abraham's aged wife Sarah had not only been barren; she was then far past the age of possibly bearing children, yet a miracle of heaven was performed. Sarah was able to conceive a child by Ibrahim in their very old ages. Ibrahim became the father of Isaac when Ibrahim was about 100 years old!

Yet with Isa al-Masih it was different. There simply was no earthly father. Sura 19.20 quotes Maryam saying "…No man has touched me…." See also Sura 3.47 Aal-E-Imran; Sura 66.12 At-Tahrīm. The Spirit of Allah [*Ruh* Allah] had "overshadowed" Maryam and she became with child. Injeel Luke 1:30-35.

"And (remember) her [Mary] who guarded her chastity: **We breathed into her of Our spirit**, and We made her and her son a sign for all peoples." Sura 21.91 Al-Anbiya

"And Mary the daughter of 'Imran, who guarded her chastity; and **We breathed into (her body) of Our spirit;** and she testified to the truth of the words of her Lord and of His Revelations, and was one of the devout (servants)." Sura 66.12 At-Tahrim

"…Mary…that which is conceived in her is of the Holy Ghost." Injeel Matthew 1:20

"And the angel answered and said unto her [Mary], The Holy Ghost shall come upon thee, and **the power of the Highest shall overshadow thee: therefore also that holy thing which shall be born of thee shall be called the Son of God.**" Injeel Luke 1:35

This is, by far, the most amazing human conception and birth ever recorded in the history of this world.

In the Taurat the ancient prophet Isaiah foretold this miracle birth of Isa al-Masih, the "holy son," giving details known only to Allah. It is amazing that Isaiah prophesied this in 742 BC, well over 700 years before Isa came: "Behold, **a virgin shall conceive, and bear a son**, and shall call his name Immanuel." Isaiah 7:14. The name "Immanuel" literally means "God with us"!

Isaiah also foretold Isa's work: "Then the eyes of the blind shall be opened, and the ears of the deaf shall be unstopped. Then shall the lame man leap as an hart, and the tongue of the dumb sing…." Isaiah 35:5-6.

All of this was fulfilled in the life of Isa al-Masih!

Notice how accurately Isa's work was recorded in the Injeel Matthew 11:5: "The blind receive their sight, and the lame walk, the lepers are cleansed, and the deaf hear, the dead are raised up, and the poor have the gospel preached to them."

Isaiah accurately related to those ancient people what Isa's work and mission would be when He would arrive. So that the Jews would not miss this important representative when He was sent down in mercy, Allah in mercy caused all these prophecies to be given to the Jews in the Holy Scriptures, yet in their stubbornness and blind misconceptions, they rejected Him.

One major reason for their rejection was that Isa did not come in the manner in which they expected Him. He came without pomp and ceremony, being born in a stable in Bethlehem. Therefore, He was disregarded by the world's great men of the time, yet humble men who were learners recognized Him as the special gift to mankind from Allah, and adored Him. Angels of Heaven rejoiced in joy at Isa's birth, and announced it:

"And this shall be a sign unto you; Ye shall find the babe [Isa] wrapped in swaddling clothes, lying in a manger. And suddenly there was with the angel a multitude of the heavenly host praising God, and saying, Glory to God in the highest, and on earth peace, good will toward men." Injeel Luke 2:12-14

It was too much for the Jews to accept that Allah would send down the gift of the Righteous One in such a humble manner. However, Isa came not to set up an earthly kingdom, as the Jews expected, but to establish a spiritual kingdom. Isa very clearly told Pilate, the Roman ruler:

"**My kingdom is not of this world**: if my kingdom were of this world, then would my servants fight, that I should not be delivered to the Jews: but now is my kingdom not from hence." Injeel John 18:36. In saying "My kingdom," Isa al-Masih is essence claimed He was a king. But not with the sword and force is the kingdom of God established, but with truth and self-sacrificing, self-renouncing love. "Then said Jesus unto him [Peter], Put up again thy sword into his place: for all they that take the sword shall perish with the sword." Injeel Matthew 26:52.

Not with the sword is the kingdom of God to be advanced and increased, but with kindness and self-renouncing love for souls. **Anything short of this is a deception.** The heart must be won, and no heart is ever won with the sword. The sword is an instrument of threat and force which, if used, will bring about only revenge and deep hatred. Allah's methods alone bring true and lasting success. When the Jews realized that Isa al-Masih would not employ the sword to advance the kingdom of Israel and deliver the hated Romans from their land, they rejected Him.

This man Isa, the "holy son," spent much time with the lowly of men, whom the Jews considered outcasts of society. He freely mixed with those whom the Jews despised and deemed unworthy of salvation:

"And it came to pass, that, as Jesus [Isa] sat at meat [to eat] in his house, many publicans and sinners sat also together with Jesus and his disciples: for there were many, and they followed him. And when the scribes and Pharisees [important Jews] saw him eat with publicans and sinners, they said unto his disciples, How is it that he eateth and drinketh with publicans and sinners? When Jesus heard it, he saith unto them, **They that are whole have no need of the physician, but they that are sick: I came not to call the righteous, but sinners to repentance.**" Mark 2:15-17.

Dear friend, today Isa al-Masih ibn Maryam is in heaven as our great High Priest and intercessor for humanity. He is ministering before the throne of God on our behalf. He took our sins upon Himself, giving in exchange His pure and unselfish life as a ransom for many. This Holy One is speaking to you and all mankind today, inviting us to come to Him. He is the channel that opens the way for us to connect with Heaven. Good works can never earn us a place in heaven; they are tainted with sin. We may be there only by the grace or goodness of Allah, through Isa. Grace is a gift, freely given to those who could never pay the price. Isa al-Masih is heaven's gift of grace. He has revealed the favor of Allah toward us. May Allah in mercy continue to guide us as we seek His will. It is time to seek Isa al-Masih, the Holy One. He is not far away!

# *The Law of Allah*

May the blessings of Allah be upon you today, dear reader. May He grant unto you His Eternal Peace.

The Ten Commandment s (Laws) of Allah are looked upon by many scholars and believers as being important for all people for all time. Others question whether these sacred laws are still binding upon humanity. They ask, "If they are indeed still binding, is it possible to dispense with one or more of them, or must we honor all of them?" Before proceeding, we shall make this serious topic a matter of *du'a* (non-formal) prayer.

## LAWS OF NATURE

The entire universe made by Allah is bound and regulated by laws, some of which keep the planets, stars, moons, nebulae, and galaxies in place, not haplessly colliding. Every believer knows that Allah has laws which govern His creation here upon earth, too. We have many laws of gravity, physics, science, health, and more. Whether we realize it or not, we are daily affected by and working with these laws, which are fixed, or unchangeable, laws of nature. The law of gravity, for example, teaches that an airplane or jet can remain aloft only so long as its power and speed exceed the earthward pull of gravity upon its mass. That is important information to the pilot and any passengers! **Living and working in harmony** with these laws—knowing and abiding by them-- is wise and beneficial for us, since we cannot change them.

## LAWS OF NATIONS

Then there are laws of the nations. Every country of the world today has laws which its people or leaders have established, in order to govern their respective nations in the interest of societal stability. No one would think of living in a nation without laws. How soon would such a condition bring chaos and destruction to all the people in the land.

Despite the wisdom inherent in just laws for a nation's people, there are some who feel that the laws of Allah are somehow different—that they are no longer binding upon His people here on earth. Imagine such a claim! Are we truly free to dispense with the sacred laws of Allah? What has Allah said about this?

## Allah's Changeless Laws

Throughout the Honored Qur'an we are reminded about Allah's Laws: "And remember We took your covenant and We raised above you (the towering height) of Mount (Sinai): (Saying): "Hold firmly to what We have given you, and **hearken (to the Law)**" [the Ten Commandments written on stone]…." Sura 2.93 Al-Baqara. Here ancient Israel was given the sacred laws of Allah, both orally and physically, as they were being led out from Egyptian slavery. Musa (Moses) was given these laws engraved in stone by Allah Himself while Musa was on Mount Sinai. The stone represents permanence.

Long before this time, the laws of Allah had been given to our first parents, for how else could they violate His law? Even during the time of Nuh (Noah), the Laws of Allah were known. Otherwise, there would be no knowledge of sin.

Abraham who lived long before Moses, knew of Allah's holy and just laws, for Allah says of Abraham: "Abraham obeyed my voice, and kept my charge, my commandments, my statutes, and my laws." Taurat Genesis 26:5.

These same laws were repeated to the followers of Allah at Mount Sinai. Moses was given a copy of the divine laws. "And We ordained laws **for him in the tablets** [Ten Commandments written on stone] in all matters, both commanding and explaining all things, (and said): 'Take and hold these with firmness, and **enjoin thy people to hold fast by the best in the precepts.'"** Sura 7.144-145 Al-Araf. For those who are unaware of what laws were given to Musa in the Mount, this chapter includes a complete list of them.

### Ten Commandments, as Given to Moses

1. "Thou shalt have no other gods before me." Exodus 20:3 *(translated from the King James Version).*

2. "Thou shalt not make unto thee any graven image, or any likeness of any thing that is in heaven above, or that is in the earth beneath, or that is in the water under the earth: Thou shalt not bow down thyself to them, nor serve them: for I the LORD thy God am a jealous God, visiting the iniquity of the fathers upon the children unto the third and fourth generation of them that hate me; And shewing mercy unto thousands of them that love me, and keep my commandments." Exodus

20:4-6.

3. "Thou shalt not take the name of the LORD thy God in vain; for the LORD will not hold him guiltless that taketh his name in vain." Exodus 20:7.

4. "Remember the Sabbath day, to keep it holy. Six days shalt thou labour, and do all thy work; but the seventh day [*Saturday*] is the Sabbath of the LORD thy God: in it thou shalt not do any work, thou, nor thy son, nor thy daughter, thy manservant, nor thy maidservant, nor thy cattle, nor thy stranger that is within thy gates: For in six days the LORD made heaven and earth, the sea, and all that in them is, and rested the seventh day: wherefore the LORD blessed the Sabbath day, and hallowed it." Exodus 20:8-11.

5. "Honour thy father and thy mother: that thy days may be long upon the land which the LORD thy God giveth thee." Exodus 20:12.

6. "Thou shalt not kill." Exodus 20:13.

7. "Thou shalt not commit adultery." Exodus 20:14.

8. "Thou shalt not steal." Exodus 20:15.

9. "Thou shalt not bear false witness [lying] against thy neighbour." Exodus 20:16.

10. "Thou shalt not covet thy neighbour's house, thou shalt not covet thy neighbour's wife, nor his manservant, nor his maidservant, nor his ox, nor his ass, nor any thing that is thy neighbour's." Exodus 20:17.

These laws are simple and easy to understand; they are good laws, just and perfect. They were given by Allah in mercy and wisdom to foster peace and stability among mankind here on earth. We wonder: Can these same laws recorded in the Taurat be found in the Qur'an? The answer is "Yes," and in many places.

## TEN COMMANDMENTS IN THE HONORED QUR'AN

1. "Thy Lord hath decreed that ye worship none but Him…" Sura 17.23 Al-Isra.

    "If there were, in the heavens and the earth, other gods besides Allah, there would have been confusion in both.…" Sura 21.22 Al-Anbiya.

2. "...But shun the abomination of idols." Sura 22.30 Al-Hajj.

   "Lo! Abraham said to his father Azar: 'Takest thou idols for gods? For I see thee and thy people in manifest error. And they set up (idols) as equal to Allah, to mislead (men) from the Path!'" Sura 6.74 Al-Anaam.

   "And he said: 'For you, ye have taken (for worship) idols besides Allah.'" Sura 29.25 Al-Ankaboot.

3. "The most beautiful names belong to Allah: so call on him by them; but shun such men as use profanity in his names: for what they do, they will soon be requited." Sura 7.180 Al-Araf.

4. "Your Guardian-Lord is Allah, Who created the heavens and the earth in six days, and is firmly established on the throne (of authority).... He created the sun, the moon, and the stars, (all) governed by laws under His command. Is it not His to create and to govern? Blessed be Allah, the Cherisher and Sustainer of the worlds!" Sura 7.54 Al-Araf.

   "And well ye knew those amongst you who **transgressed in the matter of the Sabbath**: We said to them: 'Be ye apes, despised and rejected.'" Sura 2.65-66 Al-Baqara.

   "And for their covenant we raised over them (the towering height) of Mount (Sinai); and (on another occasion) we said: 'Enter the gate with humility'; and (once again) we commanded them: **'Transgress not in the matter of the sabbath.'** And we took from them a solemn covenant." Sura 4.154 An-Nisa.

5. "Thy Lord hath decreed that ye be kind to parents. Whether one or both of them attain old age in thy life, say not to them a word of contempt, nor repel them, but address them in terms of honour." Sura 17.23 Al-Isra.

6. "...Whether open or secret; take not life, which Allah hath made sacred, except by way of justice and law: thus doth He command you, that ye may learn wisdom." Sura 6.151 Al-Anaam.

   "Kill not your children for fear of want: Verily the killing of them is a great sin." "Nor take life." Sura 17.31, 33 Al-Isra.

7. "Nor come nigh to adultery: for it is a shameful (deed) and an evil, opening the road (to other evils). Sura 17.32 Al-Isra.

   "...That they will not commit adultery (or fornication)...." Sura 60.12 Al-Mumtahina.

8. "...That they will not steal...." Sura 60.12 Al-Mumtahina.

   "Turn ye back to your father, and say, 'O our father! behold! thy son committed theft! we bear witness only to what we know, and we could not well guard against the unseen!" Sura 1.:81 Yusuf.

   "But if the thief repents after his crime, and amends his conduct, Allah turneth to him in forgiveness; for Allah is Oft-forgiving, Most Merciful." Sura 5.39 Al-Maeda.

9. "...Shun the word that is false." Sura 22.30 Al-Hajj.

   "...And if he be a liar, on him is (the sin of) his lie: ...Truly Allah guides not one who transgresses and lies!" Sura 40.28 Al-Ghafir.

   "Woe to the falsehoodmongers." Sura 51.10 Adh-Dhariyat.

   "Behold! how they invent a lie against Allah! but that by itself is a manifest sin!" Sura 4.50 An-Nisa.

   "Give full measure when ye measure, and weigh with a balance that is straight: that is the most fitting and the most advantageous in the final determination." Sura 17.35 Al-Isra.

10. "And in no wise covet those things in which Allah Hath bestowed His gifts more freely on some of you than on others." Sura 4.32 An-Nisa.

    "Come not nigh to the orphan's property except to improve it...." Sura 17.34 Al-Isra.

The truth is that the Law (Ten Commandments) given to Moses is found throughout the Honored Qur'an. Allah has commanded all men in all ages of time, regardless of who they are, to abide by these sacred and just Laws. Yet how many, even among the believers, have turned away from them. Nevertheless, those who truly know Allah as their Creator willingly keep His Holy Laws. "And hereby we do know that we know him, if we keep his commandments." 1 John 2:3.

"Let us hear the conclusion of the whole matter: Fear God, and keep his commandments: for this is the whole duty of man." Ecclesiastes 12:13.

Today, begin by asking Allah to help you to respect and keep all of His sacred Laws.

# If Scholars Lead Their Flocks Astray...

Dear reader, I greet you in the name of Allah, the most compassionate and merciful! May His peace truly be upon thee; may this be a reality. May you be blessed by Allah to inherit "the eternal home; with companions pure (and holy)...." Sura 3.15 Aal-E-Imran.

## How It All Began

Faulty leaders have abounded ever since Shatan/ Iblis (Satan) fell from Heaven. Shatan, who first was named Lucifer, had been a leader in Heaven, and under his influence many angels went astray. This history was recorded by one of the ancient prophets, so that we may know where and how Shatan (Satan) came into being. "How art thou fallen from Heaven, O Lucifer...." Isaiah 14:12. Isa al-Masih, confirmed what was said by Isaiah, and said "I beheld Satan as lightning fall from Heaven." Injeel Luke 10:18. The fallen angels Satan had led into his faulty thinking and teaching, soon became involved in Satan's great rebellion in heaven. They finally were expelled from heaven onto this earth. But why this earth?

It was in Eden, the garden of bliss, where our first parents also fell under Satan's deceptions. "Then did Satan make them slip from the (garden), and get them out of the state (of felicity) in which they had been…" Sura 2.36 Al-Baqara.

Today Satan and his fallen angels focus their evil intentions on the leaders of the people. If he can tempt and lure the leaders out of Allah's way and into his camp, then he can also lead astray the followers of those leaders. Already many leaders unknowingly are following Satan's deceptions. In other words, the special target of Satan are those who are looked upon as leaders. If he can lead the leaders astray, the sheep will all too often obey! Now for that most important question: Who is leading you?

## Who Is Leading You?

We live in a world where thousands upon thousands—yes, even millions—of religious people willingly allow themselves to be led by their leaders. These followers do little more than listen and act upon what their leaders tell them to do and say—often without serious inquiry as to whether their leaders are actually led by God. Instead of individuals inquiring of Allah for themselves, they will take the words of leaders and not even question what is being told them. Thus the leaders become the mind and thought of far too many. These leaders may be educators, scholars, even well-respected persons. Often they are well-meaning, but frequently they are not seeking direction from Allah. Far too often, the leaders will lead men astray. This has been the history ever since the beginning of time.

Should not people who were made by Allah look to Him first, rather than leaders? How is one to seek direction from Allah? The best way is to spend time in private prayer (*du'a*) and plead with Him who knows all. Allah will reveal to us His secrets if we take the time to ask and then listen for His voice. One key point is that the true leaders of Allah will always have high respect for the prior prophets and the messages they brought from Heaven, as recorded in the Taurat, Zabur and Injeel.

## Who is Your Guide?

Friends of Allah, now is the time to earnestly plead with Allah for light and direction. Men long ago, even since the days of Ibrahim, have had to do the same.

Notice that Ibrahim was given direction from Allah, while his relatives around him worshipped idols. Notice how Ibrahim pleads with his own father, who was a leader. "Lo! Abraham said to his father Azar: 'Takest thou idols for gods? For I see thee and thy people in manifest error.'" Sura 6.74 Al-Anaam.

Had Ibrahim simply followed his own father or the scholars of his day or his own relatives, he also would have followed their error. Ibrahim was different, though. He asked Allah directly for guidance, and we can do the same. "…Whosoever follows My Guidance, will not lose his way, nor fall into misery." Sura 20.123 Ta-Ha. However, if we choose to follow even well-meaning leaders and scholars, even though they appear very intelligent, yet if these lead away from the will of Allah, we may be sure that they have lost their inheritance of the eternal home, unless they change their course.

It is not only the misleading scholars and educators who will suffer, but notice what Isa al-Masih said. His words are recorded in the Injeel. "Let them [religious leaders] alone: they be blind leaders of the blind. And if the blind lead the blind, both shall fall into the ditch." Injeel Matthew 15:14.

Very clearly we are told that both false leaders and those who are led by them will fall into the ditch [of destruction]. Paul, a follower of Allah, plainly warns us not to follow false leaders, because we will be led astray from the straight path: "...From such withdraw thyself...." 1 Timothy 6:5. This is strong language, indeed!

The ancient prophet Isaiah said, "And it shall be, as with the people, so with the priest; as with the servant, so with his master; as with the maid, so with her mistress; as with the buyer, so with the seller; as with the lender, so with the borrower; as with the taker of usury, so with the giver of usury to him." Isaiah 24:2. This prophet sent from Allah for Israel clearly told the people that it was the leaders who caused Israel to err. Leaders are more responsible than others, as they are looked up to by the people. When they accept leadership, they gain a certain influence over others, for which they are accountable to Allah. They also obligate themselves to greater accountability to those higher in authority. Allah is the highest authority—the One over all. Therefore, it is very important that leaders carefully and prayerfully request from Allah to know the right way. Allah will teach them. Indeed, He will guide all those who earnestly ask for guidance.

Is this, dear reader, something that you do daily? Do you daily seek Allah for the right way? If not, you may be like many thousands who simply go on in the dark, in error down a wrong path. No matter how brilliant a scholar may appear nor how wise a man may seem, if he is teaching and living contrary to what is in Sura 3.3 Aal-E-Imran, which states that the Taurat and Injeel are the "criterion of judgment between right and wrong," then this false scholar, if he repents not of his ways, will forfeit eternity.

"...He [Allah] sent down the Law (of Moses) and the Gospel (of Jesus) before this, as a guide to mankind, and He sent down the criterion (of judgment between right and wrong)." Sura 3.3 Aal-E-Imran.

Where are you looking for guidance, dear friend of Allah? Do you heed this counsel from the Qur'an? Are you indeed looking at the Taurat and Injeel as guidance and criterion of judgment? Or are you listening to the scholars who are telling thousands that the Taurat and Injeel are falsified or corrupted? Listen, dear friend of Allah. Allah knows how to keep His Word intact from wicked minds. He is powerful enough to keep anyone from spoiling His Word which He sent down through Moses and Isa al-Masih and others.

"The word of thy Lord doth find its fulfilment in truth and in justice: **None can change His words**...." Sura 6.115 Al-Anaam.

## THE LAW OF ALLAH

Without question, the Law of Allah was mercifully given to Moses on the Mount, and written upon two tables of stone with the finger of Allah. What Moses was given, we were given. Notice the words from the Honored Qur'an regarding the sacred laws of Allah:

**"And We ordained laws for him in the tablets** in all matters, both commanding and explaining all things, (and said): 'Take and hold these with firmness, and enjoin thy people to hold fast by the best in the precepts....'" Sura 7.145 Al-Araf.

Friend, for your own eternal safety, are you holding these laws with firmness? These laws are the Ten Commandments of Allah. Now is the time to receive direction from the Taurat and Injeel. As it was true in the days of Isaiah, it is true today that the leaders cause the people to err. "For **the leaders of this people cause them to err**; and they that are led of them are destroyed." Taurat Isaiah 9:16.

Seek the Taurat and Injeel for yourself, and before opening the sacred pages, ask Allah for guidance. Remember that the Taurat came first from the hand of

Allah to Moses. In the same way that the first-born in the family is considered the most important, so that which came first from the hand of Allah must not be regarded as less important than that which followed.

In principle, everything that is brought to us must be tested by the "criterion" which was sent down. "The spirits of the prophets are subject to the prophets." 1 Corinthians 14:32. This simply means that the written teachings of later prophets must be in accord with the written teachings of the earlier prophets of God. "And remember We gave Moses the Scripture and the Criterion (Between right and wrong)." Sura 2.53 Al-Baqara. When a prophet arises with a message of Allah, that prophet may have new light, but the new light will always build upon the messages of prior prophets. A true prophet of Allah will never tear down prior existing truths.

### TIME TO START IS NOW!

How vital it is to begin now! Now is the time to begin asking Allah for guidance. He is no different now than in bygone days, when holy men sought direction from Him. He is just as eager now to listen to your prayers as when Ibrahim walked and talked with Him while on this earth. But we must ask in sincerity! "Thus saith the LORD, Stand ye in the ways, and see, and **ask for the old paths, where is the good way**, and walk therein, and **ye shall find rest for your souls**...." Jeremiah 6:16.

Unfortunately, ancient Israel refused to listen to the prophets sent from Allah. In the time of Isa al-Masih, the leaders of the Jews acted similarly. They misunderstood, misapplied, or ignored the words of the prophets. They had their own agenda, according to their own ungodly ways. Those leaders were finally rejected by Allah. They and their deceived followers perished—some when Jerusalem was destroyed. Many others were captives, enslaved in other nations.

Today, dear friend, we are in the same condition as was Israel in the past. Far too many are listening to false leaders. If they continue in these false paths, most will lose their way of the gardens of bliss in the hereafter, but "the meek will he guide in judgment: and the meek will he teach his way." Zabur Psalms 25.9. Our constant cry ought to be, "Show us the straight way." Sura 1.6 Al-Fatiha.

If you plead with Alllah, asking for guidance to the way of truth in this life, He will guide you. Keep asking, and be sincere. Be prepared; you may not anticipate where Allah will lead you.

If you would like a copy of the Taurat, Zabur, and Injeel, simply go to: www.e-sword.org for a FREE Bible download. There you can obtain a free download for your computer in the language of your choice. Be blessed by reading the Sacred Words of Allah.

# *The Rope of Hope...*

Dear reader, it is my earnest desire that we submit completely and unquestionably to Allah. May His sweet mercy and wisdom be showered upon us this day as we look into this subject ,"the Rope of Hope."

### Man Overboard!

What or who is this rope of hope? We have all heard of stories from those who have gone to sea upon vessels great and small. As often happens, some occurrence causes someone to fall overboard—perhaps a sudden shift in the ship or a strong wind gust catches him off-guard, and into the billowy deeps he falls. Then the cry rends the air, "Man overboard!"

Quickly all on board try their utmost to rescue such an unfortunate one. If far from land, then without rescue, he is at risk of death from exposure, exhaustion or sharks. The ropes are brought out and usually some floating device is attached to the end that is thrown to the person out in the waves. If the waves aren't too high, it is helpful if the person can swim to the device, but if not, often someone else risks his life by plunging into the sea to assist in the rescue. The lifeline is redirected to the stronger person and both most gratefully accept the offer to be pulled on board to safety once again.

In much the same way, amid the teeming millions of stars and planets and galaxies from the vast creation of Allah, this planet we call earth has gone awry. Adam and Eve were caught off-guard in the garden of bliss. They were deceived, though they had been warned by Allah that a deceiver was present at the forbidden tree. They chose to listen to the serpent used as a medium by Shatan. Through their fall, this earth, this small speck of His creation, has fallen overboard, so to speak, through the deceptions of Shatan or Iblis. We have been slaves of Shatan, unable in our own strength to save ourselves, almost drowning in the mire of wickedness of earth. We are struggling amidst the dark billows that almost overwhelm us, trying with all our might to cope with the trials and difficulties, temptations and troubles of life all around us. Where can we turn to find help, before we sink and die? Is there any hope for us? Any lifeline?

The Honored Qur'an tells us very specifically: "And hold fast, all together, by the rope which Allah (stretches out for you), and be not divided among yourselves; and remember with gratitude Allah's favour on you; for ye were enemies and He joined your hearts in love, so that by His Grace, ye became brethren; and ye were on the brink of the pit of Fire, and He saved you from it. Thus doth Allah make His Signs clear to you: That ye may be guided." Sura 3.103 Aal-E-Imran.

Today we can be thankful for the Grace of Allah, for by His Grace He saves us! What beautiful language is

here expressed, that Allah our Creator, by His Grace stretches out to us a "rope of hope." We were enemies but by grace we can become brethren.

## Allah Sends a Rope of Hope

What familiar and encouraging language we read in the Injeel sent down from Allah. First, from the Honored Qur'an: "He said: "Nay, I am only a messenger from thy Lord, (to announce) to thee the gift of a holy son." Sura 19:19 Maryam. It is this gift of God that made reconciliation possible. The Injeel explains, "For if, when we were enemies [with God], we were reconciled [reunited] to God by the death of his Son, much more, being reconciled, we shall be saved by his life." Romans 5:10.

"God was bringing the world back to himself through Christ [Isa al-Masih]. He did not hold people's sins against them. God has trusted us with the message that people may be brought back to him." 2 Corinthians 5:19. "For by grace are ye saved through faith; and that not of yourselves: it is the gift of God." Ephesians 2:8.

Who is this Rope of Hope? It is none other than Isa al-Masih; He is the "Rope" let down from heaven to each one of us. This is nothing but a gift from heaven to this earth. May we with gratitude cling to this "Rope."

Isa al-Masih is the rope that Allah extended to us all. He was sent for all of mankind, and not for just a select few. He plunged into the icy depths of this sin-cursed earth to seek and save the lost. Though He was One with Allah (John 10:30) and is the Word from Allah (Sura 3.39, 45 Aal-EImran), yet He tasted the depths of misery that we endure. He learned the power of temptation; we know all too well. He became the instrument sent from Allah and all heaven to draw us to safety once again.

In their Eden home, our first parents sinned, and we have all followed in their course. We have been drifting from Allah ever since—without strength to return. Isa is the One who plunged into this world of evil and degradation. From the brilliance of heaven into the dark depths of this world He came, to rescue us.

## The Ladder from Earth to Heaven

Isa can be compared to a ladder. Heaven is far above us—far above our human capabilities to reach. If we ever wish to reach heaven, we must have some kind of a ladder that spans all the distance between earth and heaven. How wonderful it would be if there were such a ladder!

Here is a true story which happened long ago about a different wonderful ladder: One dark night, a cry rang out in the streets of Liverpool, England: "Fire! Fire!" Neighbors began to cluster nearby to see the flames already shooting out from the lower windows of a home for old sailors. As the onlookers gazed at the billowing flames, they noticed several men leaning out of a window on the very top story, hoping for rescue. On the ground, a man quickly brought a long ladder and leaned it against the burning building, but alas! It was too short.

What were they to do? There was no longer ladder available. Suddenly a strong, young sailor stepped out from the crowd, rushed to the ladder and quickly climbed to the top. Balancing himself upon the uppermost rung of the ladder, he seized the windowsill with his strong hands. "Quick, men!" he shouted. "Scramble over my body onto the ladder and go down! There's no time to waste!!"

One by one the men from the burning building made their way over the strong sailor's body until all had reached safety. Finally, the sailor himself came down. His face was burned, his hair singed. His fingers were blistered from the fire, but the men were safe. .

The ladder had reached upward, but before the men could be saved, it needed the length of a man. When it came to our being saved from our lives of deadly sin, all of Heaven's resources reaching down to save us here on earth would have been too short without the length of a man: the man Isa al-Masih.

In the Injeel He is known as the Son of man. "For the Son of man [Isa al-Masih] is come to seek and to save that which was lost." Luke 19:10. "Even as the Son of man came not to be ministered unto, but to minister, and to give his life a ransom for many." Matthew 20:28.

When Isa al-Masih returns, He will come as the Son of man. "And I looked, and behold a white cloud, and upon the cloud one sat like unto the Son of man, having on his head a golden crown, and in his hand a sharp sickle." Revelation 14:14.

In the same way, our prayers, our *du'a,* our good works of charity, our good deeds may show our good intentions, but they fall short of reaching heaven without the length of a man. That man is Christ Jesus, Isa al-Masih. He is our connection with Heaven; He was sent down for us. The Holy Books say, "...Christ in you, the hope of glory." Injeel Colossians 1:27.

### Isa al-Masih and His Purity

What did He have that made Him so special? What is it about Him that makes Him also our "ladder" to heaven? The Honored Qur'an says that He had the Holy Spirit. "We gave Moses the Book and followed him up with a succession of messengers; **We gave Jesus the son of Mary Clear (Signs) and strengthened him with the holy spirit**...." Sura 2.87 Al-Baqara.

"And Jesus [Isa], when he was baptized, went up straightway out of the water: and, lo, the heavens were opened unto him, **and he saw the Spirit of God [*Ruh Allah*] descending like a dove, and lighting upon him**...." Injeel Matthew 3:16.

Isa had the *Ruh Allah,* the Spirit of Allah. Not only was He a man, born of a woman, but He was Holy and Righteous. All the rest of mankind who have ever been born of a woman were born with corruption. Since the fall of Adam, all other persons born have been born with a fallen nature. In other words, they were born separated from Allah. But it was not so with Isa al-Masih, He was born of Heaven. He was born without an earthly father, He came about through the Spirit of God.

"And (remember) her who guarded her chastity: **We breathed into her [Mary] of Our spirit,** and We made her and her son a sign for all peoples." Sura 21.91 Al-Anbiya

"And Mary the daughter of 'Imran, who guarded her chastity; and **We breathed into (her body) of Our spirit**; and she testified to the truth of the words of her Lord and of His Revelations, and was one of the devout (servants)." Sura 66.12 At-Tahrim

"He [Angel] said: "Nay, I am only a messenger from thy Lord, (to announce) to thee **the gift of a holy son.**" Sura 19.19 Maryam

Imagine that, Jesus is the gift to Mary of a 'holy or righteous son'. Such a child had never been born before, and conceived not from an earthly father, but conceived through the Holy Spirit of Allah.

"She [Mary] said: "How shall I have a son, seeing that no man has touched me, and I am not unchaste?" He [Angel] said: "So (it will be): Thy Lord saith, 'that is easy for Me: and (We wish) to appoint him as **a Sign unto men and a Mercy from Us**':It is a matter (so) decreed." So she conceived him, and she retired with him to a remote place." Sura 19.20-22 Maryam

Therefore His father was Allah, which makes him a very special person, holy and righteous.

None of the Holy Books have ever presented anyone else who was born like He was. Truly He is the second Adam.

"The similitude of Jesus before Allah is as that of Adam..." Sura 3.59 Aal-E-Imran

Much more, He is our rope of hope in this fallen world. In His purity He reaches down from Heaven and clasps our hands in His. Because He was man, He can take hold of man's hand; and because He was from heaven, He is able to reunite us with Heaven. "He became the Saviour of men." 1 Timothy 4:10. All who wish to be saved can be saved from the evils of this earth.

Dear friend of Allah, one day a sea of flames will devour this earth, yet we need not be in those flames. Those flames will completely devour all sin and all sinners who have not sought out the Rope of Hope. This is our golden day of opportunity to escape the flames and be rescued from this earth. The last days of earth are upon us. Will you allow Allah, through Isa al-Masih, to extend the rope to you? Will you gladly take hold of this rope from Heaven?

We, too, can say, "Lord, save us; we perish...." Matthew 8:25. He will hear that voice and be gracious to us in extending Isa out to us. "... And hold fast, all together, by the rope which Allah (stretches out for you)." Sura 3.103 Aal-E-Imran.

"Hold fast," and never let go! Is it any wonder that Isa al-Masih Ibn Maryam is mentioned over 90 times in the Honored Qur'an? It's time to pay attention and heed what the *Ruh* (Spirit) of Allah is trying to impress upon our minds. Our constant plea should be: "O God, be merciful to me, for I am a sinner." Injeel Luke18:13. Isa said that the one who prayed this prayer went down to his house justified. We also can be. Trust Him.

# *Jesus in the Qur'an and the Bible*

Isa al-Masih ibn Maryam (Jesus Christ the Messiah) who is he? With whom did he originate? What was his purpose in being sent to this earth? Was he a prophet? What does the Qur'an and the Bible have to say about him?

The Qur'an calls him the "Straight Way" and the "Sign of the coming of the Hour of Judgment". Sura 43.61 Az-Zukhruf This is huge! That Jesus is the Sign for the Hour of Judgment! So Jesus is tied to the Judgment according to the Qur'an.

In the Qur'an, Allah is called "the Sovereign, **the holy one**." Sura 62.1 and Isa al-Masih (Jesus the Messiah) on the other hand is the only one called in the Qur'an "**the holy son**". Sura 19.19 Maryam.

Isa al-Masih is an extremely unique person, such a person like no one else in all the history of the earth.

Who else in this world was ever born without an earthly father? Everyone knows in order to conceive a child, both the mother and father are needed, yet clearly in both the Qur'an and the Scripture, Jesus or Isa al-Masih it is recorded of him, that he did not have an earthly father. Truly a miracle from Allah!

## How was Isa al-Masih conceived?

The Honored Qur'an reveals that Isa al-Masih was conceived supernaturally in the womb of Maryam (Mary) through the Holy Spirit of Allah.

"She [Maryam] said: 'O my Lord! How shall I have a son when no man hath touched me?' He [Angel] said: "even so: Allah createth what He willeth: When He hath decreed a plan, He but saith to it, "Be" and it is! Sura 3.47 Aal-E-Imran

"And remember her [Maryam] who guarded her chastity: **We breathed into her of Our spirit**, and We made her and her son a sign for all peoples." Sura 21.91 Al-Anbiya

And again in Sura 66.12 At-Tahrim: "And Mary...who guarded her chastity: and **We breathed into (her body) of Our spirit**..."

So clearly it states that Isa came about through the Spirit of Allah or Ruh Allah. What about the Holy Books of Scripture, what do they say?

Injeel Luke 1:34,35,37 "Then said Mary unto the angel, How shall this be, seeing I know not a man? And the angel answered and said unto her, **The Holy Ghost shall come upon thee**, and the power of the Highest shall overshadow thee… For with God nothing shall be impossible."

Injeel Matthew 1:18 "Now the birth of Jesus Christ was on this wise: When as his mother Mary was espoused to Joseph, **before they came together, she was found with child of the Holy Ghost.**"

The remarkable fact is that Isa was already prophesied that he would be born unto a virgin, long before he arrived. Through several ancient prophets of Allah, and especially one by the name of Isaiah who was given information 700 years before Isa arrived. Isaiah foretold his arrival that Isa would be born of a virgin.

Isaiah 7:14 "Therefore the Lord himself shall give you **a sign**; Behold, **a virgin shall conceive, and bear a son**, and shall call his name Immanuel."

This fact alone states to us that Jesus or Isa al-Masih is a sign from Allah and a very remarkable person indeed! According to the Bible, he was somehow a blend from Mary on the human side and then from the Holy Spirit of Allah on the Divine side.

Not only was Isa al-Masih conceived by the Holy Spirit of Allah, but he was given the Holy Spirit and strengthened by Him. "…We gave Jesus the son of Mary Clear (Signs) and **strengthened him with the holy spirit**…" Sura 2.87 Al-Baqara

"…to Jesus the son of Mary We gave clear (Signs), and **strengthened him with the holy spirit**…" Sura 2.253 Al-Baqara

"Then will Allah say: "O Jesus the son of Mary! Recount My favour to thee and to thy mother. Behold! **I strengthened thee with the holy spirit**… I taught thee the Book and Wisdom, the Law and the Gospel… thou healest those born blind, and the lepers, by My leave. And behold! thou bringest forth the dead by My leave…" Sura 5.110 Al-Maeda

**If to Jesus, Allah gave the Holy Spirit (Ruh Allah) then we can ask for the gift of the Holy Spirit and be strengthened and guided as Isa was by the Holy Spirit.**

## Isa al-Masih the Mercy of Allah

Yes Isa al-Masih is termed a Mercy from Allah.

"He said: "So (it will be): Thy Lord saith, 'that is easy for Me: and (We wish) to appoint him [Isa] as a Sign unto men and **a Mercy** from Us':It is a matter (so) decreed." Sura 19.21 Maryam

In the garden of Eden, man had fallen from his lofty position, as a result of him eating the fruit of the forbidden tree, which meant that he refused to heed the words of Allah. Satan had tricked the holy pair into deception. Now man in his fallen, sinful condition needed mercy. For clearly the wages or payment for sin is death, but God not willing that any should perish, sent "Mercy" in the form of Jesus (Isa al-Masih) to bear the sin which man incurred. Man had no way of returning to God as the holy laws of God were violated and now man must face judgment. A judgment is only necessary when a law has been violated. In the case of Adam, the first pair had violated the Holy and Just Laws of Allah. Jesus was sent as the Mercy of God to redeem man from his fallen condition. Without mercy mankind would be eternally lost.

Those "…who have transgressed…Despair not of the Mercy of Allah: for Allah forgives all sins: for He is Oft-Forgiving, Most Merciful." Sura 39.53 Az-Zumar

Yes through Isa al-Masih, the Mercy of Allah, He forgives us our sins and we receive cleansing.

## Isa al-Masih the Righteous

There is another extremely important point which reveals that Isa al-Masih was a very remarkable person in that he is termed 'Righteous'.

Isa is of the 'company of the Righteous'". Sura 3.46 Aal-E-Imran

Jesus is in the ranks of the righteous, Sura 6.85 Al-Anaam

Among the ancients it had been asked:

Job 15:14 LITV "What is man that he should be clean? And he born of a woman, that he should be righteous?"

"My little children, these things write I unto you, that ye sin not. And if any man sin, we have an advocate with the Father, **Jesus Christ the righteous**:" Injeel 1 John 2:1

He shall see of the travail of his soul, and shall be satisfied: by his knowledge shall **my righteous servant** justify many; for he shall bear their iniquities. Isaiah 53:11

Both the Qur'an and the Scripture identify Isa (Jesus the Messiah) as Righteous. He was righteous from birth for a Divine purpose, to make sinful men, righteous.

"Yet God, with undeserved kindness, declares that we are righteous. He did this **through Christ Jesus** when He freed us from the penalty for our sins." Romans 3:24 NLT

To get through the Judgment we need Righteousness, because of Adam's fall we do not have this to offer, we need to be covered with the Righteousness of God which was manifested in Isa al-Masih (Jesus). He alone is our covering or righteousness.

### ISA AL-MASIH THE SIGN OF SUPREME SUBMISSION

Jesus is a Sign unto men..." Sura 19.21 Maryam  No greater sign of submission to God was ever given to men than the submission of Isa al-Masih. He is the supreme example to men of submission to the will of God.

Injeel John 6:38 "For I came down from heaven, not to do mine own will, but the will of him that sent me."

"He [angel] said: "So (it will be): Thy Lord saith, 'that is easy for Me: and **(We wish) to appoint him as a Sign** unto men **and a Mercy from Us**':It is a matter (so) decreed." Sura 19.21 Maryam

So Isa is both a Sign and a Mercy from Allah!

"Then He [Isa al-Masih] said, "Look, I have come to do Your will."... for God's will was for us to be made holy **by the sacrifice of the body of Jesus Christ**, once for all time." Hebrews 10:9-10 NLT

This 'Sacrifice" is vividly brought to our view in the story of Ibrahim being called to sacrifice his very own son. "And we ransomed him [Ibrahim's son] with a momentous sacrifice." Sura 37.107 As-Saaffat

In this account is foreshadowed and foretold the "Momentous Sacrifice" which Allah sent to this world in the Sacrifice of Isa al-Masih for the sins of humanity. The only way forgiveness and cleansing from sin could occur would be for Allah to provide the payment for sin. With humanity there was no possibility for us to save ourselves, not even by our intended good deeds.

## The Redeemer or Deliverer

God is known as the redeemer or deliverer, and the One whom He sent, was Isa to redeem/ransom us.

"O our people, hearken to the one who invites (you) to Allah, and believe in him: He will forgive you your faults, and **deliver you** from a Penalty Grievous." Sura 46.31 Al-Ahqaf

One of the ancient wise ones from the east stated:

"For I know that my redeemer liveth, and that he shall stand at the latter day upon the earth:" Ayub or Job 19:25

"Thus saith the LORD the King of Israel, and his redeemer the LORD of hosts; I am the first, and I am the last; and beside me there is no God." Isaiah 44:6

So How does Allah deliver us from this grievous penalty?

"He will forgive you your faults, and **deliver you** from a Penalty Grievous." Sura 46.31 Al-Ahqaf

And through whom is this accomplished?

The ancient prophet Isaiah foretold seven hundred years prior to the coming of the Messiah that the Messiah would come to bear the sin or iniquity of sinners.

"Surely He has borne our griefs, and carried our sorrows; yet we esteemed Him stricken, smitten of God, and afflicted. But He was wounded for our transgressions; He was bruised for our iniquities; the chastisement of our peace was on Him; and with His stripes we ourselves are healed." Isaiah 53:4-5 MKJV

"He shall see the fruit of the travail of His soul. He shall be fully satisfied. By His knowledge shall **My righteous Servant** justify for many; and **He shall bear their iniquities**. Therefore I will divide to Him with the great, and He shall divide the spoil with the strong; because He has poured out His soul to death; and He was counted among the transgressors; and **He bore the sin of many**, and made intercession for transgressors." Isaiah 53:11-12 MKJV

There is a name also given to Jesus the Messiah, that when He would come on earth, He would be known as the Redeemer.

"The Redeemer will come…to buy back those … who have turned from their sins," says the LORD." Isaiah 59:20 NLT

"For even the Son of Man did not come to be served, but to serve, and **to give His life as a ransom** for many." Injeel Mark 10:45 MKJV

"…**Blot out** our sins, and grant us forgiveness. Have mercy on us. Thou art our Protector…." Sura 2.286 Al-Baqara

To Daudi was given the Zabur which states, "…Have mercy upon me, O God, according to thy lovingkindness: according unto the multitude of thy tender mercies **blot out** my transgressions." Zabur Psalms 51:1

"So Christ was once offered to bear the sins of many; and unto them that look for him shall he appear the second time without sin unto salvation." Hebrews 9:28

"Therefore as by one offense sentence came on all men to condemnation, even so by the righteousness of One the free gift came to all men to justification of life. For as by one man's disobedience many were made sinners, so by the obedience of One shall many be made righteous." Romans 5:18-19 MKJV

Give Isa al-Masih consent and permission today, that He may Redeem you and Ransom you from the grievous penalty of sin. You see, He never forces Himself upon anyone, He has to be invited…He is pictured in the Revelation of Jesus as standing at the door of our heart, that door has no opener on the outside, that door can only be opened by you, you open the door of your heart, and invite Him in and He is more than willing to do just that.

"Behold, I stand at the door and knock. If anyone hears My voice and opens the door, I will come in to him and will dine with him and he with Me. To him who overcomes I will grant to sit with Me in My throne, even as I also overcame and have sat down with My Father in His throne." Revelation 3:20-21 MKJV

# "Raiment of Righteousness"

In the name of Allah, the most merciful and righteous, oft-forgiving and compassionate. May the *Ruh* Allah (the Spirit of God) be with you as you consider this topic, for it is exceedingly essential that all understand it! Now earnestly consider this ayat from the Honored Qur'an... "O ye Children of Adam! We have bestowed raiment upon you to cover your shame, as well as to be an adornment to you. But the raiment of righteousness,- that is the best. Such are among the Signs of Allah, that they may receive admonition!" Sura 7.26 Al-Araf.

Righteousness must be an important topic since it is mentioned over seventy times in the Honored Qur'an and well over two hundred times in the Bible. What does the word *righteousness* mean? One dictionary defines it as "purity of heart and rectitude of life; conformity of heart and life to the divine law. Righteousness, as used in Scripture/[Qur'an] and theology, in which it is chiefly used, is nearly equivalent to holiness, comprehending holy principles and affections of heart, and conformity of life to the divine law. It includes all we call justice, honesty and virtue, with holy affections; in short, it is true religion."

Surely we would want to be just and honest and virtuous, with holy affections. And surely we would desire to conform our hearts and lives to the divine law. To desire otherwise would be to desire to be evil! Yet even when we desire to be righteous, so often we fall short. Our actions or words or thoughts show us repeatedly that we have not received the "raiment of righteousness" that Allah has offered us. It is obvious that we do not naturally possess righteous characters. How, then, do we weak humans attain righteousness?-

### ADAM AND EVE

In the Garden of Eden, our first parents were blessed with possessing righteousness. They had been created righteous, and their righteousness was a wonderful gift from heaven. However, when they sinned, they forfeited that gift. In other words, when they listened to the deceptions of Iblis instead of to Allah's Word, they fell from righteousness. All their goodness/righteousness was lost. Their characters immediately revealed hearts that were no longer just and honest and virtuous, conformed to divine law. And ever since, we humans have had no goodness in ourselves. We are totally destitute of righteousness. Neither is there any goodness in our hearts, nor can we merit righteousness by our good works. Sin and self contaminate everything we do and think and say. "As it is written, 'There is none righteous, no, not one.'" Romans 3:10.

Since that fall, Adam's descendants have had no way to regain righteousness on their own. Righteousness cannot be ours unless it is given to us by God.

As mentioned before, in the Garden of Eden, both Adam and his wife were righteous. They needed no clothes to cover themselves. As a sign of their righteousness, they were covered with a garment of light. The prophet Daud wrote: "And he shall bring forth thy righteousness as the light, and thy judgment as the noonday." Zabur Psalms 37:6. Here righteousness is equal to light. So our first parents wore no artificial clothes; they were dressed in light.

When Adam and Eve fell from righteousness, they lost their heavenly covering. They then saw themselves naked and destitute of light from heaven. They had listened to Iblis' lies, and the covering of light left them. They tried to cover themselves with leaves, to hide their nakedness. The Honored Qur'an states, "In the result, they both ate of the tree, and so their nakedness appeared to them: they began to sew together, for their covering, leaves from the Garden: thus did Adam disobey his Lord, and allow himself to be seduced." Sura 20.121 Ta-Ha.

When God came looking for them, they went into hiding. "And the eyes of them both were opened, and they knew that they were naked; and they sewed fig leaves together, and made themselves aprons. And they heard the voice of the LORD God walking in the garden in the cool of the day: and Adam and his wife hid themselves from the presence of the LORD God amongst the trees of the garden. And the LORD God called unto Adam, and said unto him, Where art thou? And he said, I heard thy voice in the garden, and I was afraid, because I was naked; and I hid myself." Taurat Genesis 3:7-10.

### The Covering of God

In pity and in very important symbolism, God covered the now-naked man and wife with the skins of beasts. Innocent animals had to die; their blood had to be shed so that man could again have a covering. This was very significant, a clean animal was sacrificed so that the guilty pair could once again have a cover to cloth their shame.

This all pointed forward to the "Lamb of God" that would come one day to be sacrificed for the sin of humanity and to restore what was lost in Eden. Yahya announced clearly "…Behold the Lamb of God, which taketh away the sin of the world." Injeel John 1:29.

Christ [Isa al-Masih] is the lamb of God. He is the innocent one that would die for the guilty human race. It was His blood that was shed, so that guilty man could be forgiven of his sins and once again attain to righteousness. The covering of skins was only a temporary solution; it covered the body, but could do nothing for the heart inclined to sin. Only through Jesus could man cover his inner, heart nakedness with the righteousness of Isa al-Masih, Jesus.

Man was given a second chance to obtain that righteousness that was lost, but how would he be able to attain to the character of purity that had been lost? In Adam, man had forfeited his ability to do right. In his own strength, he could never do right or be holy in heart. What a dilemma man was in! Was there any hope? From where would help come?

## God's Plan

God had a plan. He would provide that holy covering once again. It would come through another man—the second or "last Adam"—Christ, the Son of Mary.

"…My soul shall be joyful in my God. For He clothed me with garments of salvation; He put on me the robe of righteousness…." Isaiah 61:10.

"Thy righteousness is an everlasting righteousness, and thy law is the truth." Zabur Psalms 119:142.

Righteousness is something we all lost when our forefather Adam lost it, but as we submit to God and believe in Christ, He will again clothe us with it. This is done through Isa al-Masih (Jesus), who was sent. Notice, also, that righteousness is as a robe or garment put on. Ayub, a man from among the truly wise men of the East, said, "I put on righteousness, and it clothed me: my judgment was as a robe and a diadem." Taurat Job 29:14.

…"For the sin of this one man, Adam, caused death to rule over many. But even greater is God's wonderful grace and His gift of righteousness, for all who receive it will live in triumph over sin and death through this one Man, Jesus Christ." Romans 5:17.

"This righteousness from God comes through faith in Jesus Christ to all who believe. There is no difference." Romans 3:22.

## Righteousness Is a Gift

Will you, dear reader, believe and accept the gift of righteousness from God? It is a gift. If it were earned (which it cannot be), then it would cease to be a gift. It is a gift because Allah knows we cannot earn it. "It is not righteousness that ye turn your faces towards East or West; but it is righteousness- to believe in Allah and the Last Day, and the Angels, and the Book [Bible], and the Messengers...." Sura 2.177 Al-Baqara.

We are told to seek righteousness. It obviously can be found and obtained, or else we would not be told to seek for it. "Seek ye the LORD, all ye meek of the earth, which have wrought his judgment; seek righteousness, seek meekness: it may be ye shall be hid in the day of the LORD'S anger." Zephaniah 2:3.

Isa al-Masih Himself said, "But seek ye first the kingdom of God, and his righteousness; and all these things shall be added unto you." Injeel Matthew 6:33. "Blessed are they which do hunger and thirst after righteousness: for they shall be filled." Injeel Matthew 5:6.

God's promises are certain. This counsel is for all persons of every nation on earth:Righteousness exalteth a nation: but sin is a reproach to any people." Proverbs 14:34.

The Honored Qur'an tells us that Isa al-Masih was the gift of a righteous son. (Sura 19.19) Noble Qur'an. He maintained his integrity before God and has earned the right to bestow this precious gift upon us who believe in Him. Therefore, true good works are a result of the gift of righteousness given to us. Good deeds which stem from the heart are therefore the fruit of righteousness. And once we possess this gift, we have the perfect right to enter into Heaven, for our characters will be suited to the holy peace and holy beings there. All depends upon obtaining this gift of righteousness. Truly it is like a robe woven in the loom of heaven, with no earthly devising. We must be clothed with this robe from heaven. It will allow us abundant entrance into the kingdom of bliss. "Surely, shall one say, in the LORD have I righteousness and strength..." Isaiah 45:24.

Righteousness and God's law always go together. They cannot be separated. "O that thou hadst hearkened to my commandments! then had thy peace been as a river, and thy righteousness as the waves of the sea." Isaiah 48:18.

"My tongue shall speak of thy word: for all thy commandments are righteousness." Zabur Psalms 119:172.

"But in every nation he that feareth him, and worketh righteousness, is accepted with him. " Injeel Acts 10:35. "...And this is his name whereby he shall be called, THE LORD OUR RIGHTEOUSNESS." Jeremiah 23:6.

In the last days, true Christians and true Muslims will unite and together will sound forth the praise of Allah and will accept His righteousness. "For as the earth bringeth forth her bud, and as the garden causeth the things that are sown in it to spring forth; so the Lord GOD will cause righteousness and praise to spring forth before all the nations." Isaiah 61:11.

"And they that be wise shall shine as the brightness of the firmament; and they that turn many to righteousness as the stars for ever and ever." Daniel 12:3.

## The Honored Qur'an speaks of
### two coverings...

The first is the covering of artificial clothes to cover our shame and nakedness...this is one type of covering or raiment. However this covering will not be sufficient in the Judgment. There we need another covering, the best covering...a covering of 'righteousness'. Only by the covering of 'righteousness' this second covering will we get into the Kingdom of Heaven.

### Why is the covering of Righteousness so important?

This second covering is a reflection of the character of God. This second covering is last but the best. It was forfeited in the Garden of Eden when our first parents fell in listening to the deceptions of Iblis, instead of honoring God's Word. In order to get back into God's Kingdom from where man fell, he is in need of "righteousness", which is right living and right thinking, in short... "True Religion". Allah in His abundant goodness had provided the first man and his wife with an abounding evidence of goodness by providing such a pleasant place for the first pair in Eden the Garden of God.

Every tree bearing fruit was for their needs and all that made life happy and pleasant was given to them. Thus Allah's love was seen all around them. On the other hand Iblis had given them no evidence of love nor of providing for their needs, yet his words were quickly received and believed over Allah's Word. Thus the holy pair fell from their high estate when they ate of the forbidden fruit. They lost righteousness, the blessed covering which had been given them, when they disbelieved God.

Righteousness is something which happens in the heart of the believer. Since man's fall, righteousness is something which cannot be produced by human effort. Even unbelievers can contribute to charity, (zakat) and this is very good, they can do many deeds of kindness, yet these may be outward forms of righteousness and no real motive from the heart may move them. Much is done for the purpose of being seen of men…so that men may praise your goodness. This is not righteousness. This had been a problem back in the days of Isa, [Jesus]. "But they [Jews] do all their works in order to be seen of men…" Injeel Matthew 23:5

Even today believers can say oft-repeated memorized prayers five times daily...however this can become mechanical. Almost like a machine…similar to a recording, just turn on the switch and you hear the same prayer…is that what Allah is after? A recording of our prayers? There must be something deeper, perhaps our prayers need to come from the heart.

I am privileged to have children, and when they speak to me from the heart, I can appreciate it very much. When they tell me they love me, it thrills my soul. But if they would record their love on a CD and play the same recorded message over many times to me, I would not be impressed in the least. It must be somewhat similar when we approach God. Our communion with Him must come from deep inside and expressed from a heart of appreciation.

Is there something which happens to the heart when Allah touches us inside?

True righteousness is when right actions come from deep inside a person. Actions like…refusing to take revenge and retaliate when someone has wronged you. Actions like being kind to your enemies, kind in heart…feeding them when hungry, without resentment. Refusing to hurt someone who has deeply offended you when it is in your power to do them harm. Praying private (du'a) prayers for those who persecute you. Only God can give us this type of 'righteousness'. With man this is impossible. It is a gift from Heaven through one sent down called Isa al-Masih. We need souls who will plead for this holiness of heart… Again from the great ones of the East of Ancient times, comes this promise which you can claim as your own. "He [man] shall pray to God, and He will be gracious to him; and

he shall see His face with joy, for He will restore to man his righteousness." Ayub Job 33:26

## Allah has promised to restore what was lost in Eden!

Friends this is powerful good news…though fallen and flawed, yet we are not forsaken. We can be restored to the character of Allah! He is kind to the unthankful. He cares for the heathen, provides sunshine and rain, their sores He heals…the ungrateful have food, clothing and shelter.

Allah provides salvation to the unjust. He will again cover us with the robe of His Righteousness. Do we believe it? That means "true religion" not just a form but real. Something real from the heart and expressed in the daily life! When this happens our prayers take on a completely different form. No longer some recorded prayers we mumble and hurry through as though accomplishing some duty, but rather a heart response to what Allah means to us.

Friends is that what you desire in your heart? You can have it and it is free! It all comes through the gift of the "Righteous Son" sent down from Allah. Sura 19:19 Maryam.

This is the state of every person…"I know there is nothing good in my sinful nature. I want to do what is good, but I can't." Romans 7:18 But we like Ibrahim can believe the promises… "Abram believed the LORD, and he credited it to him as righteousness." Taurat Genesis 15:6 Regardless of the defects of the people of God, Christ does not turn away from the objects of His care. He has the power to change their raiment. He removes the filthy garments [all selfishness and sin], He places upon the repenting, believing ones His own robe of righteousness, and writes pardon against their names on the records of heaven. He confesses them as His before the heavenly universe. Iblis their adversary is shown to be an accuser and deceiver, but Allah will do justice for His own elect. Our God says…

"Take away the filthy garments from him [the sinner]. And unto him He said, Behold, I have caused thine iniquity [sin] to pass from thee, and I will clothe thee with change of raiment..." Zechariah 3:4, 5.

Even so God will clothe you with "the garments of salvation," and cover you with "the robe of righteousness." Isaiah 61:10.

Remember this raiment of righteousness is a sign from Allah… "But the raiment of righteousness,- that is the best. Such are among the Signs of Allah…" Sura 7:26 Al-Araf

Surely this raiment or covering of Allah is the righteousness of Christ, His own unblemished character, that through faith is imparted to all who receive Him as their personal Saviour. The white robe of innocence was worn by our first parents when they were placed by God in holy Eden.

They lived in perfect conformity to the will of God. A beautiful soft light, the light of God, enshrouded the holy pair. This robe of light was a symbol of their spiritual garments of heavenly innocence. Had they remained true to God it would ever have continued to enshroud them. But when sin entered, they severed their connection with God, and the light that had encircled them departed. Naked and ashamed, they tried to supply the place of the heavenly garments by sewing together fig leaves for a covering. Nothing can man devise to supply the place of his lost robe of innocence. Only the covering which Christ Himself has provided can make us fit to appear in God's presence. This covering, the robe of His own righteousness, Christ will put upon every repenting, believing soul. "I counsel thee," He says, "to buy of Me . . . white raiment, that thou mayest be clothed, and that the shame of thy nakedness do not appear." Revelation 3:18. He says "buy", it will cost you everything to obtain it, yet it is free.

This robe, woven in the loom of heaven, has in it not one thread of human devising. Christ in His humanity wrought out a perfect character, and this character He offers to impart to us. "All our righteousness are as filthy rags." Isaiah 64:6.

Everything that we of ourselves can do, is defiled by sin. But the Son of God "was manifested to take away our sins; and in Him is no sin." Sin is defined to be "the transgression of the law." 1 John 3:5, 4.

The righteousness of Christ will not cover one cherished sin. Only that which is in accord with the principles of God's law will stand in the judgment. There will be no future probation in which to prepare for eternity. It is in this life that we are to put on the robe of

Christ's righteousness. This is our only opportunity to form characters for the home which Christ has made ready for those who obey His commandments. The days of our probation are fast closing. The end is near. "Blessed is he that watcheth, and keepeth his garments, lest he walk naked, and they see his shame." Revelation 16:15.

Dear friends we have no time to delay and neglect this most important topic. Now is the time to earnestly pray and plead that Allah may grant unto us this blessing. Make no mistake, to miss here is to miss eternity. May Allah grant unto His sign…the Raiment of Righteousness.

The ancient prophet Isaiah stated under inspiration, "Surely, shall one say, in the LORD have I righteousness and strength: even to him shall men come; and all that are incensed against him shall be ashamed. " Isaiah 45:24

# The Forgiveness of Allah

Greetings in the name of Allah, who loves us with an everlasting love.

Dear reader, many uninformed Christians say that, based on the words and deeds of Allah as recorded in the Honored Qur'an, He is unloving. Others claim that in Islam His love is seldom mentioned. Yet there is a most profound ayat in Sura 3.31 Aal-E-Imran:

"...Allah will love you and forgive you your sins: For Allah is Oft-Forgiving, Most Merciful."

I am a Seventh-day Adventist, and I find that His love is mentioned over fifty times in the Honored Qur'an! I find also that the term "forgiveness" and close derivatives of the same word are found there well over two hundred times! Is forgiveness not a clear aspect of love? Amazing, to say the least!

The topic I want to review today is how Allah's love is shown in His forgiveness of sin. Truly, if we had no forgiveness from Allah, we would be eternally lost.

Our review will begin back in those far-off days of Adam when he was in the Garden of Bliss. Adam sinned and lost his way. We are the children of Adam—his descendants— and we, too, have lost our way. Because of his choice to sin, we have inherited from him a nature destitute of true love. Our hearts are at enmity with Allah. We can look forward only to eternal death. "When Adam sinned, sin entered the world. Adam's sin brought death, so death spread to everyone, for everyone sinned." Injeel Romans 5:12.

However, eternal death need not be our end. The Honored Qur'an contains man's urgent plea for the blotting-out of sins: "...Our Lord! Forgive us our sins, blot out from us our iniquities...." (Sura 3:193 Aal-E-Imran.) The Lord's gracious affirmation comes two ayats later: "...Verily, I will blot out from them their iniquities....." See also Sura 4.43, 99, 149 An-Nisa. The trustworthy forgiveness of Allah is plainly referred to in Sura 2:286 Al-Baqara, as well.

Surely those ayats bear good news! Because of these things, we have a hope which we can hold onto—a hope that unbelievers do not have. There is a "way" out of our dire predicament.

This little tract will present this wonderful old truth in new ways. We should count ourselves blessed to make this information known to all around us.

The Honored Qur'an tells us that "We did bestow on some prophets more (and other) gifts than on others: and We gave to David [Daud] (the gift of) the Psalms." Sura 17.55 Al-Isra.

In the Psalms, Zabur, we read David's inspired words to Allah: "But there is forgiveness with thee, that thou mayest be feared." (Psalms 130:4.) Daud also pleads, "Hide Your face from my sins, and blot out all my iniquities." Psalms 51:9.

## The Cost of Forgiveness

Allah has gone to great lengths to give us forgiveness and yet uphold His holy law. For many, little thought is given regarding the cost He incurred in giving us forgiveness for our sins. Remember that when a person sins and does a wrong deed, there is always a cost, or payment. When someone has wronged you—for example, he's stolen a valuable item from your home, such as a big-screen TV—and the thief is caught, several things can happen:

- You forgive the thief and voluntarily suffer the loss of your big-screen TV, without expectation of compensation.
- The thief can be jailed; he suffers the loss of his freedom. You may or may not be compensated for your loss.
- Someone else offers to replace your TV out of the kindness of his heart. The thief goes free and you endure no loss. In this option, this other person bears the loss personally, even though he was neither victim nor perpetrator.

Remember, forgiveness always comes with a cost. Someone always pays. When it comes to our sins, we can suffer the cost; we can pay the price for our sins. The price is the loss of eternal life, because the "wages," or cost, of sin is death. "For the wages of sin is death…." Romans 6:23.

The third option above is what Allah has done for us. If we should bear the cost for our sins, we would lose our lives for eternity, but because of Allah's love, kindness and mercy for us, He has willingly taken our case upon Himself. He has offered One who was in the bosom of Allah to pay the price for our sins. So that we need not suffer eternal loss, He offered the life of His only-begotten Son in our stead.

He was One who was nearest to Allah and called the Word of Allah—*Kalimatu* Allah. Sura 3.39; 3.45; 4.171 Aal-E-Imran.

"Behold! the angels said: "O Mary! Allah giveth thee glad tidings of a Word from Him: his name will be Christ Jesus, the son of Mary, held in honour in this world and the Hereafter and of (the company of) those nearest to Allah." Sura 3.45 Aal-E-Imran.

"But Allah commended his love toward us, in that, while we were yet sinners, Christ died for us." Romans 5:8.

"For since our friendship with God was restored by the death of His Son while we were still His enemies, we will certainly be saved through the life of His Son." Romans 5:10.

Yes, dear friends, this fact we often overlook. Someone had to pay the price for our sin! Otherwise, our whole human race would have been eternally lost. The cost of forgiveness was high—extremely high: death!

"The God of our ancestors raised Jesus from the dead after you [the Jewish leaders] killed Him by hanging Him on a cross. Then God put Him in the place of honor at his right hand as Prince and Saviour. He did this so the people … would repent of their sins and be forgiven." Acts 5:30-31.

So the cost of our forgiveness was death—paid in full forever by the death of Isa al-Masih. In this way justice was met and mercy was extended to the family of man. Man could go free on condition that he abide by the terms of redemption. Those terms are neither complicated nor numerous. Man simply needs to believe and receive in what Allah has done. "We have been set free because of what Christ has done. Through his blood our sins have been forgiven. We have been set free because God's grace is so rich." Injeel Ephesians 1:7.

## Forgiveness Demonstrated

So close was Isa al-Masih to Allah, and so clearly and fully did Isa represent Allah, that Isa stated, "He who has seen Me has seen the Father." Injeel John 14:9.

Here is a clear statement that describes His closeness with Allah: "The Son radiates God's own glory and expresses the very character of God, and He sustains everything by the mighty power of His command."

We get a much better picture of the forgiveness of Allah when we see how Isa treated those who were hanging Him upon the cross for execution. When the Roman soldiers nailed Isa to the rough cross at the request of the Jewish leaders, there was only profound love and humility in the blameless heart of Isa. No hatred was shown; no curses came from His lips. While they were doing their fearful work, Isa was praying for them, "Father, forgive them, for they don't know what they are doing...." Injeel Luke 23:34.

Here is profound forgiveness, displayed in the life and death of Isa in such magnitude as had never before been conceived or witnessed in the entire universe. And remember, Isa is the "express image" of Allah. Hebrews 1:3.

That prayer of Isa for forgiveness embraced the entire world. To all, forgiveness from Allah through Isa is freely offered. Whosoever will, may find peace with God and inherit eternal life. No vengeance was invoked upon those soldiers, priests, or rulers involved in Isa's agonizing death. Isa breathed only a plea for their forgiveness, because He pitied them in their ignorance and guilt. He pities us today, too, because "His compassions fail not." (Lamentations 3:22.) Thus that earnest prayer from the cross embraces every soul that has ever lived; it embraces each person from the family of Adam throughout earth's history. Dear friends, today you can make it possible that the prayer of Isa al-Masih be answered in your life, too.

"...When He had cleansed us from our sins, He sat down in the place of honor at the right hand of the majestic God in heaven." Injeel Hebrews 1:3.

It was Allah who had sent Isa into the world to redeem man from sin and its effect. Through His death on behalf of mankind—the innocent for the guilty—Isa earned the right to forgive us, and now we stand with this sacred opportunity and privilege—not only to be delivered from the loss of eternal life, but even more—to be reinstated into the paradise of God. Wondrous love and forgiveness!

Some may think it was a small thing for the Father to send Isa into the world to pay the penalty for man's transgression, but it was not small. Though the plan of salvation had been set in place long before the creation of the earth, yet it was a struggle, even with the King of the universe, to yield up His only-begotten son to die for the guilty race.

Oh, the mystery of redemption! The love of God for a world that did not love Him! Through endless ages immortal minds, seeking to comprehend the mystery of that incomprehensible love, will wonder and adore.

Now, at this moment, we can respond by repentance toward God and faith in Christ. Thus the fallen children of Adam might once more become "sons of God" through adoption.

Injeel 1 John 3:2-3 explains God's love for us: "Behold what manner of love the Father has given us, that we should be called children of God. Therefore the world does not know us, because it did not know Him. Beloved, now we are children of God, and it has not yet been revealed what we shall be. But we know that when He shall be revealed, we shall be like Him, for we shall see Him as He is."

Today, dear friend of Allah, you can make that choice to accept and believe that Isa al-Masih is the One Who was sent into this dark world to purchase our ransom from sin with His own life and blood. To reject such an expensive offer would keenly insult Allah, Who is so willing to forgive us and blot out our sins through Isa. Today, may you choose to have peace through the sacrifice of Isa al-Masih.

# Pure and Holy Wine, or the Wine of Babylon?

Today many souls are confused. They have been drinking alcoholic beverages that Allah never intended that mankind should consume. Through the wisdom He gave King Solomon, we know that "Wine is a mocker, strong drink is raging: and whosoever is deceived thereby is not wise." Proverbs 20:1. However, Iblis (Satan) deceives the minds and hearts of people with fermented or alcoholic drink, causing them to make decisions they would not make if they had clear minds.

Thousands have gone down into ruin because they disregarded the admonition of Allah, when obedience to Allah would have protected them from such mental and moral confusion. Is it any wonder that such clear instruction has been given in the Honored Qur'an and in the Holy Books of the Taurat and Injeel, that fermented wine or drink is not a suitable beverage for man.

Allah has been trying to warn us of this danger "…concerning wine and gambling…. In them is great sin…." Sura 2.219 Al-Baqara. "It is not for kings to drink wine, or for rulers to desire strong drink." Proverbs 31:4.

There is wine, however, that is pure and holy. It is the pure juice of the grape or other fruit. The unfermented (non-alcoholic) juice of fruit was meant to be a blessing to mankind. "…Their Lord will give to them to drink of a Wine Pure and Holy." Sura 76.21 Al-Insan. "Thus saith the LORD, As the new wine is found in the cluster [of grapes], and one saith, destroy it not; for a blessing is in it…." Isaiah 65:8.

Iblis has deceived man into manufacturing alcohol. He hopes to confuse and even destroy the minds, hearts and lives of the many souls who drink it. We would be wise to heed the counsel and examples from the Holy Books. For example, when Isa al-Masih was offered vinegar (a by-product of alcohol) while thirsting immensely upon the cruel instrument of torture, He refused to drink it—even in His suffering condition.

"There they offered Jesus wine [vinegar] to drink, mixed with gall (myrhh); but after tasting it, he refused to drink it" (Injeel Matthew 27:34) lest His holy purpose become subverted through dulled senses.

What a grand example we have from prophet Isa al-Masih to refuse anything corrupted.

## THE DECEPTIVE CUP OF DEVILS

Another wine is even more destructive and deadly than alcoholic wine. This wine is spoken about in the Taurat and Injeel. This wine comes from the vineyards of Satan himself, for it is called the "cup of devils." The Injeel says, "Ye cannot drink the cup of the Lord, and the cup of devils: ye cannot be partakers of the Lord's table, and of the table of devils." I Corinthians 10:21.

This wine is a deceptive mixture of true doctrines with false doctrines. Corrupt teachings are taught alongside true teachings, and by association made to appear as truth. This adulterated "wine" comes tainted with a sting and bite, as the color or appearance alone will not determine whether the wine is pure or corrupt. So it is with the teachings of religion. All teachings must be investigated to see if they are holy or corrupt. For every truth of Allah, Iblis or Satan has a counterfeit that appears like the real, but the taste reveals its corruption. If his wine is imbibed, loss of life—eternal life—often follows.

In all things, we need to be wise not only to refuse the corrupt, but also to accept that which is pure and holy. There are teachings that are pure and holy and that leads to life everlasting. There are also deceptive teachings that are corrupt and impure. They lead to eternal destruction. Iblis holds out to each of us his deceptive "cup of devils," which he tries in various ways to induce us to drink. We need to be warned of his devices. Warning about them is the purpose of this publication that you hold in your hand.

Allah, in mercy, is making known to the listening ear the secret and evil workings of Iblis. Allah's love for souls is such that He wishes all to be aware and take every precaution against the wiles of Satan.

## THE WINE OF BABYLON

At this point we want to separate the true from the false. The Taurat and Injeel have much to say about the false doctrine or teachings that Iblis has been feeding millions of souls. In God's Book, ancient prophecies of the Injeel warn of the last days, when corrupt wine or doctrines will be accepted, instead of the pure. That time has come; the last days are upon us.

"For the time will come when people will not put up with sound doctrine. Instead, to suit their own desires, they will gather around them a great number of teachers to say what their itching ears want to hear." Injeel 2 Timothy 4:3.

But God has told us to "...speak thou the things which become sound doctrine." Titus 2:1.

This deceptive cup of devils is also called the wine of Babylon, or the "wine of her fornication." Revelation 17:2. The Bible says: "For all nations have drunk of the wine of the wrath of her fornication, and the kings of the earth have committed fornication with her, and the merchants of the earth are waxed rich through the abundance of her delicacies." Injeel Revelation 18:3.

Bible prophecy warns that in the last days, the great ones of earth will become corrupted and manipulated by the false wine of deception. In great symbolic and figurative language, inspired words sent by Allah reveal the present situation: "With her [the most powerful religious system] the kings of the earth [powerful, wealthy men] committed adultery [made alliances for profit and power], and the inhabitants of the earth were intoxicated [misled] with the wine of her adulteries [her unfaithfulness to Allah's principles of righteousness]." Revelation 17:2.

You may say, "I am Muslim, so surely this will not affect me," but the Injeel states: "...**And all the world wondered after the beast [world power].**" Revelation 13:3. "And **all that dwell upon the earth** shall **worship** him [the world power]." Revelation 13:8. One obeys whom one worships. The Bible speaks of national and religious leaders of earth who have accepted the wine or teachings of Satan as taught by the fallen apostate churches, which constitute spiritual Babylon, which itself is headed by the "mother of harlots."

## Beware These Teachings of Iblis

The Injeel warns of a particular deception: "This know also, that in the last days perilous [dangerous] times shall come..., [religious people] having a form of godliness [acting religious], but denying the power thereof [rejecting Allah]: from such turn away." Injeel 2 Timothy 3:1, 5. All over the world, these people have spread their convincing but misleading doctrines that lead to eternal death. Today we wish to expose a number of these false teachings that the Bible calls the intoxicating "wine of Babylon."

1. It is widely taught that those who die and are buried in their graves can still communicate with the living. This is called "spiritualism." It is based on the belief that the dead continue to live on in spirit form after their bodies die. But the Word of God tells us that when a person dies, he ceases to exist. No further communication can exist between the dead and the living. "For the living know that they shall die; but the dead do not know anything, nor do they have any more a reward; for their memory is forgotten." Ecclesiastes 9:5; also Psalms 6:5, 146:4.

2. The use of images and idols in the worship of God is strongly forbidden by Allah and explained in the Taurat in the second commandment. "You must not make for yourself an idol of any kind or an image of anything in the heavens or on the earth or in the sea. You must not bow down to them or worship them...." Exodus 20:4-5.

3. Many religious people worship Maryam, the mother of Isa al-Masih, as if she were divine, but she is only a human being. Allah's Word says, "You shall have no other gods before Me." Taurat Exodus 20:3.

4. Millions claim that the pope in Rome is the vicar, or representative, of God on earth. Papal policy claims that only the Catholic Church has authority to interpret Scripture for mankind. But the Holy Word says, "But the Comforter, the Holy Spirit [*Ruh* Allah] whom the Father will send in My name, He shall teach you all things and bring all things to your remembrance, whatever I have said to you." John 14:26. The true "vicar or representative of Allah" is the Holy Spirit, or *Ruh* Allah.

5. Multitudes are being taught that the traditions or teachings of some religions are to be believed above the Bible. However, Isa al-Masih, who was sent from Allah, unmistakably reminded the people that this was "vain worship." "But in vain they worship Me, teaching for doctrines the commandments of men." Injeel Matthew 15:9. Isa al-Masih always upheld the Word of Allah, the Bible, as truth. "Sanctify them through thy truth: thy word is truth." John 17:17.

6. Masses of people confess their sins to a religious authority or priest, but the Word from Allah says, "I acknowledged my sin unto thee [God], and mine iniquity have I not hid. I said: 'I will

confess my transgressions unto the LORD; and thou forgavest the iniquity of my sin.'" Zabur Psalms 32:5. Sins (broken laws of Allah) are to be confessed to God, and confession is to be made to those who have been wronged by your actions.

7. Bible prophecy foretells of a movement in the last days to exalt Sunday, the first day of the week, as Allah's holy day of rest. The Word of God, however, says clearly that the Sabbath (Saturday, the seventh day) is the day of rest instituted by Allah at the beginning of time. We must remember that Allah's holy and just laws do not change. "Remember the Sabbath day, to keep it holy. Six days shalt thou labour, and do all thy work: But the seventh day [Saturday] is the sabbath of the LORD thy God…." Taurat Exodus 20:8-10

Allah, in mercy to mankind, set aside the seventh day of every week (Al-Sabt) as a day of rest or cessation from our earthly labors, so that we can praise and acknowledge God as the Creator of all. Allah designated that specific day to give mankind the world over a time to rest from their wearying labor.

8. Scores are being taught that salvation (eternal life) can be earned through good deeds or payment of money, yet the Bible states, "Not by works of righteousness which we did ourselves, but in the measure of his mercy, he gave us salvation, through the washing of the new birth and the giving of new life in the Holy Spirit, Which he gave us freely through Jesus Christ our Saviour." Injeel Titus 3:5-6. Salvation is free; all that is needed is faith.

9. In many false religions, no difference is made between clean and unclean foods. Pork or "swine's flesh," and the flesh of many other animals which have been forbidden by Allah, are eaten, even though they have been strictly forbidden by Allah. "And the swine, …he is unclean to you." Taurat Leviticus 11:7; see Leviticus chapter 11 for more admonitions about food.

10. It is being taught through a major false religion that forgiveness of sins can be obtained only through the Roman Catholic Church, but Allah says "For there is one God, and one mediator between God and men, the man Christ Jesus," 1 Timothy 2:5. "…If any man sin, we have an advocate [intermediary, pleader] with the Father, Jesus Christ the righteous." 1 John 2:1

These ten errors that Satan holds out to the world to drink constitute only a few of the errors taught. Allah, however, urges us to "drink the pure blood [juice] of the grape" (Deuteronomy 32:14), the pure doctrines or teachings of Bible truth. Allah promises to "...give you good doctrine, forsake ye not my law." Proverbs 4:2. Our prayers ought to be, "Ever give us the pure doctrines." May Allah grant unto you His eternal peace.

# "The Hour of Judgment"

The honored Qur'an clearly speaks of an Hour of Judgment: "And (Jesus) shall be a Sign (for the coming of) **the Hour (of Judgment)**: therefore **have no doubt** about the (Hour), but follow ye Me: this is a Straight Way." Sura 43.61 Az-Zukhruf.

How often have imams recited and discussed that sura! For a great many, the thought of divine judgment strikes fear into their hearts. So much is unknown about it. Should it be a day to fear? Can we know when it is near? Is it possible to prepare for it? Is there anything we can do to escape the final verdicts from that grand court?

Dear friends of Allah, as we look into the great judgment of Allah, may He guide us, and give us grace and wisdom to understand.

### The Investigative Judgment

We may be confident that Allah is always just and fair in His dealings with humanity. Therefore, it is not surprising to read in the Holy Scriptures, in the Taurat, that an investigative phase of the great judgment occurs before the irrevocable decisions of the heavenly tribunal are announced. In all conceivable fairness, the verdicts are based on what is revealed during heaven's investigation of each individual's life record.

It is perhaps best explained this way. In any earthly court, when someone is accused of a crime, there is a time when the court sits. At that time, all the evidence from both the accusing and defending sides is examined and weighed by the court. In any fair trial, during this time of investigation into the guilt or innocence of the accused, witnesses and experts are questioned, records of all types are scrutinized, and all other factors related to the investigation are carefully looked into. During this investigative time, the court especially reviews the actions of the accused. Close efforts are made to discern what motives prompted the individual to do the actions he is charged with doing. After both sides have completed the presentation of their cases, then comes the final verdict, pronounced by the judge or magistrate. The verdict is final, unless the losing side can successfully appeal the verdict in a higher court.

In much the same way, every human who has ever lived is the "accused" in a massive investigative judgment in heaven. Each one of us will be on trial, whether we are aware of it or not. Not only that, Allah, through an ancient, long-forgotten prophecy in the Bible, has revealed to us that the day of His investigative judgment has already begun for people of earth. It is later truly than we think for planet earth!

## A Heavenly Sanctuary

One of the Bibles' longest time prophecies was recorded by the ancient prophet Daniel. It is called the "2300-year/day prophecy," and it reads, "And he said unto me, Unto two thousand and three hundred days; then shall the sanctuary be cleansed." Daniel 8:14. In biblical prophecies, when speaking of time, the Bible has established that a day equals a year.

Daniel 8:14 refers to the investigative phase of the great judgment event occurring near the close of earth's history. Calendar calculations based on the dates of specific events foretold by Allah in His prophecy reveal the ending year of the 2300-year prophecy to be 1844. In that year, according to the prophecy, the prophecy of Daniel ended, and "*then*" the sanctuary began to be cleansed. That was over 170 years ago. In other words, when the 2300- day/year prophecy of Daniel 8:14 came to a close in 1844, the great investigative judgment in heaven began in the heavenly sanctuary. The hour had arrived when the sanctuary cleansing would begin. We are now living in the final days of earth.

What is this sanctuary of which the prophet Daniel spoke, and how is it associated with the judgment? The Bible speaks of three physical sanctuaries—or tabernacles/temples, as they are also called. After God's people had been led out of Egypt by Allah's appointed man Moses, it wasn't long before Allah called Moses up to Himself into the towering heights of Mount Sinai. When the prophet Moses was with God there in the mount, Allah gave him a view of the glorious heavenly sanctuary, or tabernacle. This sanctuary was not built by man's hand. Injeel Hebrews 8:2 tells us, "...In the heavenly Tabernacle, the true place of worship that was built by the Lord and not by human hands."

The honored Qur'an mentions God's instruction to Moses in the Mount: "And remember We took your covenant and We raised above you (the towering height) of Mount (Sinai): (Saying): 'Hold firmly to what We have given you, and hearken (to the Law).'" Sura 2.93 Al-Baqara.

In the mount, Allah instructed Moses to build a portable, earthly replica of that heavenly sanctuary. "And let them make me a sanctuary...." Exodus 25:8. It was to be placed in the very center of every camp of God's people. This desert sanctuary was to be a mini-model of the one in heaven—a miniature version of the real, much larger, and more beautiful one in heaven. Moses was admonished by God, "Be sure to make everything just like the pattern I showed you on the mountain." Taurat Exodus 25:40. "Everything" included the sanctuary structure itself with its open courtyard area and two enclosed, adjoining rooms; the furniture, utensils and curtains (veils) used inside and outside; and the white linen "wall" that enclosed it all.

Allah intended that the sanctuary would be the primary means through which His people would understand the great judgment hour that would come upon the earth—primarily because of the significance of the actions that were to be done therein. Those actions, done in specifically appointed areas of the sanctuary, reveal how the process of salvation is carried out in heaven. It gives us, in micro-fashion, a view of what has been, and is now, taking place in the sanctuary in heaven.

## A Courtroom Scene: Our Mediator

After God's people had settled in the land of Canaan, where God directed them, the movable desert sanctuary built by Moses was replaced by a much larger, permanent structure built by King Solomon, King David's son. That sanctuary or temple, built in Jerusalem, was destroyed by the Babylonians, then later rebuilt, then destroyed again in AD 70 by pagan Rome. It has not been rebuilt. Since the prophecy takes us down through time to 1844, when there is no longer an earthly sanctuary of Allah's design, there can be no doubt that the sanctuary and its cleansing spoken of in Daniel 8:14 refers to the sanctuary in heaven, where God's throne is, and where the heavenly judgment court sits. "A glorious high throne from the beginning is the place of our sanctuary." Jeremiah 17:12. It is to this heavenly sanctuary that we must look for the fulfillment of Daniel 8:14.

In addition to a view of the heavenly sanctuary, to the ancient prophet Daniel was given a grand view of the coming judgment of God: "I watched until the thrones were set in place, and the Ancient of Days [Allah] sat, whose robe was white as snow, and the hair of His head like the pure wool. His throne was like flames of fire, and His wheels like burning fire. A stream of fire went out and came out from before Him. A thousand thousands served Him, and ten thousand times ten thousand stood before Him. [*In vision the prophet Daniel saw…*] **The judgment was set, and the books were opened.**" Daniel 7:9-10 MKJV. What an awesome, solemn scene is here pictured to us by the prophet! Many centuries ago, he saw what was to transpire in our day!

The records of all of the deeds, both good and evil, of every single person on earth, have been collected in that sanctuary above. Those "ten thousand times ten thousand" that stand before the Ancient of Days (Allah) are heavenly angels, whose duty it has been to keep a record of our acts and deeds. They present the evidence of our characters, in our physical absence. The court sits in session, our lives are reviewed, and eternal decisions are made as to whether or not each individual may receive eternal life. No appeals can be made to a higher court. This is the highest court in the universe, and its decisions are perfect, just, and irrevocable and final—but this is not something to be feared!

All praise to Allah, we have an advocate in that heavenly courtroom—someone who will speak on our behalf, someone who has our best interests in His heart and mind. Daniel describes His arrival to the courtroom: "One like the Son of man [that is, One in human form] came with the clouds of heaven, and came to the Ancient of days, and they brought him near before him." Daniel 7:13. In this heavenly court setting, Isa al-Masih ibn Maryam is our intercessor. An intercessor is one who comes between and mediates between two or more parties in order to reach an agreement between or among them. He will speak and act in our behalf—something we sinners desperately need, for we are indeed guilty, and most of us will admit that.

Scripture clearly tells us, "For there is only one God and one Mediator who can reconcile God and humanity--the man Christ Jesus." 1 Timothy 2:5. Isa al-Masih is the only one worthy to be our intercessor, as He alone earned the right to do this by taking upon Himself our humanity when He was "sent down" to this earth. He so unselfishly 2000 years ago gave up His life near Mount Moriah, where the temple back then stood. (Today the sacred "dome of the rock," or "Noble Sanctuary," stands as a constant reminder of that event long ago. Here, tradition tells us, is the very site where Ibrahim was called upon by Allah to sacrifice his son.)

"And We ransomed him [Abraham's son] with a momentous sacrifice:"Sura 37.107 As-Saaffat

This is sanctuary language and testifies of the great sacrifice of Isa al-Masih which this 'momentous sacrifice' in Abraham's day stood for.

## The Sanctuary and the Judgment

In the earthly sanctuary in Moses' day and beyond, when someone sinned, and then sought forgiveness from God brought into the courtyard of the sanctuary a healthy, (halal) unblemished animal. That (halal) animal represented Isa al-Masih, the only sinless One of humanity. There in the courtyard the sinner confessed his sin against Allah as he pressed his hands on the animal's head to symbolically transfer his sin(s) to the innocent animal, which he then slew in his own guilty stead. In Allah's teaching model of the sanctuary, His sin would not be forgiven without the death of the innocent in his place; that was to illustrate that the sins of all humanity necessitated the death of Isa in our places, for the remission of sins. Isa al-Masih is called the "Lamb of Allah".

In reference to the "Momentous Sacrifice" of Allah, the Taurat speaks of the same event in Genesis 22.

And the son, "…spake unto Abraham his father, and said, My father: and he said, Here am I, my son. And he said, Behold the fire and the wood: but **where is the lamb for a burnt offering**? And Abraham said, My son, **God will provide himself a lamb for a burnt offering**: so they went both of them together." Taurat Genesis 22:7-8

Many years later when Isa al-Masih was sent from Allah, Yahya made this profound announcement…"the Lamb of God."

"The next day John seeth Jesus coming unto him, and saith, Behold the Lamb of God, which taketh away the sin of the world." Injeel John 1:29

In the Injeel, Isa al-Masih is often referred to as the Lamb. Revelation 5:6, 7:17, 14:10, 15:3,19:9, 21:22,23, 22:1,3.

In the ancient Hebrew system it was the lamb which typified or foretold the coming One who was to be sacrificed for humanity's sins. That is why Isa al-Masih, was called the "Lamb of God".  Jesus alone was "Halal". He was clean and righteous and never sinned.  He alone could fulfill this sacrifice of Allah.

Today, our sins are forgiven only because a way was made for someone else (Isa) to bear our sins and punishment.

In the ancient Hebrew sanctuary system, after the halal animal was slain, the officiating priest made atonement for the sinner by applying a small portion of the blood to the altar of incense that stood in the first enclosed apartment of the sanctuary. In symbol, through the blood, the priest transferred the sin from the substitutionary animal to the sanctuary. The priest represents Isa's present reconciling work in the heavenly sanctuary; the fragrant incense represents the reuniting mediation of Isa al-Masih between Allah and the sinner. He takes our sins from us, and bears the guilt and consequences for us, so that we may have another chance to live aright. "The next day John seeth Jesus coming unto him, and saith, Behold the Lamb of God, which taketh away the sin of the world."

The location of that altar of incense was significant. It stood before a heavy curtain that hung between the first apartment and the second, wherein was the ark of the testimony containing the tablets of stone upon which Allah wrote the ten commandments with His own finger. The covering or top of the ark was pure gold, and was called the "mercy seat." Between two angels at either end of the mercy seat was a brilliant light called the "shekinah glory." It was a manifestation of the glory of God. No one but the high priest could enter that second apartment and live, and only on the Day of Atonement could he do that.

The once-a-year Day of Atonement, in the teaching or "type" of the earthly sanctuary, was the very special day each year on which the sins of every believer were "cleansed" from the sanctuary. After appearing before the presence of God's glory with incense (dua' prayers of the believers), the high priest then transferred all confessed sins from the sanctuary to another, called the "scapegoat," a goat chosen to represent Iblis or Satan. All the sins that Satan has caused people to commit over the centuries and millennia—all the *confessed* sins that believers no longer have attributed to them, since they accept that Isa al-Masih took the consequences for them—are now transferred in symbol back to Satan. The goat is led away to perish in the wilderness, and the sanctuary was cleansed of the defilement of sin. This pointed forward to a time not far hence when the judgment is completed, all have received their rewards, and the entire universe is free of sin forevermore. Those who, in the earthly Day of Atonement, had unconfessed sins could not benefit spiritually from this symbolic cleansing, for they had retained their sins. Only those who trusted in the sacrifice and confessed their sins would have them forgiven. Those who refused the offer of God, would forfeit eternity.

Jesus (Isa) is the innocent, spotless lamb (or other animal) slain in the courtyard (the earth) for the sinner's sin. He is the priest in the heavenly sanctuary, mediating our prayers with the incense of His sinless life, and today He is the high priest on the true Day of

Atonement, fulfilling the symbolic one of the ancient system of Moses. He is standing in the presence of our Father God in the current cleansing of the heavenly sanctuary. He is presenting His blood, evidence of the sacrifice of Himself, interceding for us with the Father, so that those who have faith in Him may live eternally. Our good deeds earn us nothing; it is all of faith.

## Final Decisions

Not only is Isa now our intercessor, but we also need to understand that Isa al-Masih is the One who was sent down from Heaven to ransom all from this sin-stricken earth. "...[Isa] Who gave himself a ransom for all." 1 Timothy 2:6. It is this same Isa al-Masih to whom the final judgment of all persons is entrusted, "for the Father judges no man, but has committed all judgment to the Son, so that all should honor the Son, even as they honor the Father. He who does not honor the Son does not honor the Father who sent Him." Injeel John 5:22-23. The final decisions are His, and they are justly based upon the records in heaven which clearly reveal the choices we have made, either for or against God and the One whom was sent down for us. (It is never too late to sincerely repent and ask for forgiveness, no matter how horrible our sins may be.) Our own choices will determine the outcome of the verdict; they determine our eternal reward. We basically choose our own future by our acceptance or rejection of the means Allah has provided for our salvation. Isa sets His seal to our decision; we will either be granted eternal life or eternal death. We have earlier discussed what happens during the "investigative judgment," and now the bestowal of what each person has chosen is called the "executive judgment," when the verdict of the heavenly court of justice is "executed" or carried out or put into effect toward the individual.

Solemn indeed is this time in which we are living! Never has there been a more sobering era in human history, as it nears its close. Such things ought to make us appeal with earnest *du'a* (prayers) to be found without fault in that day when our names are called for heavenly consideration. Now, as the judgment proceeds in the heavenly sanctuary, Isa al-Masih pleads His own blood in our defense. He urges that His death for our sins be accepted as a covering for our sins, if we believe in His substitutionary death for us. Friend, we cannot help but realize that it is time that we give deep thought to what is going on in heaven above. It is now, while this searching investigation of human lives is steadily proceeding, that we need to seriously consider all that God in mercy has revealed to us.

Allah is making known these things all around the world. This is such good news! You, dear reader, are greatly loved by Allah. His compassion and mercy for you is far greater than any human can offer. His compassion and mercy for you is measureless, and he earnestly longs to save your soul from eternal ruin. The primary reason for this publication is to tell you of His infinite compassion and mercy and His plans for you. There is more light to be revealed to the people of Allah, too. We must plead for a revelation of truths which have long been hidden from many minds. Today, while you hear His voice speaking to you, respond to Him with a positive "Yes!" Earnestly ask Allah in private prayer (*du'a*) to reveal truths to you which are essential for you to know in this time of the investigative judgment.

## COURT ADJOURNED

As the cases of all upon earth come up before the court in heaven, each case is closely investigated, as if there were no other person on earth except that one. When Isa al-Masih and the court finish, the investigative work will have been completed, the cases of all will have been decided. He returns in the clouds of heaven ("clouds" of bright angels) to this earth with His reward for the righteous and the unrighteous. Ancient writers of the Taurat foretold the event: "Behold, the Lord GOD will come … and behold, his reward is with him…." Isaiah 40:10.

The same thought is revealed in the Revelation of Isa al-Masih. It clearly foretells the time when Isa returns for the faithful people of earth, to take them to be with Him forever. Isa promised that when He was living on earth as a man: "I go to prepare a place for you. And if I go and prepare a place for you, I will come again, and receive you unto myself; that where I am, there ye may be also." John 14:2-3.

It's obvious He could not come "with rewards" for each person if the judgment were still future. "And, behold, I come quickly; and my reward is with me, to give every man according as his work shall be." Revelation 22:12. The "reward" of the unrighteous is eternal death. The reward of the righteous, however, is the very best that unlimited divine compassion and mercy can give. It is eternal life in a kingdom of peace and joy—unending happiness in the company of other happy beings. Eternal life will be given to the faithful; the others living at that time will be destroyed by the brightness of His coming.

Friends, we are living in the great "Hour of Judgment." The announcement of the beginning of the "hour of His [God's] judgment" was clearly given in the years of 1843-44, when the special message of Revelation 14:6-7 was sounded by messengers all over the world. To be both just and merciful, Allah will cause this same message to continue to sound until the judgment is over. Today you can be ready for this judgment hour; you need not fear, if you have faith. It is decision time for each one of us, and Allah be praised, we have a heavenly Helper. Isa al-Masih is your Intercessor. Appeal to Him in private prayer. He listens!

# *Preparation for the "Day of the Lord"*

In both the Honored Qur'an and in the Holy Books, the subject of the judgment hour often arises. In fact, it is referred to in the Honored Qur'an seventy-seven times as "Day of Judgment" or "Day of Resurrection." In the Holy Books of the Scriptures, this event is often referred to as the "Day of the Lord."

"Seek ye the LORD, all ye meek of the earth, which have wrought his judgment; seek righteousness, seek meekness: it may be ye shall be hid in the day of the LORD'S anger." Zephaniah 2:3.

"Son of man, prophesy and give this message from the Sovereign LORD: 'Weep and wail for that day, for the terrible day is almost here--the day of the LORD! It is a day of clouds and gloom, a day of despair for the nations.'" Ezekiel 30:2-3 NLT.

Upon this day all sinners, unless they beforehand seek to "repent and believe, and work righteousness" (Sura 19.60 Maryam), will receive their reward: "the penalty of the fire." Sura 22:4 Al-Hajj.

These words could be so frightening, and they could fill us full of fear and despair, if it weren't for the fact that Allah, in His love and mercy, has told us ahead of time how to come out alive and clean in the heavenly judgment.

## WARNINGS ALWAYS PRECEDE PUNISHMENT

Throughout human history, as recorded in the Holy Scriptures, always before God sent judgments upon rebellious nations, cities or men, He sent warnings as to how to avoid the judgments. If souls turned from their wicked ways, the judgments were turned aside, or perhaps deferred. But when men continued to transgress God's holy laws, the judgments finally fell. The judgments came in the form of famines, droughts and other natural disasters, destructive foreign invaders, captivity, plagues and pestilences or insect infestations, for example.

We find examples of warning before judgment in the ancient account of Jonah. Allah sent Jonah (Yunus) to the wicked city of Ninevah. "Now the word of the LORD came unto Jonah the son of Amittai, saying, Arise, go to Nineveh, that great city, and cry against it; for their wickedness is come up before me." Jonah 1:1-2. The king and the inhabitants believed Jonah and repented, and the destruction warned about was delayed for over 100 years, when the Ninevites returned to wicked ways.

Long before Allah sent Jonah, He sent Noah (Nuh) to warn the inhabitants of earth of a coming flood due to man's exceeding sinfulness. Noah was instructed to build an ark for those who believed the warning and repented; the ark building demonstrated Noah's own conviction that the Flood was coming, as God had warned. Of those alive at the time of the Flood, only Noah and his family believed the judgment of the Flood was coming. They entered into the safety God had arranged for them. Genesis 6 and 7.

After repeated appeals to repent and warnings of the consequences of continued sin, judgments were the only means our long-suffering God had left to try to turn their hearts to seek Him in repentance, so they could be saved eternally. (The same applies to us today; we are no different.) At one point, God appealed to them with these words: "If my people, who are called by My name, would humble themselves and pray, and seek my face, and turn from their wicked ways, then will I hear from heaven, and will heal their land, and will forgive their sin." 2 Chronicles 7:14.

Unfortunately, often God's people—those who thought themselves His followers—refused to honor and obey Him until they finally suffered the judgments God had warned them of. Then they realized they had brought their suffering upon themselves and their children through their own stiff-necked sinfulness. Confessing their sins, they sought the Lord for forgiveness and restoration of peace.

The Holy Scriptures tell us, "Now all these things happened unto them for ensamples: and they are written for our admonition, upon whom the ends of the world are come." 1 Corinthians 10:11. Now, so close to the Day of the Lord, when it will forever be too late to repent, and lest we repeat their history of rebellion and suffering of judgments, it is so very vital that we understand and know the Laws of Allah, the ten commandments, and live according to them.

## Allah's Question!

Allah's heartfelt appeal to sinners over two thousand years ago applies equally to us today: "Why will ye die, thou and thy people, by the sword, by the famine, and by the pestilence, as the LORD hath spoken…." Jeremiah 27:13. "Get rid of all of the evil things you have done. Let me give you a new heart and a new spirit. Then you will be faithful to me. Why should you die…?" Ezekiel 18:31.

When you come to God asking for that new heart and mind, you will be made aware of how evil sin is, and how much you need forgiveness and cleansing: "Then you will remember your evil ways and wicked deeds, and you will loathe yourselves for your sins and detestable practices." Ezekiel 36:31. You will loathe (abhor or despise) your former way of corrupt living and thinking, and earnestly desire that new heart and mind that Allah desires to give you!

We will find that Allah is amazing, if we will allow Him to work freely in our lives. This is all part of the cleansing that is going on in believers while Isa al-Masih is yet in the heavenly sanctuary above. It is a cleansing of our hearts and lives from sin and its devastating results. Does not this tender appeal from Allah reach your heart?

"As surely as I live, says the Sovereign LORD, I take no pleasure in the death of wicked people. I only want them to turn from their wicked ways so they can live. Turn! Turn from your wickedness, O people of Israel! Why should you die? " Ezekiel 33:11.

## On Trial before Allah

There is a time when with all the inhabitants of earth will have to stand trial before God. It will then be seen if they are worthy to receive eternal life. The announcement of just such a trial is recorded in the last book of Revelation: "And I saw another angel fly in the midst of heaven, having the everlasting gospel to preach unto them that dwell on the earth, and to every nation, and kindred, and tongue, and people, Saying with a loud voice, Fear God, and give glory to him; for **the hour of his judgment is come**: and worship him that made heaven, and earth, and the sea, and the fountains of waters." Revelation 14:6-7

From the lonely Isle of Patmos, John, or Yahya, the writer of Revelation, clearly stated, "And I saw a great white throne, and Him sitting on it…And I saw the dead, the small and the great, stand before God. And books were opened, and another book was opened, which is the Book of Life. And the dead were judged out of those things which were written in the books, according to their works. And the sea gave up the dead in it.... And each one of them was judged according to their works." Injeel Revelation 20:11-13.

None can escape this judgment, "for we must all appear before the judgment seat of Christ, so that each one may receive the things done through the body, according to that which he has done, whether good or bad." 2 Corinthians 5:10. "For God shall bring every work into judgment, with every secret thing, whether it be good, or whether it

be evil." Ecclesiastes 12:14.

Allah's plan is to cleanse and save you, in preparation for the final judgment. "Whoever has the Son [Isa] has life; whoever does not have God's Son does not have life."1 John 5:12.

Allah's plan is to vindicate you in this judgment—to clear your name—to have you found "not guilty." He is there to hold your hand. Look at this verse from Isaiah. "Come now, and let us reason together, saith the LORD: though your sins be as scarlet, they shall be as white as snow; though they be red like crimson, they shall be as wool." Isaiah 1:18.

This good news gets even better, Allah has sent Isa al-Masih not only as the halal sacrifice but also to grant unto us His righteousness. Being acquitted is not enough we also need to be righteous. And that is the very thing that Allah does through Isa, as we are to reflect the character of God which comes only through Isa.

"The law of Moses was unable to save us because of the weakness of our sinful nature. So God did what the law could not do. He sent His own Son in a body like the bodies we sinners have. And in that body God declared an end to sin's control over us by giving His Son as a sacrifice for our sins." Injeel Romans 8:3.

All of this means that now is the time for us to confess our sins and send them beforehand into judgment: "Some men's sins are open beforehand, going before to judgment. And some they also follow after." 1 Timothy 5:24. When sins go 'beforehand," it means they are repented of and confessed. Unless we turn away from obedience to our compassionate and merciful God, those sins will have "pardoned" written next to them in the record books of heaven. If we have confessed and forsaken all our known sins—not in our own strength but in faith in the promised strength of heaven—then there will be no sin that can condemn us during the courtroom investigation of our lives.

Furthermore, we need not fear any consequence for sins we committed in the past, for (Isa) Jesus has already suffered the consequence of death for us. Dear friend, isn't that good news about the judgment?

Today is the day to accept Isa al-Masih as your sacrifice for sin! Isa is fully able to acquit you in the final judgment, but only if you have accepted Him as your personal Saviour. God's wish is to save all; He "will have all men to be saved, and to come unto the knowledge of the truth. For there is one God, and one mediator between God and men, the man Christ Jesus; Who gave himself a ransom for all, to be testified in due time." 1 Timothy 2:4-6.

## No More Stony Hearts

Here is a view of what Allah is going to do with those who are willing! Friends of Allah, are you willing? "For I will take you from the nations and gather you out of all the lands and bring you into your land. Then I will sprinkle clean waters on you, and you shall be clean. I will cleanse you from all your defilement and from all your idols. And I will also give you a new heart, and I will put a new spirit within you. And I will take away the stony heart out of your flesh, and I will give to you a heart of flesh. And I will put My Spirit [*Ruh* Allah] within you and cause you to walk in My statutes, and you shall keep My judgments and do them. And you shall dwell in the land that I gave to your fathers. And you shall be a people to Me, and I will be God to you. I will also save you from all your defilements…." Ezekiel 36:24-29.

Friends, we all have defilements. We all have things in our lives that need cleansing. This is what Allah is trying to do in each of us while Isa is yet in the Heavenly sanctuary, before it is too late. Will we allow Him to perform His heavenly task? Will we constantly say "yes" to Him?

## Man's Intercessor is Isa

It is the plan of Allah to save you. Will you work with Him, trusting that His way is wisest and best? Will you allow Him to save you in His appointed way? "There is salvation in no one else! God has given no other name under heaven by which we must be saved." Acts 4:12.

That worthy name is none other than Isa al-Masih, the Saviour of all men. Will you accept Him into your life? Long ago it was foretold by Allah through the ancient prophets that Allah would send One who would justify or pardon the sinner. "After he [Isa al-Masih] has suffered, he will see the light of life and be satisfied; by his knowledge my righteous servant will justify many, and he will bear their iniquities." Isaiah 53:11.

## Day of Atonement

Anciently it was called the Day of Atonement. This yearly event was closely tied to the sanctuary, as explained previously. On this day all Israel were to assemble themselves before Allah. All Israel were to be intelligently involved in the services of the high priest for them in the sanctuary. Before this day arrived, they were to search their hearts and put away all sin from their lives. Those who didn't were to be separated from God's people; they could not share in the blessing. This is what Allah had promised to ancient Israel on that special day:

"For on this day he [the high priest, who now is Isa al-Masih] shall atone for you, to cleanse you from all your sins; you shall be clean before Jehovah." Taurat Leviticus 16:30.

This annual event, carried out in the desert model sanctuary as well as in the two successive sanctuaries that once stood in Jerusalem, was the culmination, or concluding event and high point, in the teachings of the sanctuary. It pointed forward (foreshadowed) a much greater event at the end of time. From the events of this yearly Day of Atonement—from the actions and duties of priest and people on that day—we may learn of the heavenly and final Great Day of Atonement it foreshadowed, that is even now proceeding in heaven. It is during this critical time that Allah wants to do something very special. He wants to separate His people from their sins once and for all—a cleansing from sin the likes of which we have not yet seen on earth. Will you and I receive of that heavenly cleansing? If we are willing, it will be done in and for us. You have read Allah's promise.

In conclusion, then, we need not fear the judgment! If Isa al-Masih is in our hearts and we allow Him to cleanse our lives from our sins, we may rejoice that "if God be for us, who can be against us?"

May the sweet peace of Heaven be upon thee.

# Ibrahim, "Imam to the Nations"

Abraham (Ibrahim) was a great man of Allah. Highly regarded by God, he was chosen as a type or example for others to follow. He is called the "Imam to the nations" in the Honored Qur'an. Sura 2.124 Al-Baqara.

We wish to look into the life of this remarkable man who chose to follow God at great odds. There is much we can learn from his example. As Ibrahim experienced, following God without reserve on our part always bears a cost. Those who closely follow Him will often be looked upon as strange. Often we will be misunderstood by those around us, and especially by those of our own family, or *ummah*. Following God's voice can bring us into conflict even with those of our own religion. It is stated in the Honored Qur'an that Ibrahim's own father opposed him, and most likely his other relatives, as well.

"And remember that Abraham was tried by his Lord with certain commands, which he fulfilled: He said: 'I will make thee an Imam to the Nations.' He pleaded: "And also (Imams) from my offspring!" He answered: "But My Promise is not within the reach of evil-doers." Sura 2.124 Al-Baqara.

How did this "Imam to the Nations" live? What is his example for us? The Holy Books, the Taurat and Injeel, provide a number of details as to how Ibrahim conducted his life. From these sources we can gain a better understanding of why Allah called him an Imam, a leader of those who seek Allah with all their hearts.

Allah said, "For I know him, that he will command his children and his household after him, and they shall keep the way of the LORD, to do justice and judgment; that the LORD may bring upon Abraham that which he hath spoken of him." Taurat Genesis 18:19.

Even the heathen at the time of Ibrahim recognized that Allah was with him. "Now at that time, Abimelech and Phicol (the captain of his army) said to Abraham, I see that God is with you in all you do." Genesis 21:22.

As it was with Abraham, Is it apparent to the heathen today that God is with you and me? If the heathen cannot see that, is it because we fail to connect with God as we ought? The Taurat says of him, "… Abraham obeyed my voice, and kept my charge, my commandments, my statutes, and my laws." Taurat Genesis 26:5.

## Ibrahim's Example

There are various lessons from Ibrahim's life which we would do well to learn, and some character traits of his that stand as examples for us to follow. First of all, Ibrahim had a very humble opinion of himself. "And Abraham answered and said, Behold now, I have taken upon me to speak unto the Lord, which am but dust and ashes." Taurat Genesis 18:27.

Next we wish to consider Ibrahim's liberality—in other words, his manner of giving his wealth back to Allah. As is too often the case today, the wealthy are as they are because of hoarded wealth.

However, Ibrahim did not keep his wealth to himself. As incredible as it sounds, He graciously gave back to Allah a full tenth of his increase (profits or income); in returning that portion, he humbly acknowledged that all that he possessed had come from the hand of Allah.

This example of a ten-percent return is often overlooked by believers. They settle for a much smaller percentage, such as two or three percent of their income. They say that is sufficient— but what does the Taurat say about the amount which Ibrahim returned to Allah? In times past, Allah had made known through early prophets what He expects from His people throughout earth's history; He was specific as to what He asks that we return to Him: a tenth of our increase. This beneficial requirement, established long ago, is what Ibrahim and others willingly gave. "And concerning the tithe of the herd, or of the flock, even of whatsoever passeth under the rod, the tenth shall be holy unto the LORD. Leviticus 27:32.

Here in clear language that no one can miss, we are instructed that the Lord expects a "tithe," or a "tenth," which is what "tithe" means. The Taurat continues:

"And all the tithe of the land, whether of the seed of the land, or of the fruit of the tree, is the LORD'S: it is holy unto the LORD." Leviticus 27:30.

Ibrahim obeyed this admonition. The record states that after a military victory, Ibrahim was met by Melchizedek, a priest of God. Melchizedek said to him, "And blessed be God Most High, who has defeated your enemies for you." Abram then gave Melchizedek a tenth of all the goods he had recovered." Taurat Genesis 14:20. So important—so significant—was this deed that Ibrahim did, that it was recounted many years later in the Injeel. "But Melchizedek, who was not a descendant of Levi, collected a tenth from Abraham. And

Melchizedek placed a blessing upon Abraham, the one who had already received the promises of God." Injeel Hebrews 7:6.

Ibrahim's example is for us. Returning a tithe, or a tenth, is simply grateful and obedient recognition of God's faithful provision for our needs, and evidence of our trust in Him for the future.

## Allah Asks a Question

In Taurat Malachi 3:8, there is a very serious question from Allah to those who professed to follow Him: "Should people cheat God? Yet you have cheated Me! But you ask, 'What do You mean? When did we ever cheat You?' You have cheated Me of the tithes and offerings due to Me." Malachi 3:8.

Why did Allah ask that question of those who believed themselves to be His people? Anciently, the people of Allah cheated Him by refusing to return the tithe or tenth back to Him. They kept the tenth for themselves; they made themselves rich, but God considered their act to be robbery of Him.

The same holds true for us today. Allah has abundantly given to us of His wealth, and He requests that we not only return a tenth of our increase, but also give offerings. Today, we who are living at the close of earth's history need to take this matter very seriously and follow that example.

Ibrahim's life was one of liberality—of unselfish generosity—as he strove to be in harmony with Heaven. The spirit of liberality is the spirit of Heaven. Heaven has the spirit of giving, and this spirit displayed its highest manifestation in Isa al-Masih's supreme sacrifice on the cross. On our behalf, Allah gave His only-begotten Son. Christ, having given up all that He had, then willingly gave Himself, that man might be saved. What took place near Mount Moriah two thousand years ago demonstrates that Heaven gave its best for mankind, in order to redeem and ransom us from eternal death. That great event—Isa giving His life on behalf of all mankind— should stir the heart of every child of Allah to grateful benevolence.

On the other hand, the spirit of selfishness is the spirit of Iblis, or Satan. The principle illustrated in the lives of worldlings is to "get, get, get." Thus they hope to secure happiness and ease, but the fruit of their sowing is misery and death. Not until God ceases to bless His children will they cease to be under bonds to return to Him the portion that He claims.

## Allah's Claim of Our Tithe, or Tenth

"Bring the whole tithe into the storehouse, that there may be food in my house. Test me in this," says the LORD Almighty, "and see if I will not throw open the floodgates of heaven and pour out so much blessing that there will not be room enough to store it. I will prevent pests from devouring your crops, and the vines in your fields will not drop their fruit before it is ripe," says the LORD Almighty." Malachi 3:10-11.

Allah is asking us to test or prove Him. In order to do so, we need to take Him at His word. I would highly recommend that the reader prove these promises of Allah to be true! Return a tithe, or a tenth of your increase, to Him, as well as additional offerings, and see if the windows or "floodgates of heaven" will open for you! The promise is that there will not be room enough to store it. He also promises to protect our goods and crops from being devoured.

I have tested Allah by doing this, and I can truthfully say that I have more than I can carry! The blessings outweigh the returns which I give back to Him. "The LORD shall command the blessing upon thee in thy storehouses, and in all that thou settest thine hand unto; and he shall bless thee in the land which the LORD thy God giveth thee." Deuteronomy 28:8.

Dear friends, would you like Allah to command a blessing upon you? This is what the Taurat says He will do if we comply with the conditions. Are you ready to comply by returning a tenth? Then fear not to ask for the blessings which Allah will command upon you!

Friends, where is your treasure? Isa al-Masih states a principle: "For where your treasure is, there will your heart be also." Injeel Matthew 6:21. We will be blessed if we follow the example of Ibrahim, the Imam to the nations, in returning a tenth of our increase to Allah.

## Prophecies at the End of Time

Lastly, there are ancient prophecies in Isaiah 60 that include the Children of the East (Islam today) in end-time settings, that reveal their involvement with Allah and the faithful "people of the Book." These people "of the East" will bring forth of their wealth to bring glory to Allah and advance the last-day message before the world ends and Isa returns. Dear friend of Allah, He wants you to be a part of the closing work on earth!

"The multitude of camels shall cover thee, the dromedaries of Midian and Ephah; all they from Sheba shall come: they shall bring gold and incense; and they shall shew forth the praises of the LORD. All the flocks of Kedar shall be gathered together unto thee, the rams of Nebaioth shall minister unto thee: they shall come up with acceptance on mine altar, and I will glorify the house of my glory." Isaiah 60:6-7.

"Surely the isles shall wait for me, and the ships of Tarshish first, to bring thy sons from far, their silver and their gold with them, unto the name of the LORD thy God, and to the Holy One of Israel, because he hath glorified thee." Isaiah 60:9.

"And I will shake all nations, and the desire of all nations shall come: and I will fill this house with glory, saith the LORD of hosts. The silver is mine, and the gold is mine, saith the LORD of hosts." Haggai 2:7-8.

In this life, as we await the soon return of Isa al-Masih Ibn Maryam, may we follow the example of Ibrahim closely in all aspects of our lives. May we devote much time to prayer and contemplation of the things of Allah, and may we return faithfully that portion that belongs to Him. May we be among those who are righteous in hearts and lives. The time is now for us to do what Ibrahim did. Let us be faithful.

# "Sincere Repentance"

May the sweet peace of Allah and His grace be with you, dear friend of Allah, as together we consider a subject that is seldom addressed. There is a promise in the Honored Qur'an that comes to those who repent. "(A voice will say:) 'This is what was promised for you,- for every one who turned (to Allah) in sincere repentance, who kept (His Law)'" Sura 50.32 Qaf.

What was promised? "The Garden will be brought nigh to the Righteous." "Enter ye therein in Peace and Security; this is a Day of Eternal Life!" Sura 50.31, 34.

But notice the condition for fulfillment of the promise: "sincere repentance." Without "sincere repentance," nothing will be received. Therefore, we need to know what "sincere repentance" is. Who must "sincerely repent"? How does a person repent?

One type of repentance involves a sorrow for something that was done or said that caused grief or pain to another person. It involves regret or affliction of conscience that a person experiences on account of his past conduct. Often this repentance stems from a fear of punishment or undesirable consequences that may come as a result of one's actions; then it is more concerned with self than with others. But none of this is true or sincere repentance.

## SINCERE REPENTANCE BRINGS CHANGE

Sincere repentance is a deep sorrow or contrition for sin because it is an offense and dishonor to Allah. It is acknowledged in humility as a violation of His divine holy law, the ten commandments, whether in specific act or in principle. Through the power of Allah, through His Holy Spirit, true repentance brings about a change in one's life. There is a change of mind and heart, of thoughts and motives, which is the essence of conversion from sin to Allah.

True repentance is the relinquishment, from conviction, of any practice that offends Allah. Even though the wrong deed or word may have been against a person, yet it is still understood to be an offense against Allah. This is because the foundation of Allah's law and His kingdom is love toward God and love toward our fellow men. It is also because we have sinned against someone God loves—which means every sinner on earth. The blow intended at another also lands on God.

Sincere repentance always has with it a desire to obey Allah's holy laws, the ten commandments. The Injeel tells us that "godly sorrow brings repentance that leads to salvation and leaves no regret, but worldly sorrow brings death." 2 Corinthians 7:10.

The prophet Isa al-Masih had much to say about repentance. In the Injeel it is written, "When Jesus heard, He said to them, They who are strong have no need of a physician, but the ones who have illness. I did not come to call the righteous, but sinners to repentance." Injeel Mark 2:17. Clearly it says that Isa al-Masih called upon sinners to repent. That includes all of us, for all men and women have need of repentance, as do children of an age to understand.

Sincere repentance is when a person, through the power of the Holy Spirit or *Ruh* of Allah, becomes convicted that he is thinking or acting in violation of Allah's Laws. Under deep conviction, he then makes a decision—a commitment—to follow Allah completely, to live his life completely under God's beneficent rule, for it is the only way to live without godly regret and guilt. The sinner turns away from all known evil in heart and in life through strength given him by Allah. This is true repentance.

The sincere repentance spoken of in the Honored Qur'an involves a turning-around from a life of sin to a life of godliness. John (Yahya), the forerunner of Isa al-Masih, preached repentance: "And he came into all the country about Jordan, preaching the baptism of repentance for the remission of sins." Injeel Luke 3:3.

Powerful indeed was John's message: "Prove by the way you live that you have repented of your sins and turned to God. Don't just say to each other, 'We're safe, for we are descendants of Abraham.' That means nothing, for I tell you, God can create children of Abraham from these very stones." Injeel Luke 3:8.

More than once, Isa al-Masih confirmed that He came to call sinners to repentance. "I came not to call the righteous, but sinners to repentance." Luke 5:32.

"And that repentance and remission of sins should be preached in his [Isa's] name among all nations, beginning at Jerusalem." Injeel Luke 24:47.

The same message was given to ancient Israel: "Therefore, I will judge each of you, O people of Israel, according to your actions, says the Sovereign LORD. Repent, and turn from your sins. Don't let them destroy you!" Ezekiel 18:30.

## Signs of Sincere Repentance

The Taurat speaks of the people of ancient Nineveh who became very wicked. They had departed so far from the ways of Allah that He sent them a stirring message through the prophet Jonah (Yunus). "Now the word of the LORD came unto Jonah … saying, Arise, go to Nineveh, that great city, and cry against it; for their wickedness is come up before me." Jonah 1:1-2.

In the following account, look for specific behaviors that indicate that the people of Nineveh truly repented.

"Jonah began by going a day's journey into the city, proclaiming, 'Forty more days and Nineveh will be overthrown.' The Ninevites believed God. They declared a fast, and all of them, from the greatest to the least, put on sackcloth [burlap]. When the news reached the king of Nineveh, he rose from his throne, took off his royal robes, covered himself with sackcloth [burlap] and sat down in the dust [ashes]. Then he issued a proclamation in Nineveh: 'By the decree of the king and his nobles: Do not let people or animals, herds or flocks, taste anything; do not let them eat or drink. But let people and animals be covered with sackcloth. Let everyone call urgently on God. Let them give up their evil ways and their violence. Who knows? God may yet relent and with compassion turn from his fierce anger so that we will not perish.' When God saw what they did and how they turned from their evil ways, he relented and did not bring on them the destruction he had threatened." Jonah 3:4-10.

The people of Nineveh showed true signs of repentance by their earnest change in life. Jonah's message had caused them to earnestly seek God. The mightiest ruler down to the humblest beasts were clothed in burlap. The king proclaimed a fast for the entire city, and all the people sat in ashes as a sign of their humiliation before God. They were urged to forsake their wicked ways and pray to Allah to spare them. History reveals that Allah spared that ancient city for Nineveh for another 140 years. Thus we know God in mercy will hear our prayers and see our repentance.

## Allah Promises a New Heart

Allah hates sin, for it can cause the sinner He loves to lose eternal life. Therefore, Allah loves repentance, because it means the sinner rejects the power of sin and seeks instead the power of God to refrain from sin.

"'So I will judge you people. I will judge each of you in keeping with what you have done,' announces the LORD and King. 'Turn away from your sins! Turn away from all of the evil things you have done. Then sin will not bring you down. Get rid of all of the evil things you have done. Let me give you a new heart and a new spirit. Then you will be faithful to me. Why should you die, people of Israel? When anyone dies, it does not give me any joy,' announces the LORD and King. 'So turn away from your sins. Then you will live!'" Ezekiel 18:30-32.

Allah's call of repentance comes to all people of every nation. He earnestly pleads with every person to turn to Him. His heart of kindness seeks only to save, not to destroy, yet He will not force us to repent. To be sincere, repentance must be our own decision. Dear friend of Allah, will you not accept His offer?

"'For I will take you out of the nations; I will gather you from all the countries.... I will sprinkle clean water on you, and you will be clean; I will cleanse you from all your impurities and from all your idols. I will give you a new heart and put a new spirit in you; I will remove from you your heart of stone and give you a heart of flesh. And I will put my Spirit in you and move you to follow my decrees and be careful to keep my laws." Taurat Ezekiel 36:24-27.

Now some may ask, "How is it that a man will repent? Does repentance come from deep inside him?" No, it doesn't, because the natural heart is at enmity with God. It values the things of the flesh, not of the spirit. How, then, can the natural heart stir itself up to repentance when it has no inclination or power to do so? What is it that brings man to repentance?

## ALLAH'S GIFT OF REPENTANCE

In a thousand ways, it is Isa al-Masih that leads men to repent. He knows they will be lost if they do not, so He is tireless in His many efforts in our behalf:

"Opponents must be gently instructed, in the hope that God will grant them repentance leading them to a knowledge of the truth." 2 Timothy 2:25.

"The Lord is not slow in keeping his promise.... Instead, he is patient with you, not wanting anyone to perish, but everyone to come to repentance." 2 Peter 3:9. "...God's kindness is intended to lead you to repentance...." Romans 2:4.

"(And to preach thus), 'Seek ye the forgiveness of your Lord, and turn to Him in repentance; that He may grant you enjoyment, good (and true), for a term appointed, and bestow **His abounding grace** on all who abound in merit! But if ye turn away, then I fear for you the penalty of a great day." Sura 11.3 Hud.

How true it is, then, that it is simply the abounding grace of Allah that leads us to repentance. We, as humans, don't even know how to repent on our own. We definitely sense the sorrow or guilt of sin, but how to turn around, how to make that u-turn in life to hate and forsake sin, we don't know and can't do. Many, in their outward conduct, appear to shun evil and many sins, but if their hearts were examined, it would be found that in heart they still desire some evil deed. As long as a cherished sin is not relinquished, it holds us captive unto death. Sin must be removed from the heart before the soul is free.

The ability to change the course of our lives comes only from Allah. Even if we don't truly feel sorry, we must realize that our sin condemns us, and we must seek help to even desire repentance. It will be given.

When we ask for the gift of true repentance, Allah will deliver. When Isa lived on earth, not one believing soul was denied his or her request for healing. So, too, in cleansing our hearts from sin, if we would but ask Allah, He who sustains the galaxies in their orbits has promised, "He shall call upon me, and I will answer him...." Zabur Psalms 91:15. Not one soul escapes His notice; no one is too small for Him to see. He is waiting to bestow His grace on even the least. Dear friend of Allah, ask Him today for the gift of repentance, that our lives may be cleansed from the filth of sin through the blessed gift of Isa al-Masih which was sent down. Ask for the gift of repentance now.

# The Eternal Home and Great Salvation

Greetings dear friend of Allah! What prospect stands before us! Imagine that our future lives can link with the life of the Infinite One! This subject is so grand and incomprehensible that our minds fail to take it in. That mortal beings can one day live in the sight of Allah with "companions pure and holy", (Sura 3:45 Aal-E-Imran) in His Eternal Home, is a most precious thought. There the "doors will ever be open" Sura 38:50 Sad. What great salvation it is for Allah to save us from this fallen world of sin, suffering, and sorrow, and grant us an eternal home with "gardens of bliss", Sura 5:65 Al-Maeda.

It is almost too much to consider! And why should He offer this to us? It is only His Infinite Love for the fallen sons and daughters of Adam. And to think it was all done through the One sent down for us! Isa al-Masih the Great Ransom for man! Is it any wonder that Eid al-Adha is the greatest celebration ever made? The "momentous sacrifice" Sura 37:107

As-Saaffat, was made for not only Ibrahim's beloved son, but for every son and daughter of Adam which was born on this world. Truly Allah has made this immense sacrifice on behalf of all humanity! Dear friend of Allah, never allow anyone or anything to get you to set aside these thoughts.

## The Garden forfeited is restored

The Honored Qur'an speaks of the "Gardens of Eternity" Sura 16:31 An-Nahl which is the home of ransomed souls from this earth! The Taurat tells of how man was driven from the Garden of Eden when he disobeyed Allah. "And the LORD God planted a garden eastward in Eden; and there he put the man whom he had formed." Genesis 2:8

As a simple test, Adam was told: "approach not the tree, or ye run into harm and transgression [sin]. Sura 2:35 Al-Baqara. However Adam listened as "Satan whispered evil to him" Sura 20:120 Ta-Ha, and they both fell from their lofty position. Adam "allowed himself to be seduced" Sura 20:121

Ta-Ha. After man sinned the... "LORD God banished him from the Garden of Eden to work the ground from which he had been taken. After he drove them out, he placed on the east side of the Garden of Eden cherubim [holy angels] and a flaming sword flashing back and forth to guard the way to the tree of life." Genesis 3:23-24 What a sad and terrible day when man was driven out of his Eden home!

## Glad Tidings to Man

These 'glad tidings' are that man who is ransomed and who asks for repentance and forgiveness can be made righteous, and will again be restored to the Gardens. Sura 3:15 Aal-E-Imran

In the Revelation of Isa al-Masih the ransomed will be returned to the very Garden lost in the beginning. The Garden Eden with the beautiful fruit lost in the book of Genesis is restored to man in the book of Revelation. "Then the angel showed me the river of the water of life, as clear as crystal, flowing from the throne of God and of the Lamb down the middle of the great street of the city. On each side of the river stood the tree of life, bearing twelve crops of fruit, yielding its fruit every month. And the leaves of the tree are for the healing of the nations. No longer will there be any curse. The throne of God and of the Lamb will be in the city, and his servants will serve him." Injeel Revelation 22:1-3

## Descriptions of the Garden

The Honored Qur'an speaks of "Saints to be on raised thrones"... Sura 18:31 Al-Kahf The Injeel promises that those who are overcomers in the battle against self, sin, and Satan will rule upon thrones. "I saw thrones on which were seated those who had been given authority to judge. And I saw the souls of those who had been beheaded because of their testimony about Jesus and because of the word of God. They had not worshiped the beast or his image and had not received his mark on their foreheads or their hands. They came to life and reigned with Christ a thousand years." Revelation 20:4

"To him who overcomes I will grant to sit with Me in My throne, even as I [Isa al-Masih] also overcame and have sat down with My Father in His throne." Revelation 3:21 Thrones are promised to those who overcome the devil and his deceptions, and refuse to receive the mark of the beast.

Here upon earth, our homes are often taken from us, by wars, by violent covetous hands, or by the elements of nature, but our homes in paradise will be sure. We are promised: "They will build houses and dwell in them; they will plant vineyards and eat their fruit. No longer will they build houses and others live in them, or plant and others eat…" Isaiah 65:21-22

"Your gates will always stand open, they will never be shut, day or night, so that people may bring you the wealth of the nations-- their kings led in triumphal procession." Taurat Isaiah 60:11 In that place: "On no day will its gates ever be shut, for there will be no night there." Revelation 21:25

## WHO MAY ENTER THERE?

The Honored Qur'an says the "Eternal Home" is for the "Righteous" Sura 3:15 Aal-E-Imran. In clear words spoken from the ancient prophet Daud is laid out in detail who may once again dwell in the Holy Sanctuary or the 'Eternal Home" of Allah? "LORD, who may dwell in your sanctuary? Who may live on your holy hill? He whose walk is blameless and who does what is righteous, who speaks the truth from his heart and has no slander on his tongue, who does his neighbor no wrong and casts no slur on his fellowman, who despises a vile man but honors those who fear the LORD, who keeps his oath even when it hurts, who lends his money without usury [interest] and does not accept a bribe against the innocent. He who does these things will never be shaken." Zabur Psalms 15:1-5

In Sura 3:15 the "righteous" will live in that Eternal Home. Who are the Righteous? The Righteous are those who honor and keep the Eternal Law of Allah the Ten Commandments. They have given Allah complete permission to write His Holy and Sacred Laws into their very hearts and minds.

"This is the covenant that I will make with them after those days, says the Lord; I will put My Laws into their hearts, and in their minds I will write them," Injeel Hebrews 10:16

The Righteous are such because of what was given to them… Righteousness. Which means they were granted the gift which they had forfeited in Eden! In order to go through the Judgment we need Righteousness and that naturally we do not possess.

This gift of righteousness comes only thorough One, and that One is Isa al-Masih the Righteous! In Sura 19.19 it clearly tells us that Isa was Righteous. He had no earthly father, as Maryam confessed to the Messenger angel that she was not unchaste and had not touched a man, how could she have a son? The Messenger angel announced that she would conceive through the Spirit of Allah, that the son given to her would be Righteous.

"The angel said: 'I am only a Messenger from your Lord, to announce to you the gift of a righteous son'". Sura 19.19 Maryam

It is quite obvious that Isa al-Masih did not have an earthly father, thus He came from a Heavenly origin, and since He was conceived through the Spirit of Allah.

Sura 21.91 Al-Anbiya "…We breathed into her [Maryam] of **Our spirit**…"Sura 66.12 At-Tahrim "And Mary…who guarded her chastity; and we breathed into (her body) of **Our spirit**…"

Isa al-Masih or Jesus, son of Mary was conceived through the spirit of Allah. That makes it crystal clear that He came forth from Allah, making Him the Son of Allah through the spirit of Allah.

Isa al-Masih was born from Allah, and was Righteous, and He is willing to give His Righteousness to all who will accept Him as their redeemer from sin and Satan.

"My little children, these things write I unto you, that ye sin not. And if any man sin, we have an advocate [*intercessor*] with the Father, Jesus Christ the righteous: " 1 John 2:1

## Yahya saw the Eternal Home

Almost 2000 years ago the Prophet Yahya (John) was given a view of the Eternal Home. Here in the Revelation of Isa al-Masih he gives us a description of what he saw. This gives us hope in this fallen world of suffering, sin, and sorrow. "After this I beheld, and, lo, a great multitude, which no man could number, **of all nations**, and kindreds, and people, and tongues, stood before the throne, and before the Lamb, clothed with white robes, and palms in their hands;" Revelation 7:9

They regain their lost raiment (covering), the white robes which was 'stripped [off] them' in the Garden of Eden'. Sura 7:27 Al-Araf, for it says they were again 'clothed with white robes'. "And one of the elders answered, saying unto me, What are these which are arrayed in white robes?... And he said to me, These are they which came out of great tribulation, and have washed their robes, and made them white in the blood of the Lamb. Therefore are they before the throne of God, and serve him day and night in his temple: and he that sitteth on the throne shall dwell among them. They shall hunger no more, neither thirst any more; neither shall the sun light on them, nor any heat. For the Lamb which is in the midst of the throne shall feed them, and shall lead them unto living fountains of waters: and God shall wipe away all tears from their eyes." Revelation 7:13-17

Oh precious peace, oh blessed hope, warmest of all thoughts, the blessings which Allah holds out to each soul who in humbleness submits his entire life into the hands of the living God and accepts by faith the One whom was sent down to save our souls from eternal ruin! Isa al-Masih. Dear friend of Allah, His desire is that you be among that throng! It is a vast company which no man could number. "After this I beheld, and, lo, a great multitude, which no man could number, of all nations, and kindreds, and people, and tongues, stood before the throne, and before the Lamb, **clothed with white robes**, and palms in their hands…" Revelation 7:9

In that Eternal Home, "God shall wipe away all tears from their eyes; and there shall be no more death, neither sorrow, nor crying, neither shall there be any more pain: for the former things are passed away."

Revelation 21:4 Dear friend it is the wish of Allah that you are among those to enter the Eternal Home.

# The Baptism of Allah

Dear friends, I greet you in the name of Allah.

In the Honored Qur'an is mentioned the "Baptism [or Colouring] of Allah." Sura 2.138 Al-Baqara, Noble Qur'an. What is this "Baptism of Allah"? We know the people of the Book believe in baptism, but what about those in Islam? What kind of baptism is it? Did Allah go through a baptism? Please read on! The full sura says,

"(Our religion is) the Baptism of Allah: And who can baptize better than Allah? And it is He Whom we worship." Sura 2.138 Al-Baqara. The commentary on this topic in the Yusef Ali version of the Honored Qur'an is worth reading. It says "baptism" in Arabic is *Sibghah* or *Sihgat*: "the root-meaning implies a dye or colour; apparently the Arab Christians mixed a dye or colour in the baptismal water, signifying that the baptized person got a new colour in life...." Comment on Sura 2.137 Al-Baqara, page 56.

Why would the Honored Qur'an mention this baptism? It is obviously important, for it says the Baptism of Allah is the best! What is it that Allah will do in this baptism? What is this colouring? We can see why Yusef Ali mentions that the Arab Christians added a dye to the baptismal water. That was significant, in that it showed that the person who was baptized was coloured--yes, coloured for life! This baptism was significant because when one submitted to Allah, his whole life changed, or became "newly coloured"!

We find that John, or Yahya, the son of Zachariah who announced the coming of Isa al-Masih, was calling for people to renounce their lives of sinful living and be baptized. During that time period he was preaching at the river Jordan and baptizing all classes of people. Baptism was and is an outward sign, a symbol of a change or "new colouring" in life, reflecting what had happened in the heart of the one baptized.

In truth, it is Allah who baptizes or colours a person, as only He can cleanse the soul of defilement and change the heart. In baptism there is water involved. In Biblical baptism, a person who consents to baptism is fully immersed in water and is taken back up out of the water alive. This is done as a sign of submission to Allah and gives public testimony that this person has surrendered his or her life completely to Allah.

## Baptism of Water

There are three baptisms mentioned in the Holy Books. One is the baptism of water, the one administered by Yahya (John the Baptist). "John came baptizing in the wilderness and proclaiming the baptism of repentance for the remission of sins." Injeel Mark 1:4. That baptism meant a heart surrender to Allah; it results from a conviction in the human heart of sin. There is a desire of the soul to repent of all sin and turn fully to Allah for forgiveness and cleansing from sin. The life is changed, or coloured, to one of obedience to God. Joy replaces sorrow and regret.

We read that Yahya was baptizing in the river Jordan. Similarly, in the Honored Qur'an, in Sura 5.6 Al-Maeda, water is the agent to be used for cleansing before prayer, unless no water is available. Since baptism is a sign of a complete change or colour in life, so it is fitting that the person be completely immersed in water as a sign of a complete cleansing.

Yahya preached "…the baptism of repentance to all the people of Israel." Injeel Acts 13:24. The symbolism is this: When a person comes under conviction that he is a sinner and in need of cleansing from sin, he decides to seek Allah for help. He acknowledges in his own heart that he is helpless to change, and he knows that not only is Allah all-powerful to help him, but also that Allah desires to cleanse him so he can receive an eternal inheritance. The person's own desire is to be cleansed from all sin and wickedness, so as an outward sign of his surrender and submission, he is baptized in water. This is a fitting sign of complete trust in and dependence upon God—a surrendering of the will to Allah's will. There is a death to self, and as the person rises from the water, he rises in newness of life. Allah has pledged that all heaven will look after this person who has dedicated himself to Allah in this world of sin, suffering, and degradation.

## Baptism of the Holy Spirit

The second baptism mentioned is of the Holy Spirit or *Ruh* Allah. It is also known as the baptism by fire. It means a person who has come to complete submission to Allah receives not only water baptism, but he also is given the Holy Spirit and is "baptized," or covered, by the Spirit of Allah. As a sign of acceptance with God, the person is given the gift of the Holy Spirit, which is received by faith. "Peter replied, 'Repent and be baptized, every one of you, in the name of Jesus Christ for the forgiveness of your sins. And you will receive the gift of the Holy Spirit.'" Injeel Acts 2:38.

Yahya mentioned the One who would come after him, who would baptize with fire, or the Holy Spirit. "...'As for me, I baptize you with water; but One is coming who is mightier than I, and I am not fit to untie the thong of His sandals; He will baptize you with the Holy Spirit and fire.'" Injeel Luke 3:16. Yahya was referring to Isa al-Masih as the One coming after him.

### BAPTISM OF BLOOD

The third baptism mentioned in the Holy Scriptures is not only of water, but also of blood, or suffering. Like the others mentioned, it follows a complete surrender to Allah. It also includes a self-renouncing love for perishing souls of earth. This baptism was consummated near Mount Moriah when Isa al-Masih gave His Holy life to ransom all sinners from earth. It was manifested by Isa al-Masih by totally giving of Himself for humanity.

In the last days of the life of Isa al-Masih, He was cruelly abused by the temple priests, the religious leaders, and the heathen Romans. All these were following the agenda of Iblis, or Shatan. Prior to His suffering and death, Isa al-Masih had asked His followers, "...Can ye drink of the cup that I drink of? and be baptized with the baptism that I am baptized with? And they said unto him, We can. And Jesus said unto them, Ye shall indeed drink of the cup that I drink of; and with the baptism that I am baptized withal shall ye be baptized." He was referring to the baptism of suffering which He, and later they, in lesser degree, would have to endure. Injeel Mark 10:38-39.

Isa al-Masih willingly took upon Himself the responsibility of paying the ransom for our sins. He willingly suffered the wrath of God on behalf of all sinners of earth. Hear Him while suffering upon the instrument of torture, while hanging upon the Roman cross, crying out to His Father: "And at the ninth hour Jesus cried with a loud voice, saying, Eloi, Eloi, lama sabachthani? which is, being interpreted, My God, my God, why hast thou forsaken me?" Injeel Mark 15:34.

The Father had hid His face from His beloved, and though sinless, on our behalf Isa suffered the vengeance of an offended God. Out of pity for helpless humanity, Isa voluntarily suffered this baptism of blood for all nations of earth. It matters not, dear friend of Allah, where you were born, or under what conditions. Allah sees you and knows your situation. Through the One He sent, He has already paid the redemption price for your soul, and He wants you in His eternal kingdom of bliss. In your heart, will you receive Isa, who was sent down to us?

Remember the near-sacrifice of Ibrahim's son on Mount Moriah? Remember how, right before Ibrahim's knife ended the life of his son, Allah Himself provided a substitute "ransom"—a "momentous sacrifice." Sura 37.100-113 As-Saaffat. Today this occasion is yearly celebrated as Eid al-Adha! Only from the Torat in the Holy Books can we learn that for Ibrahim and his son, the "ransom" was a ram caught in a nearby thicket. That ram was hardly a "momentous sacrifice," but *what it symbolized was indeed momentous*. It would die that day as a sacrifice, so that a man need not die. Its symbolic, substitutionary death foreshadowed a future time when Isa, the Lamb of God, would die to ransom all mankind, so that each one of us might live eternally.

That event of the ancient past was a foreshadowing of the time when God would send His own Beloved to the same area to perish for the sins of humanity. It is only Someone of infinite love that would attempt such a "baptism of blood" and suffering. How easily Allah could have wiped out all of sinful humanity, but no. He chose to suffer on a much greater scale than Ibrahim endured when called upon to sacrifice His son on Mount Moriah! Allah endured the suffering and loss of His own dear Beloved.

In Ibrahim's case, his hand holding the knife was stopped from slaying his son Isaac on the altar of sacrifice on Mount Moriah. This was not the case with Isa. His own Father had to allow the agonizing death of His Beloved, who felt Himself forsaken of the Father. From the beginning they had been together, but then He had to see Him perish. What profound love for humanity! God loved us so much that He surrendered His Son to humanity, which slew the guiltless Isa. Yet those who believe in Him will receive eternal life.

So we see that Allah suffered immensely with His Son. We may truly say that Allah was baptized with suffering. He was coloured in ways and depths that we will never comprehend throughout all eternity. We realize only in small part what Allah gave when He gave Isa al-Masih to this earth. This was the most costly gift which heaven could bestow upon us. In this venture of Allah, we see that Allah Himself submitted to the baptism of blood, or suffering, for the sinful race of humanity, through the giving of His Son.

He would rather suffer the loss of His own dear Son than see us perish for eternity! Words cannot describe accurately this thought. It will take all eternity to try to understand the deep and compassionate love of Allah for His created beings! Oh, dear friend, this is truly the "baptism [or colouring] of Allah." Sura 2.138 Al-Baqara. Instead of vengeance upon the human race for their disobedience, He allows vengeance to fall upon His One and only Beloved Isa al-Masih! The thought is too much for us to grasp. All eternity is needed to take it in!

### BAPTISM, THE SIGN OF SUBMISSION TO ALLAH

Dear friend of Allah, will you make that decision to follow Allah by allowing yourself to be baptized by immersion in water? This is truly what God wishes for us to do as a sign that we have accepted the sacrifice of Isa al-Masih as payment of the penalty for our sin and as our ransom from sin. He undertook this costly venture for each one of us personally—for you personally! To reject this is spurning infinite Grace!

Right now, Allah is asking you to believe and be baptized, as a sign of your submission to Him.

"And He [Isa al-Masih] said to them, Go into all the world, proclaim the gospel to all the creation. He who believes and is baptized will be saved, but he who does not believe will be condemned." Mark 16:15-16.

May we say with the eunuch, "...See, here is water, what hinders me from being baptized? Philip said, If you believe with all your heart, it is lawful. And he answered and said, I believe … and he baptized him." Acts 8:36-38. Friend, be blessed and follow the example of the eunuch. It will be the most blessed day of your life.